I0810533

IMAGES
of America

TILLAMOOK ROCK LIGHTHOUSE

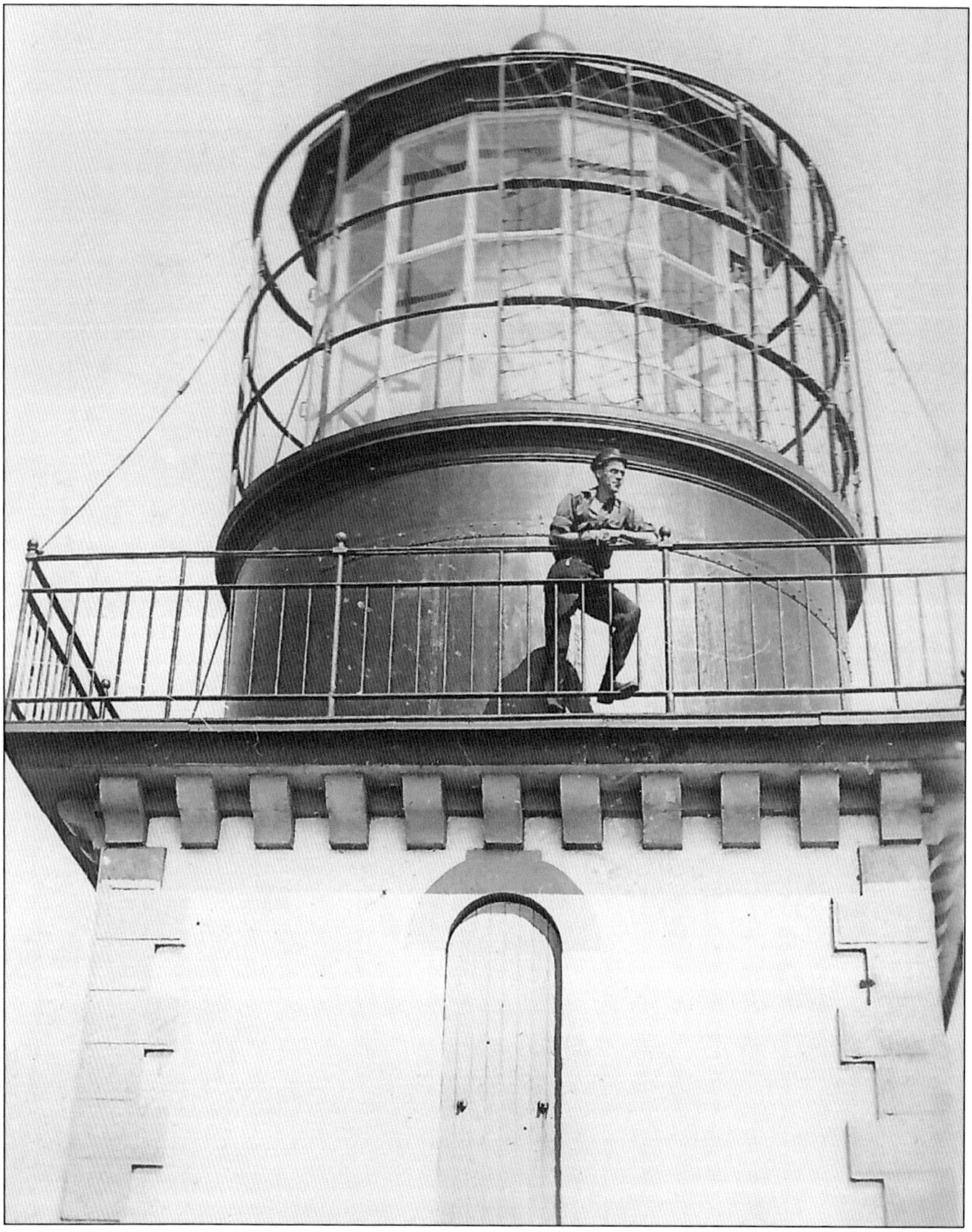

Second assistant keeper Walter T. Lawrence keeps a lookout on the lantern deck of Tillamook Rock Lighthouse in 1920. Above his head, a bent bar in the welded wire protective screen covering the lantern glass attests to the powerful force of the boulders thrown up toward the light during severe storms. (Walter T. Lawrence collection, courtesy Brian Bay.)

On the Cover: In an official 1943 naval report, Tillamook Rock Lighthouse was described as being "one of the most famous as well as one of the most exposed light stations in the United States." It is easy to understand how it gained the nickname "Terrible Tilly" due to its precipitous location and vulnerability to the elements, as shown in this post-1935 photograph. (Clatsop County Historical Society.)

IMAGES
of America

TILLAMOOK ROCK LIGHTHOUSE

Debra Baldwin
Lighthouse Digest Magazine

ARCADIA
PUBLISHING

ISBN 978-1-4671-2832-2

Published by Arcadia Publishing
Charleston, South Carolina

Printed in the United States of America

Library of Congress Control Number: 2018941669

For all general information, please contact Arcadia Publishing:
Telephone 843-853-2070
Fax 843-853-0044
E-mail sales@arcadiapublishing.com
For customer service and orders:
Toll-Free 1-888-313-2665

Visit us on the Internet at www.arcadiapublishing.com

To all the thousands of lighthouse keepers who selflessly served to save lives while at times even sacrificing their own. May we honor each one.

Contents

Foreword 6

Acknowledgments 7

Introduction 8

1. Rocky Start 11

2. Halcyon Days 23

3. Tilly's Wrath 59

4. Tender Mercies 85

5. Changing Tides 103

6. Silent Sentinel 119

Known Keepers of Tillamook Rock Lighthouse 126

Foreword

For more than 25 years, *Lighthouse Digest Magazine* has played an integral part in the lighthouse preservation movement across America. We are proud of the role we have assumed by taking solid stands in helping to save lighthouses and lighthouse artifacts, and uncovering and reporting stories and history that otherwise might never have been told.

In doing so, we have built a massive archive. We have helped found a lighthouse museum and donated numerous artifacts to various organizations. We were among the first to join the innovations of the World Wide Web with our Lighthouse Explorer database. We have helped start several lighthouse groups, supported their early development, and donated to numerous lighthouse restoration projects.

More recently, we have tried to lead the way in honoring our nation's lighthouse keepers with ceremonies to place memorial lighthouse service markers at their gravesites in hopes that others will follow suit. All of the author's proceeds from the sales of this book will be used toward that end.

In our ongoing research efforts, we have found, archived, and published for the first time many rare, historic photographs that have been buried in the vaults of time, unlabeled and forgotten. Through traveling the country and contacting keeper family descendants, we have been able to put names with faces once again and give context to events to recreate the full story of life at many lighthouses. The photographs and narrative that appear in this book are a prime example of those efforts.

Although each and every lighthouse has its own distinct history, none is more dramatic than that of Oregon's Tillamook Rock Lighthouse. Now, for the first time, this book offers the most complete visual record and unique perspective of Terrible Tilly that has ever been assembled in hopes that not only will the history be preserved for future generations, but it will motivate others to compile similar visual histories of their lighthouses for the benefit of all. We hope you enjoy seeing these images as much as we have enjoyed gathering, identifying, and sharing them with you.

Timothy Harrison, Editor
Kathleen Finnegan, Managing Editor
Debra Baldwin, Historian

Acknowledgments

We are deeply indebted to the staff of the museums, archives, government agencies, and societies, as well as several keeper family descendants who have allowed us access to their cherished photographs and documents that they have carefully preserved through the years. Many of them have spent long hours scanning photographs for us and hunting amidst dark corners and high shelves to find these images. To this end, we especially wish to thank Brian Bay, Nora Chidlow, Gene Davis, Marcy Dunning, Jeff Gales, Rich Gales, Anna and Bryce Gray, Lon Haynes, Roy Lowe, Ray and Deb Pedrick, Liisa Penner, Jeff Smith, Shawn Stephensen, Darrell van Ness, Dale Webber, and Jean Hayward Wilkinson for their inestimable help. We also express gratitude for the technical expertise rendered by Jim Claflin, Josh Greene, Chad Kaiser, and Ted Panayotoff. Thank you all for your generosity and efforts spent to help us compile this visual history.

Key to Courtesy Line Abbreviations:

BB	Walter T. Lawrence collection, courtesy Brian Bay
CCHS	Clatsop County Historical Society
CGHO	Coast Guard Historian's Office
CGNW	Coast Guard Museum of the Northwest
CRMM	Columbia River Maritime Museum
JGC	Jim Gibbs collection, courtesy Ray and Deb Pedrick
JHW	Hayward Family collection, courtesy Jean Hayward Wilkinson
LHC	Lon Haynes collection
LHD	*Lighthouse Digest* Archives
NARA	National Archives and Records Administration
USFWS	United States Fish and Wildlife Service
USLHS	United States Lighthouse Society

Introduction

Of all the lighthouse station assignments on the Pacific coast, Oregon's Tillamook Rock Lighthouse was deemed the worst. It was not uncommon for a keeper to feel he was being punished by being sent there. It was "the most God-forsaken, nastiest chunk of rubble anywhere . . . a pint-sized Alcatraz that took on the aspects of an insane asylum where its inmates had been exiled forever," according to historian and former keeper Jim Gibbs in his reminiscence of when he was first stationed there.

In fact, in 1890, keeper Louis C. Sauer was indeed hauled off to spend his remaining days in an insane asylum after rushing toward his fellow keepers like a raving maniac, threatening to kill them. A 1900 newspaper declared that a man "not only risks his life in accepting the position, but his reason as well." Most of the early keepers decided not to take the chance and resigned instead. The first head keeper, Albert Roeder, only lasted three months.

Terrible Tilly earned its moniker from the unleashed furies of the fiercest of storms with waves that regularly broke over the 134-foot height at the top of the lantern. Hurricane force winds that exceeded 100 miles per hour and pounding surges would sheer off chunks of the basaltic rock, which were thrown upward by the eruption of a geyser formed out of the adjoining crevice on the south side. These hurtling missiles shattered panes of glass and damaged prisms of the first order Fresnel lens, all the while letting in the swirling waters, which would cascade down the stairs to flood the rooms below carrying seaweed, fish, dead seabirds, and debris. The fog-signal trumpets would be full of rocks, and original ventilators were flattened by the onslaught.

A storm in 1913 threw so many rocks into the lighthouse that, according to Gibbs, "a gunboat firing a full broadside could not have done more damage." The keepers thought they would surely be swept into the sea during the 15 hours that it lasted.

The horrendous storm of 1934 was so intense that it chipped and cracked the lens prisms, which had to be replaced with an aero-marine revolving beacon. Iron railings were crushed by large boulders, and the three-foot deeply anchored iron bolts of the huge derrick and boom-lifting apparatus were unearthed from solid rock, and all was swept away into the raging seas. Keepers who endured these storms talked of feeling the rock shudder beneath them with every wave that crashed into its sides, yet the lighthouse still stood and the keepers were undaunted in the performance of their duties, many times receiving heroes' commendations from their superiors as a result.

The newspapers accurately stated that, because of its perilous situation, it was the most avoided lighthouse on the government list, and that only through a long and careful search could men be found who were willing to go there as keepers. It took a special type of man to be able to withstand such horrendous conditions, but amazingly enough, many were found who were willing to endure the wrath of Tilly for decades—and some even relished it!

Charley Bearman, who later served as head keeper at Smith Island Lighthouse in Washington, was one such man. He recalled with fondness his days at Tillamook Rock right before the Great War. Based on a recording he made shortly before his death, his wife later noted,

> He enjoyed every minute of the five years he spent on the Rock, and they were among the very happiest of his life—tending the light; making furniture from the hard wood crates in which their supplies were lowered on the Rock from cranes on the tender; experimenting with cooking for the crew of four always on the Rock while the fifth was on shore leave; playing cribbage and pinochle with the men; and [having] precious time to read.

In 1919, Robert Warrick, superintendent of the 17th Lighthouse District, reported in the Eugene, Oregon, *Morning Register* that "Tillamook Lighthouse is regarded as a desirable post and applications have come from distant points, some of them in Europe for assignment to work there."

There were many keepers who had long tenures on the Rock, refusing any transfer opportunities, thus showing their acceptance of and outright preference for it. Head keepers George H. Wheeler and Oswald "Ozzie" Allik served 21 and 20 years, respectively, while William Dahlgren completed 18. But perhaps the most famous keeper who was known for his devoted love of Tillamook Rock was Robert Gerlof. He faithfully served at Tilly for 25 years—from 1903 until 1928, at which point he was forced to leave, having reached the mandatory retirement age of 70.

In a 1928 *Oakland Tribune* interview, Gerlof remarked, "I do not want to leave my rock. I have no family. The sea is my friend. I do not want to go ashore." In fact, Gerlof did not like to take shore leave at all if he could help it. The Rock was truly his home.

During Gerlof's long residence there, many keepers came and went, but none were more memorable than the four young men he served with in 1920. Howard L. Hansen, Walter T. Lawrence, Orlo E. Hayward, and Raymond Bay became the "Fearless Foursome" of Tillamook Rock. They truly enjoyed their time there together, and in their off-duty hours chose photography as a hobby. They captured their daily activities through several hundred photographs that survive in family albums today.

The photographic legacy these four left offer further visual proof that mitigates the harsh reputation of the West Coast's most loathsome lighthouse assignment. It shows a human slice of normalcy and calmer times, along with camaraderie and high-spiritedness of youth in lighthouse service. It's not that the relentless storms raged any less. But whatever the hardships, they still maintained an upbeat attitude during their service there.

Even Jim Gibbs came around to a more favorable view of his time on the Rock, mixed with some obvious sentimentality. In summary, he wrote,

> Despite my early hatred of the Rock, I had gradually grown very fond of it and had learned a whole new side to life, that of being in a lonely place and yet finding fulfillment in the natural wonders of God's world. Where else could you be on a small islet with a perfect 360-degree view of the ocean in all of its varied moods, a place with a grandstand seat for the most beautiful sunrises and sunsets of any place in the world? Where else could you better see the endless string of sea birds flying south in the fall or watch the vast aquarium of mammals and fish cavorting about? I became hooked on lighthouses, and Old Tillamook, despite its scars, was the hallmark.

Maybe the real truth of the matter is that Terrible Tilly was not so horribly "terrible" as history has branded her—it just took the right person to appreciate all she had to offer.

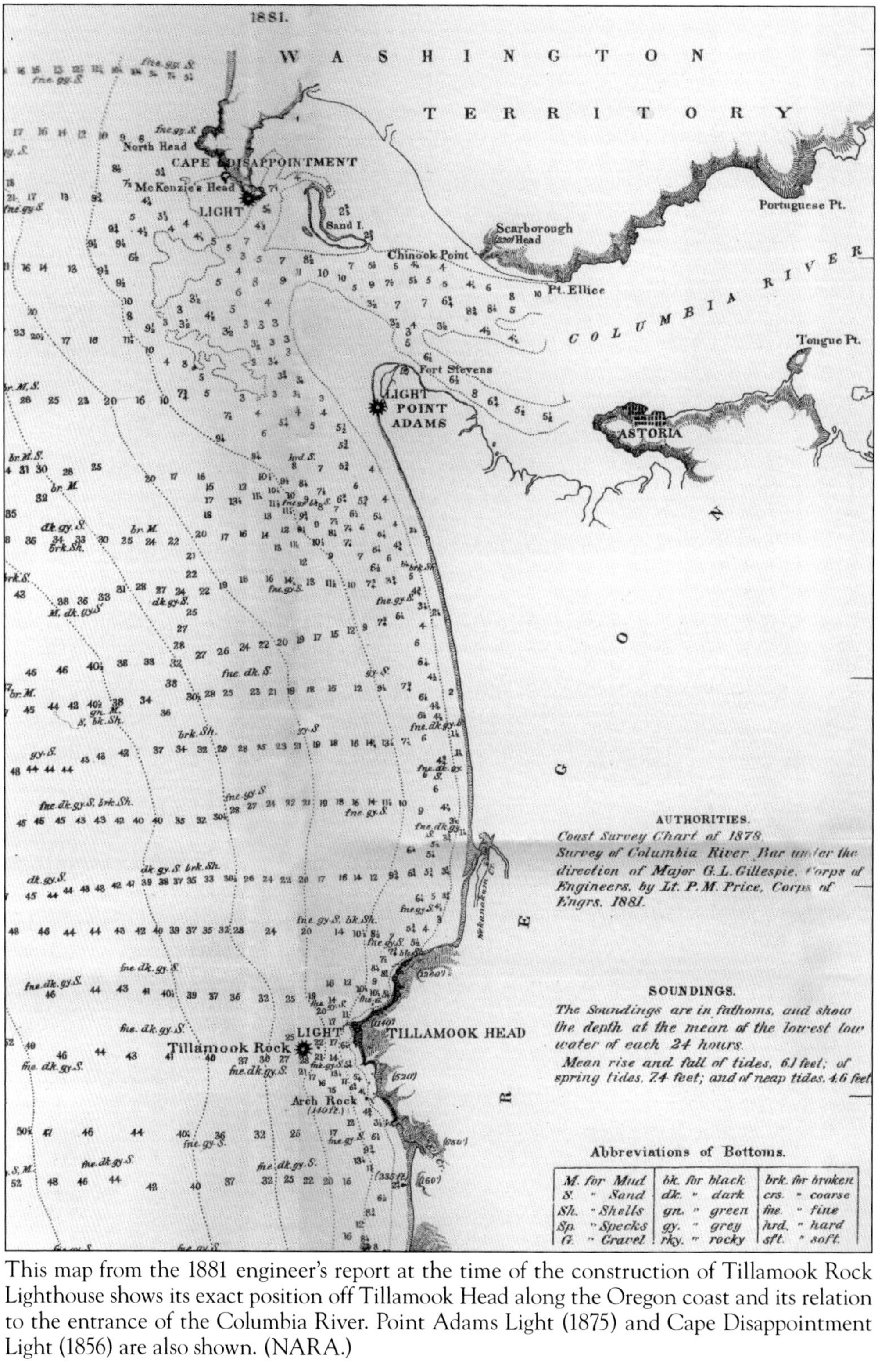

This map from the 1881 engineer's report at the time of the construction of Tillamook Rock Lighthouse shows its exact position off Tillamook Head along the Oregon coast and its relation to the entrance of the Columbia River. Point Adams Light (1875) and Cape Disappointment Light (1856) are also shown. (NARA.)

One

Rocky Start

Along the dangerous stretch of the Oregon coastline known as the "Graveyard of the Pacific" rises a one-acre basaltic rock located a mile offshore of Tillamook Head. Legend relates that the Clatsop Indians, who inhabited the region in the early 19th century, believed the rock to be inhabited by spirits who traversed from shore through the use of secret underwater tunnels. The Clatsops shunned the rock, fueled by their respectful awe and superstitious fear of consequence.

With increased settlement by white men and successive shipping growth, it was deemed a necessity to have a lighthouse along the hazardous approach to the Columbia River bar. At first, a light on top of Tillamook Head was considered, but because of the rugged terrain, frequent landslides, and low-lying fog, it was decided that a lower location offshore would be better.

In 1879, a survey party was sent out to Tillamook Rock to assess its potential. According to the *Annual Report of the United States Light-house Board*, "The light should be placed as low as possible, and the rock is its proper site. Though the execution of the work will be a task of labor and difficulty, accompanied by great expense, yet the benefit, which the commerce seeking the mouth of the Columbia River will derive from a light and fog-signal located there, will warrant all the labor and expense involved."

Plans were drawn and approved, but before construction could commence, detailed measurements for leveling the rock were required, and master mason John R. Trewavas was sent to do the job. Tragically, he fell at the rock's base while attempting to land and was sucked down in the undertow to his death.

Although this was seen as a bad omen, leveling crews were immediately dispatched under the direction of a newly appointed foreman, Alexander Ballantyne, Trewavas's partner. The crews eventually achieved their goal over the next six months, notwithstanding many harrowing experiences due to winter storms. Construction of the actual lighthouse began in June 1880 under the capable leadership of superintendent H.S. Wheeler, and 201 days later, on January 21, 1881, the light at Tillamook Rock Lighthouse was first displayed.

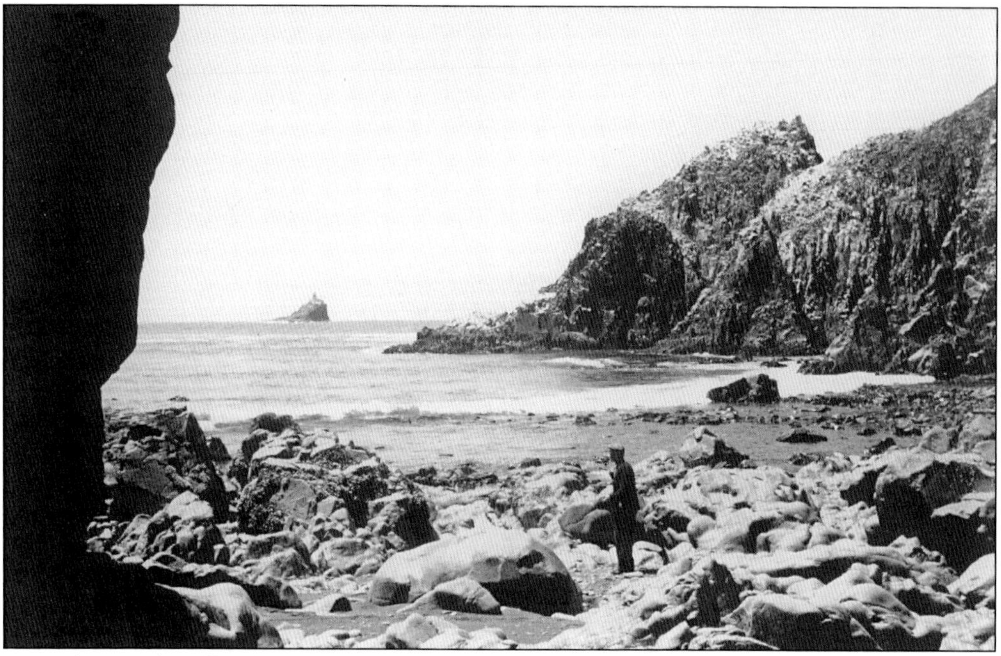

According to the official government deed drawn up in 1879, the State of Oregon conveyed the title of "an isolated basaltic rock, known as Tillamook Rock, standing in the Pacific Ocean, one mile approximately seaward of the most Westerly point of Tillamook Head, Clatsop County, Oregon, and 20 miles approximately south of the Columbia River bar." (LHD.)

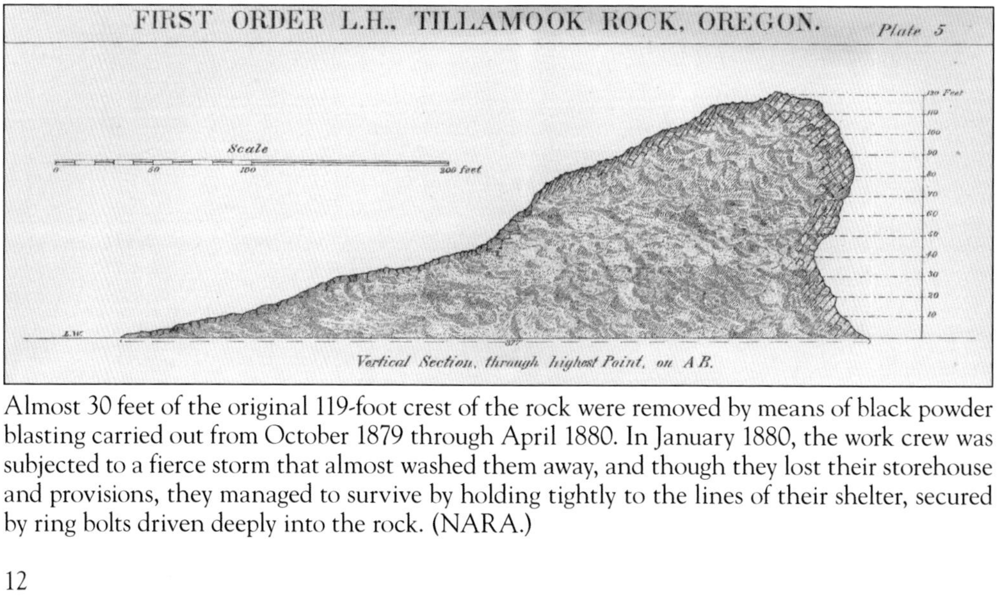

Almost 30 feet of the original 119-foot crest of the rock were removed by means of black powder blasting carried out from October 1879 through April 1880. In January 1880, the work crew was subjected to a fierce storm that almost washed them away, and though they lost their storehouse and provisions, they managed to survive by holding tightly to the lines of their shelter, secured by ring bolts driven deeply into the rock. (NARA.)

Brig. Gen. George Lewis Gillespie Jr., a highly decorated and revered Civil War veteran, served as chief engineer of the 13th Lighthouse District in 1879. He drew up the architectural plans and oversaw the construction of Tillamook Rock Lighthouse. Regarding the finished project, in his report to the US Lighthouse Board, Gillespie commended both foreman Alexander Ballantyne and superintendent H.S. Wheeler for meeting his expectations and "distinguishing themselves by diligent, energetic and intelligent service." (Library of Congress.)

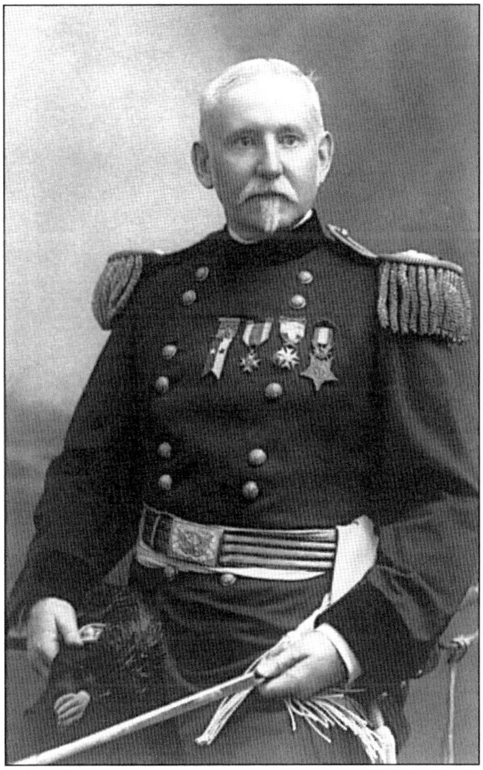

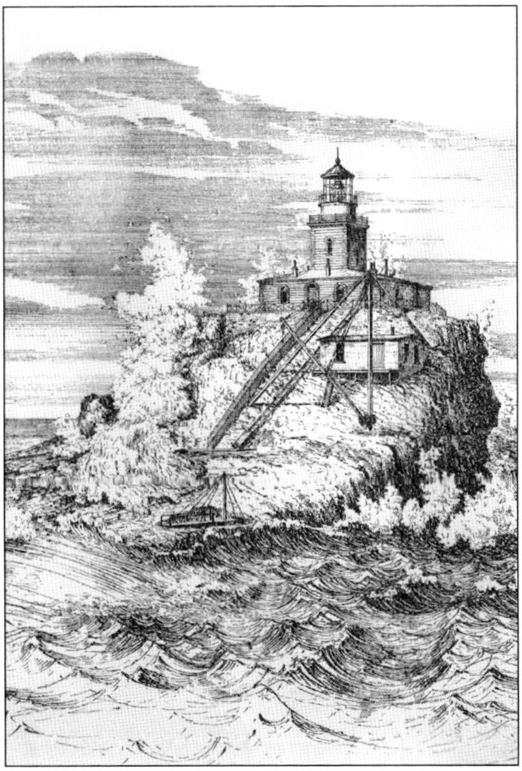

Gillespie wrote that landing on the rock was accomplished "by means of a derrick with a long swinging boom which reaches out very nearly over the deck of a steam tug lying at the moorings. At the outer end of the boom is suspended a car which accommodates two persons. This car is hoisted or lowered by hand or steam power." Notice the small swing bridge at the base of the rock that did not survive past the first few years of storms. (NARA.)

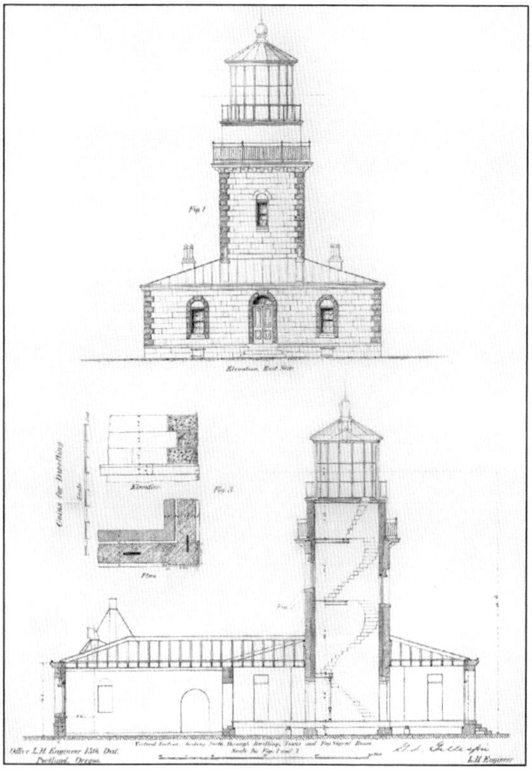

The plans called for a structure with two-foot-thick walls and a tower rising from the roof of the keeper's dwelling reaching 48 feet in height from the rock to the focal plane of the lens. The tower was 16 feet in diameter, constructed of stone lined with brick, and contained an iron stairway that passed through four landings to the lantern deck. The iron lantern supported a dome roof covered in sheet copper. (NARA.)

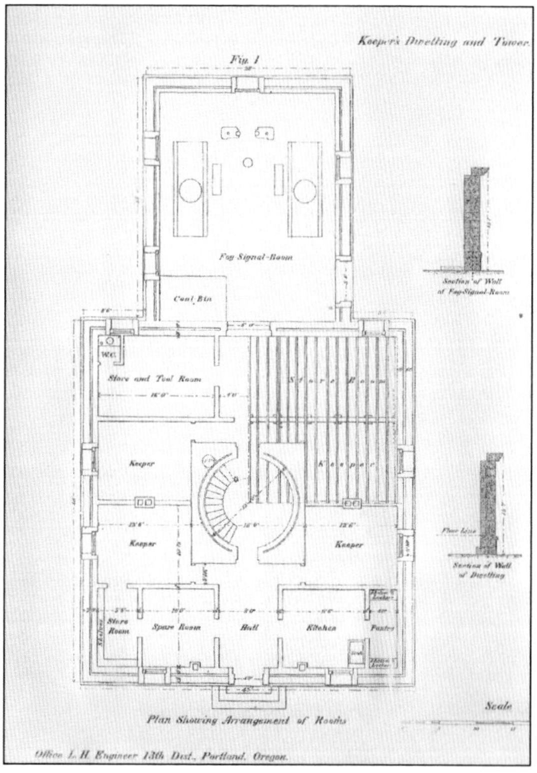

The 45-by-48-foot keeper dwelling was divided into eight large room spaces with some smaller storage areas. Room allocations were for lighthouse supply storage, pantries, a kitchen, four keeper bedrooms, and a spare room used as an office. Outbuildings included a fog-signal room attached to the west end of the dwelling, a small brick storehouse for oil storage, a winch house for the hoisting engine, a water closet, and a 13,000-gallon cistern to collect rainwater from the roof. (NARA.)

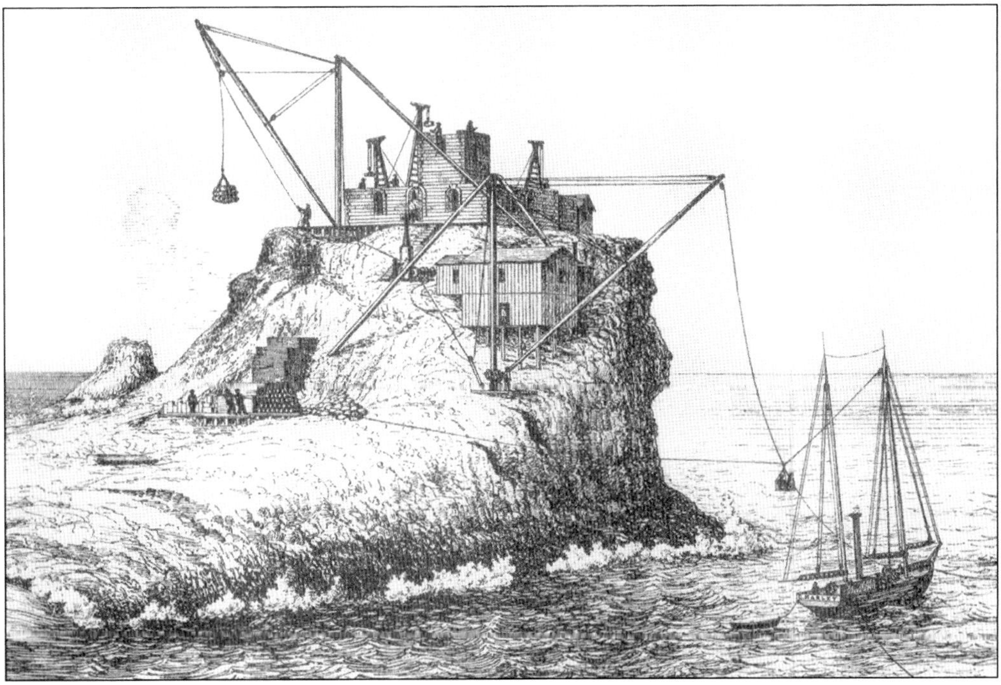

The ashlar stone used to build the lighthouse was quarried from Mount Tabor, six miles east of Portland. The revenue cutter *Thomas Corwin*, steam tug *Mary Taylor*, wrecking vessel *George Harley*, schooner *Emily Stephens*, and lighthouse tender *Shubrick* were all employed in transporting materials during construction. It was 575 days from when the rock was first examined for suitability to the time the light was first displayed on January 21, 1881. (NARA.)

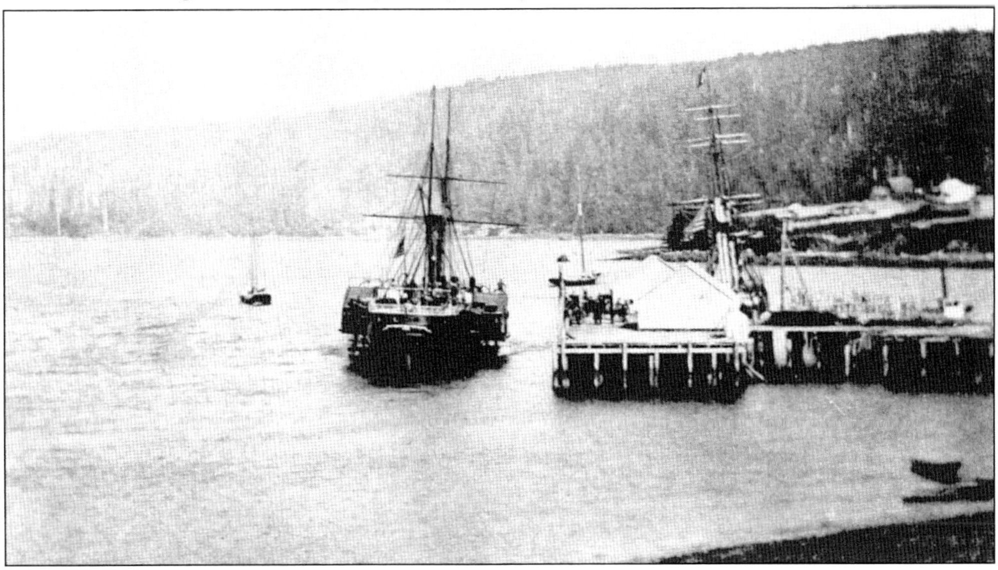

This very early photograph shows the lighthouse tender *Shubrick* at Flavel's dock in Astoria, Oregon, in the 1860s. It is an interesting view of the stern, showing the wide paddle boxes on either side that housed the paddle wheels. The *Shubrick*, commissioned in 1857, was the first lighthouse tender on the Pacific coast and was used to transport stone for the construction of Tillamook Rock Lighthouse in 1880. (CRMM.)

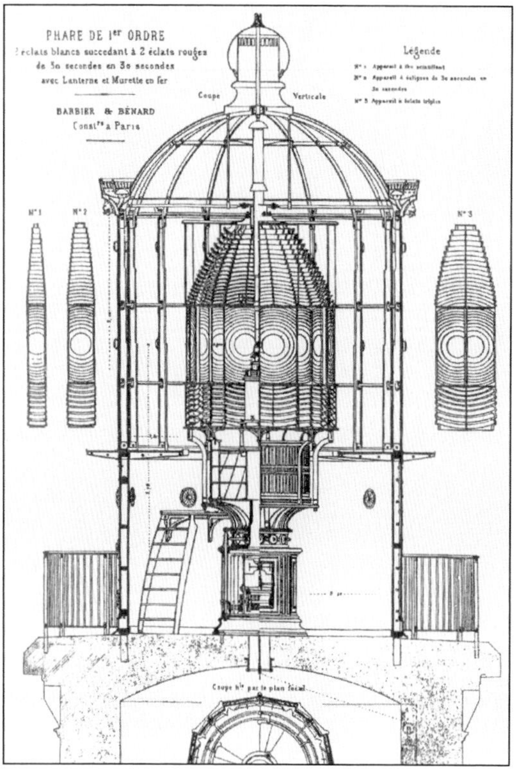

This page from an 1894–1901 Barbier and Bernard catalog shows a very similar style and assembly to the Henry-Lapaute lens that was ordered for Tillamook Rock Lighthouse. The first order flashing Fresnel lens had 24 bulls-eye dioptric lens panels, 18 upper catadioptric prisms, and eight lower catadioptric prisms that rotated on a clockwork pedestal. Fully assembled on its pedestal base, the lens was 12 feet in height. (USLHS.)

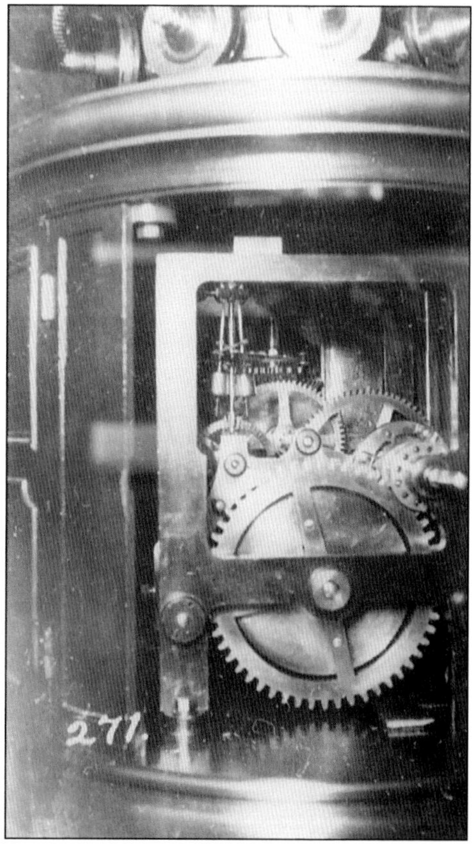

The cast-iron lens pedestal base utilized clockwork gearing and a 500-pound weight as part of the winding apparatus for rotation. The revolving cord fed down through the watch room floor to a drift tube running down the length of the tower. After being fully wound, the clockwork rotated the lens for a little over two hours. (CRMM.)

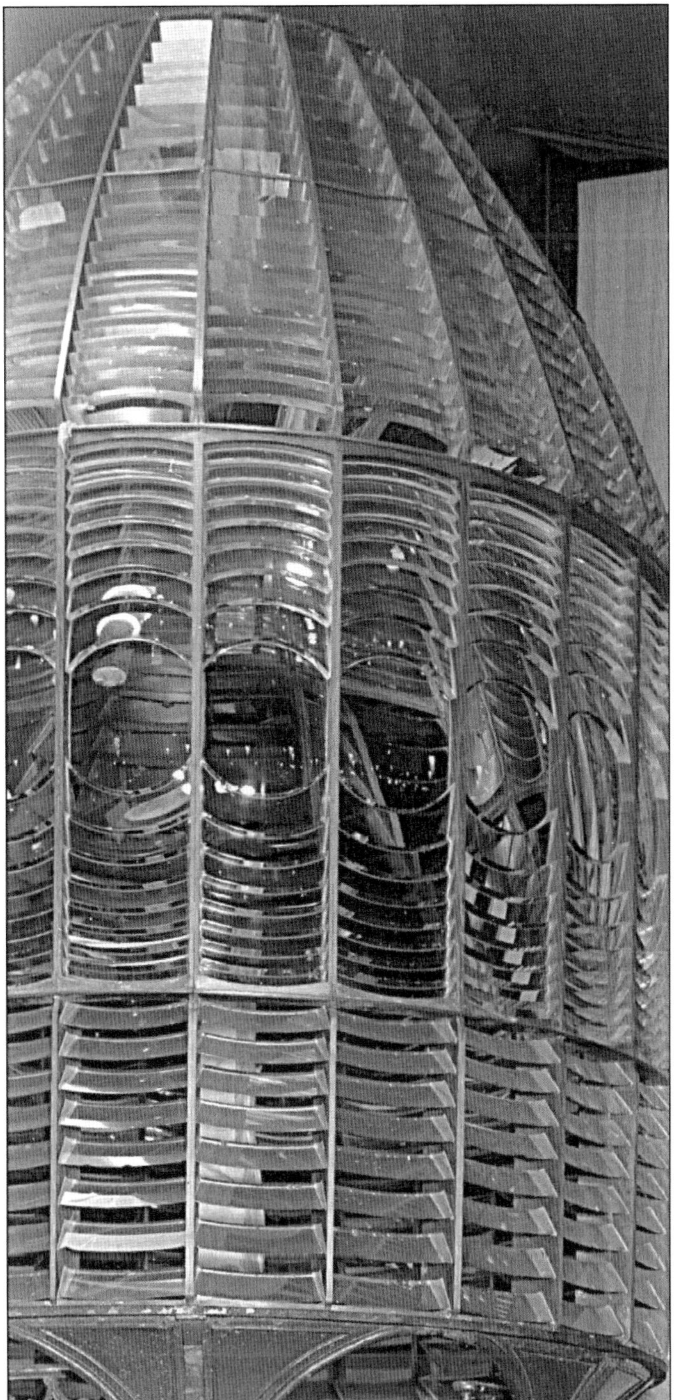

The first order Fresnel lens had a focal plane of 133 feet above sea level that could be seen for approximately 18 nautical miles. The signature was a single white flash every five seconds, with one complete revolution of the lens taking place every two minutes. A Funk's hydraulic float lamp was the illuminant initially used in 1881. (CRMM.)

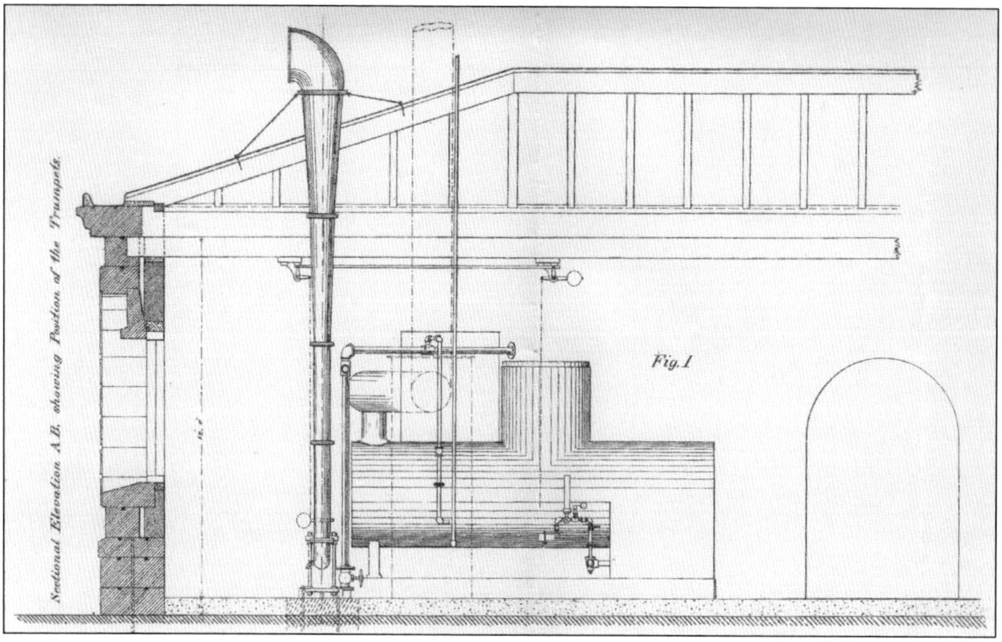

The 28-by-32-foot fog-signal room housed two A. and F. Brown's steam siren foghorns that required water from three iron cylindrical tanks located outside the dwelling to run them. The blast of the siren was five seconds long at 90-second intervals. (NARA.)

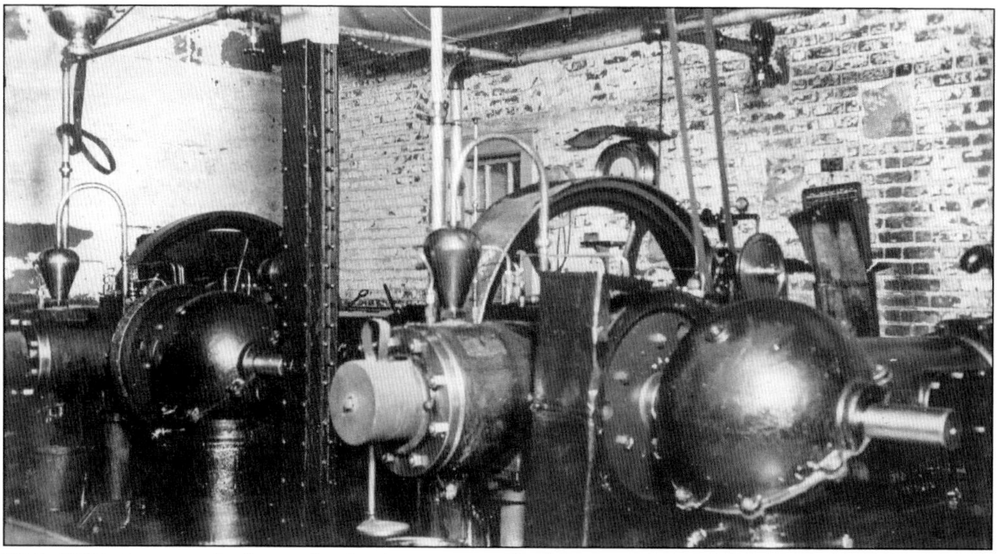

This 1920 photograph shows the duplicate sets of foghorn engine and compressor assembly used at that time. There were many contentions over the years between keepers about running the foghorn. First assistant Teofil Milkowski wrote a letter to the district superintendent in 1924 to complain about another keeper not turning it on when necessary, which resulted in a fistfight. Milkowski wrote, "I turned around and he grabbed me so we went at it and I gave him plenty." It was not easy for keepers to be in such cramped quarters with a loud foghorn only a few feet away. (BB.)

The two units were run on alternating days so there would always be a functioning backup in case one failed. That meant the foghorn trumpets were alternated daily as well, with the non-used trumpet being capped off when not in operation to keep out rocks, salt spray, and debris. (CRMM.)

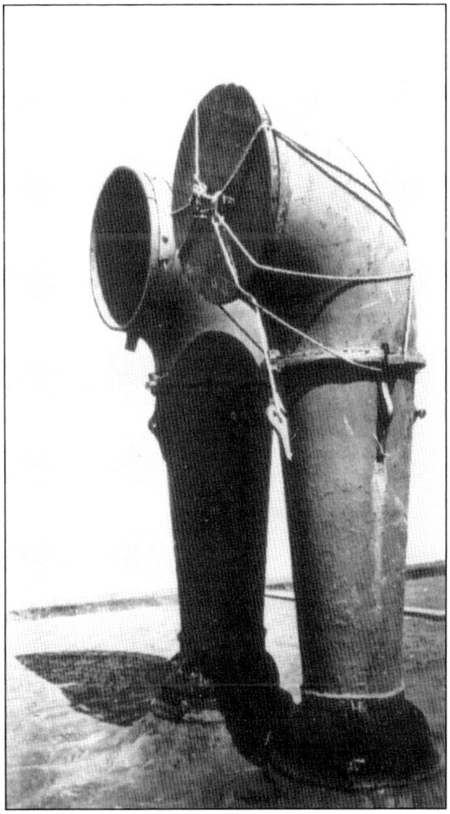

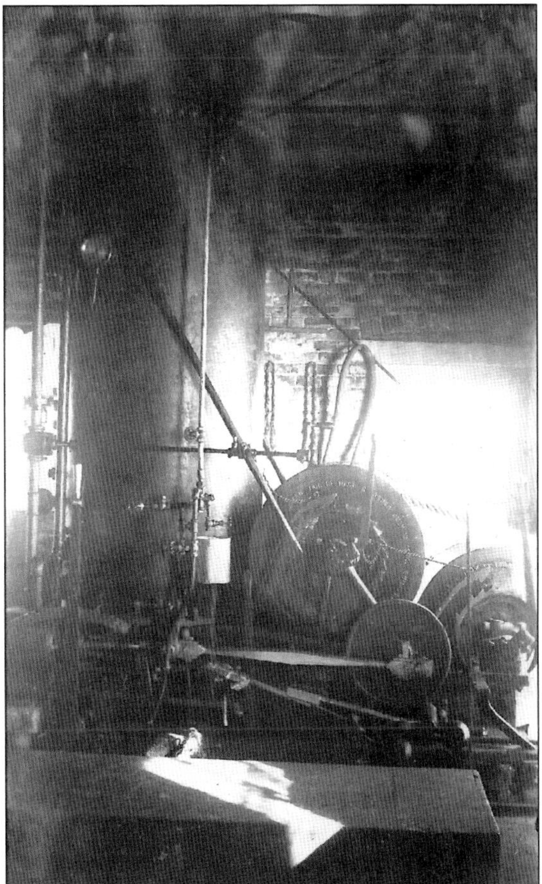

This rare photograph, also taken in 1920, shows Tillamook Rock's winch engine and assembly that was used to operate the derrick and boom. It was located in the winch house about a third of the way down the northeast side of the Rock, where the keeper who operated it could see both the cargo boat and landing platform clearly. There are many tales of mishaps in operating the boom with dunking people in the basket—both unintentional and otherwise. (BB.)

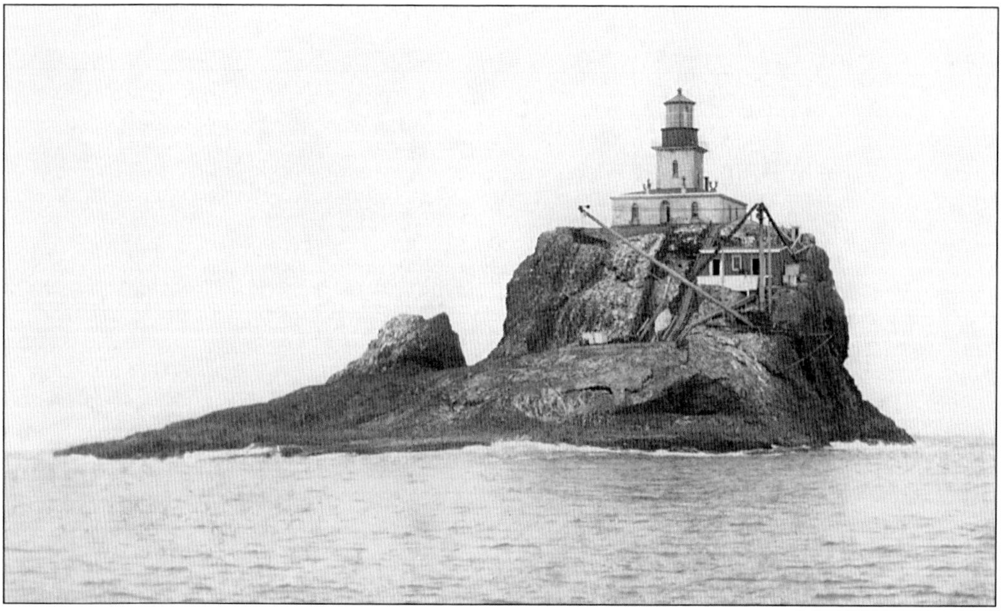

This c. 1883 photograph taken by I.G. Davidson is the earliest known view of the completed Tillamook Rock Lighthouse. The twisted chimney vent tops, darkly painted winch house with white trim, and lack of a second-story attic help date the photograph. It is also interesting to compare this photograph with later ones showing how much of the rock on the left front-facing side of the foundation of the lighthouse was broken off by storms over the ensuing decades. (LHD.)

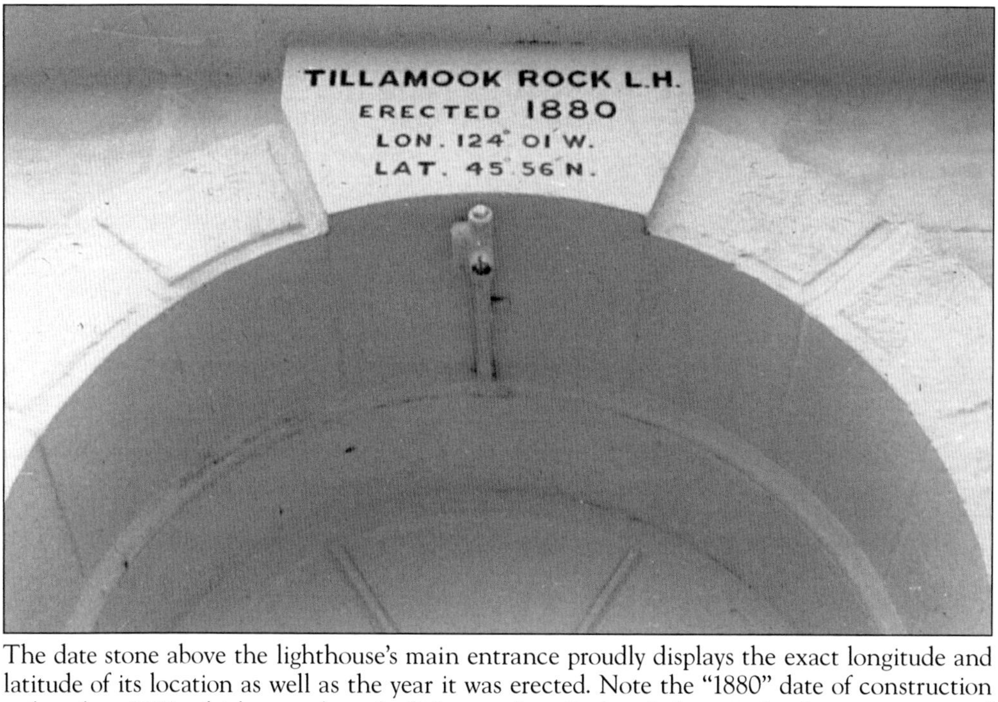

The date stone above the lighthouse's main entrance proudly displays the exact longitude and latitude of its location as well as the year it was erected. Note the "1880" date of construction rather than 1881, which was when the light was first displayed. Amazingly, this stone is one of the few things that remain totally intact in good condition at the lighthouse today. It is unknown if it was ever replaced. (JGC.)

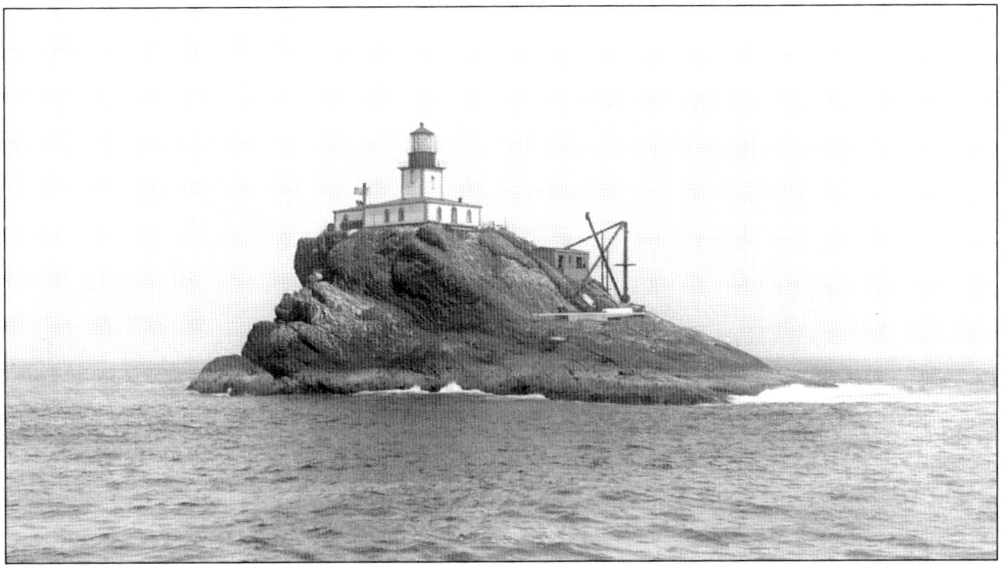

In December 1886, during a huge storm, heavy seas crushed sections of the roofs on the fog-signal room and dwelling. The galvanized-iron vent tops from two chimneys were broken off, and some of the concrete and brick parapet on the southeast corner of the foundation was washed away. A new partial roof was put on in 1887, as is clearly shown in this 1891 S.B. Crow photograph. Note the totally painted winch house. (Library of Congress.)

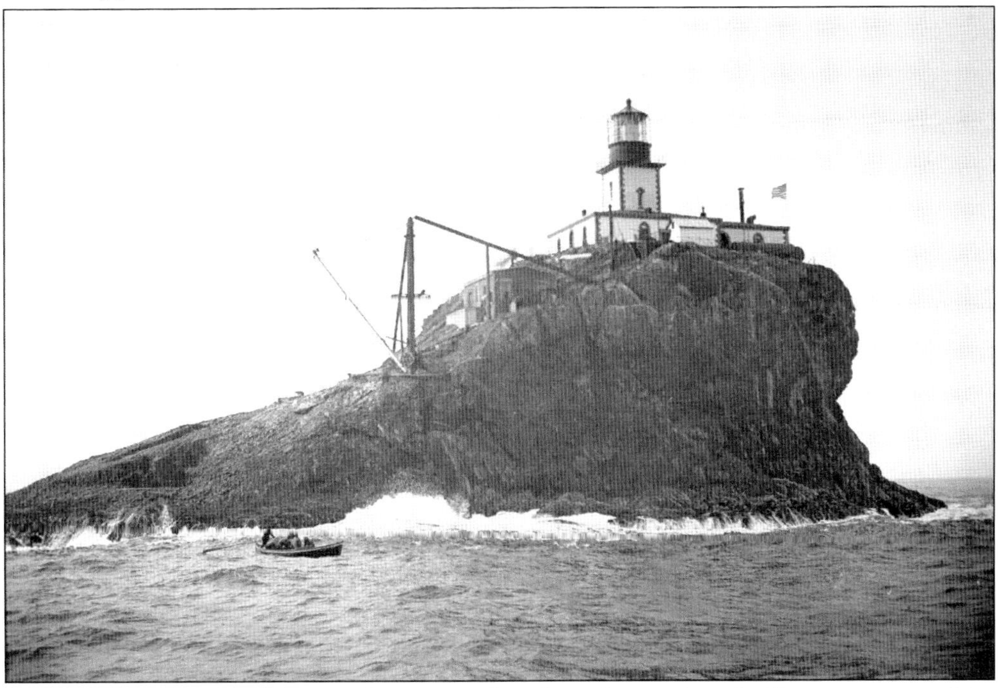

This pre-1898 photograph by J.H. Bratt was taken from the north and offers nice views of the small white oil house as well as the boom wheel at the base of the derrick. A close look reveals a second small derrick mast that is situated near the northeast corner of the lighthouse and rises barely above the roofline. The small boom was attached to hold a telegraph cable line away from the rock to avoid damage. (CCHS.)

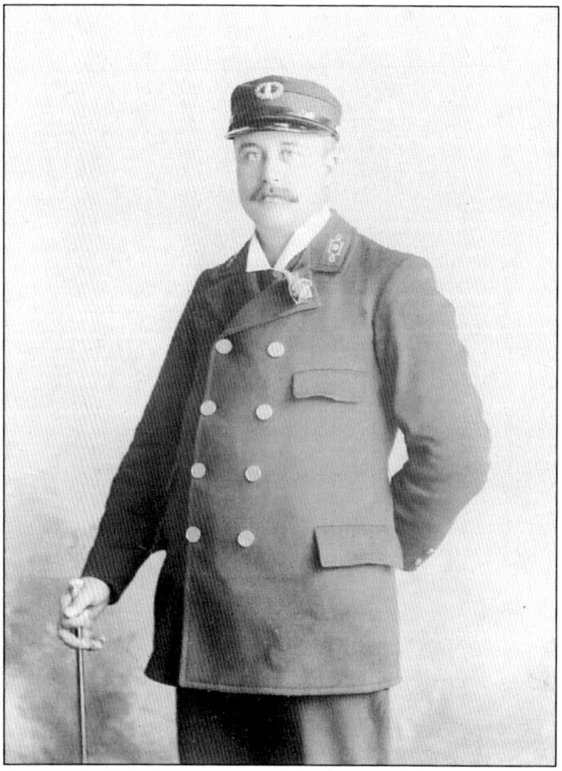

This portrait, thought to be William T. Langlois (b. 1874), would have been taken sometime between 1896 and 1899, when he served as a second assistant at Tillamook Rock Lighthouse, as shown by the number two on his lapel insignia. He later returned to serve for seven years as head keeper from 1903 to 1910. His father was famous keeper James S. Langlois of Cape Blanco Lighthouse who served there continuously for 42 years. (CRMM.)

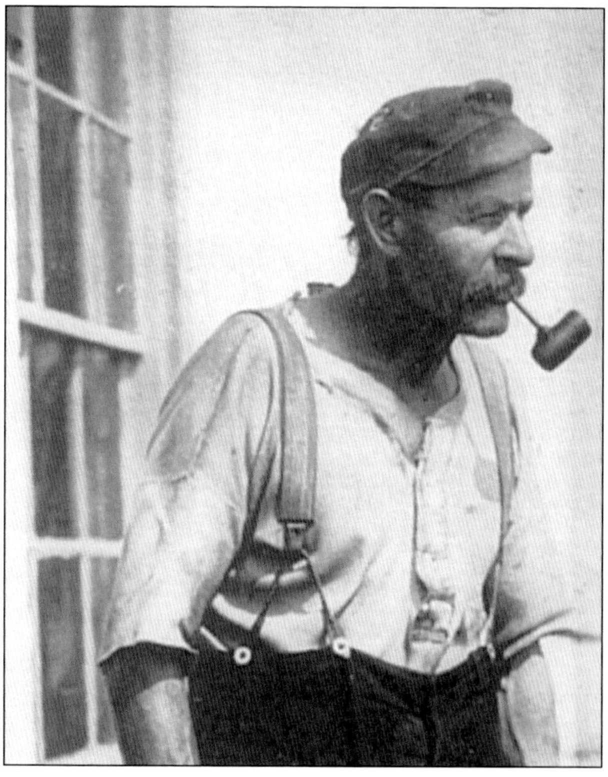

This is one of only two known photographs of Robert Gerlof (b. 1860), who was the most famous keeper of Tillamook Rock. He was on the Columbia River Light Vessel No. 50 and the tender *Columbine* before transferring to the Rock in 1903; there he stayed until his forced retirement in 1928, making him the longest-serving keeper. He had a body bag sewn so he could be dropped off the west end of the Rock to be near it when he died, but his request was denied. (Webb Research Group, Publishers.)

Two

Halcyon Days

During his exceptionally long 25 years of service on the Rock, keeper Robert Gerlof later reminisced that his best time was in 1920, when he served with four young men who made life thoroughly pleasant and entertaining. There were still the fierce storms and isolation, but first assistant Howard L. Hansen, age 19; second assistant Walter T. Lawrence, age 23; third assistant Orlo E. Hayward, age 18; and assistant Raymond Bay, age 18, truly made it a hallmark year in the history of Tillamook Rock Lighthouse.

Perhaps it was so much more enjoyable because the four were friends and family before they ever served together. Lawrence and Bay were half-brothers. Bay and Hansen had been raised together in part at Heceta Head Lighthouse, as their fathers were stationed there along with Hayward's father, who was serving at the same time. Orlo Hayward even lied about his age to get onto the Rock with the other three. They had to be 18 to serve; at the time of Hayward's enlistment, he was only 17, but he clearly did not want to be left behind.

Having been around lighthouse life and raised as lighthouse kids, they all seemed indifferent to the negative aspects of the confinement and isolation on the Rock. While serving there, the four found plenty of diversions to keep them occupied outside of the normal expected light-tending routine. Photography was the most prominent of these pastimes. They set up a developing room inside the lighthouse, purchased new cameras, and spent a lot of time experimenting with both photographic aesthetics and developing techniques of 1920s-era photography.

The "Terrible Tilly Photograph Studio" was in high production mode in 1920, and any keeper who had shore leave was to purchase and shoot as many rolls of film as he could, then bring them back to the lighthouse to develop. Additionally, several hundred photographs of life on Tillamook Rock during this time were also captured in the best tradition of vernacular photography. It is through them that we see the calmer, more pleasurable side of life on Tillamook Rock, as shown in this chapter.

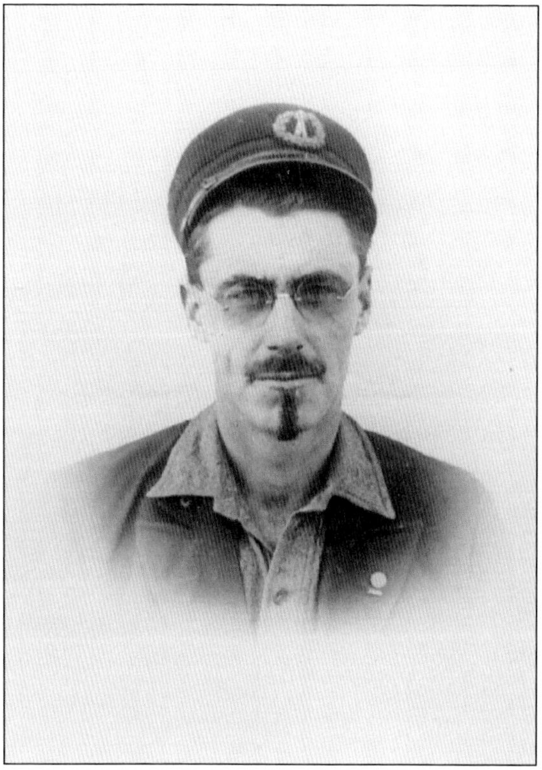

Walter Tillman Lawrence (b. 1896), stepson of Heceta Head Lighthouse keeper Robert Bay, served at Tillamook Rock from 1919 to 1921. He then transferred to Umpqua River Light until 1924, after which he left lighthouse service to work with the fire and water departments in Newport, and then went on to Portland to work as a naval shipyard guard. He remained an avid photographer, at times doing work for other people up through the 1940s. (CRMM.)

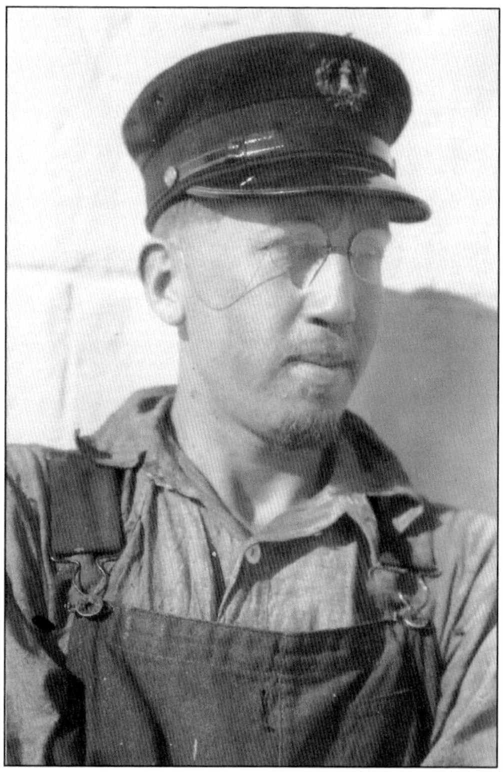

Howard L. Hansen (b. 1901), son of Heceta Head keeper Olaf L. Hansen, was only in lighthouse service for the two years he was at Tillamook Rock from 1919 to 1921. He went on to become a crab fisherman in Empire, Oregon. Tragically, he died in a boating mishap on the Coquille River bar in 1936. He was married with three children at the time. (JHW.)

Orlo Hayward (b. 1902), son of Heceta Head keeper Eugene O. Hayward, had an amazing lighthouse career after serving at Tillamook Rock from 1920 to 1921. He was transferred ten times to eight different lighthouses in Oregon and Washington over the next 25 years. His longest stint was at Cape Blanco Lighthouse from 1933 to 1944. (JHW.)

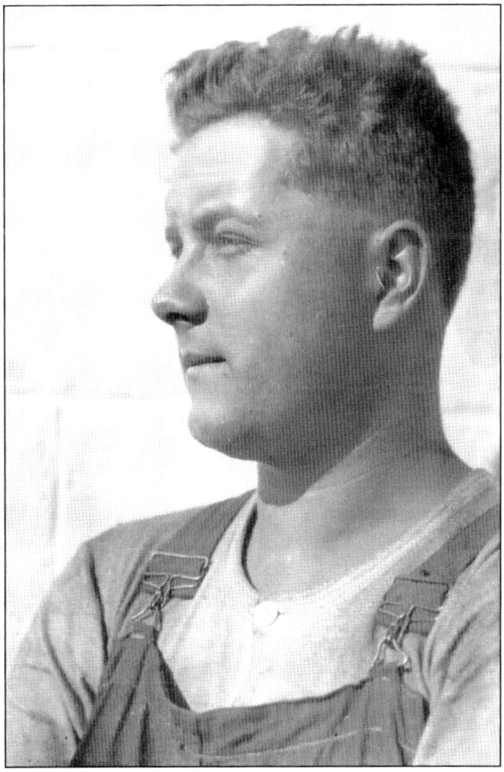

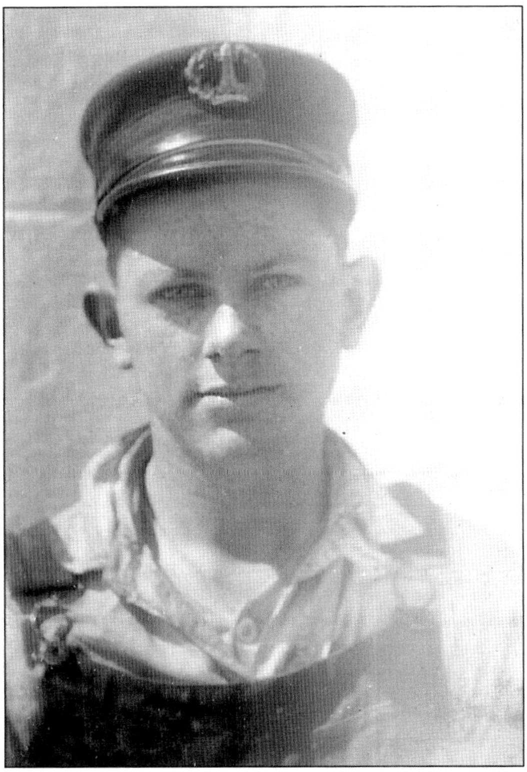

Raymond Bay, son of Heceta Head keeper Robert Bay, was stationed at Tillamook Rock from 1920 to 1921, after which he transferred to Cape Blanco Lighthouse until at least 1924. He then left lighthouse service and is shown in the 1940 census as living with his family at the Point Arguello Coast Guard station in California and working in the fishing industry. He went on to serve as a ferryboat captain in Eureka, California, for many years. (JHW.)

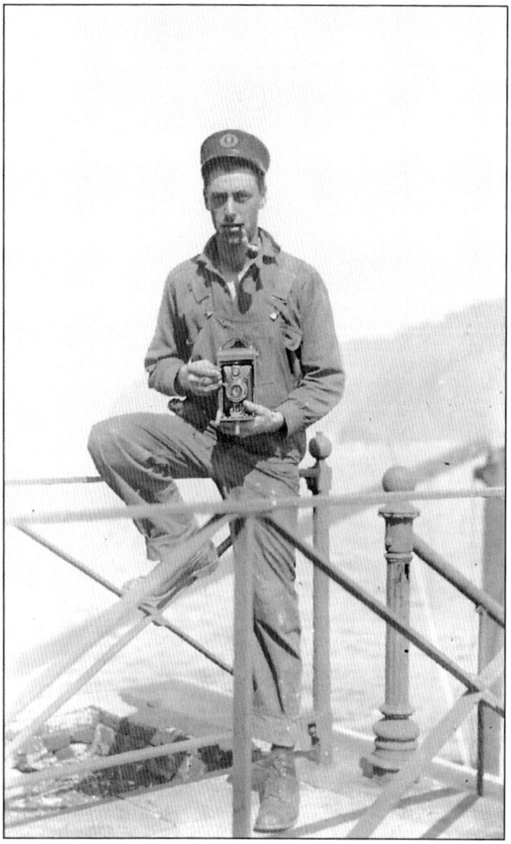

Of the four keepers, Walter T. Lawrence was the most interested in the photographic medium. He was continually experimenting with developing processes, and many of his prints show enhancements in creating the negatives as well as the prints. It was easy to see why the interest turned into something professional for him in later years. (JHW.)

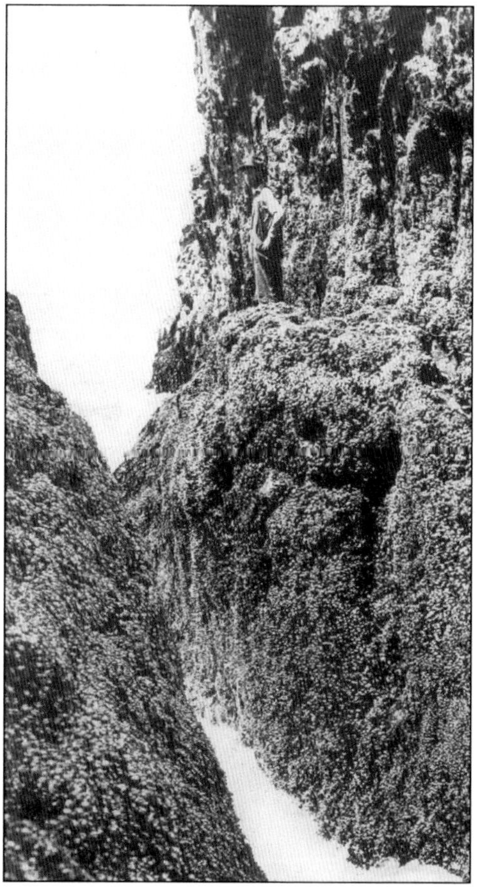

Walter T. Lawrence loved to alter the textural appearance and tonal values of the rock surfaces in the crevice on the south side of the lighthouse. He made them look almost alive in the lower part of this photograph below the ledge where keeper Howard Hansen is standing. Lawrence experimented with the manipulation of contrast and the principles of sensitometry, which later became the "zone system," as codified by famous photographer Ansel Adams in the 1940s. (BB.)

Walter T. Lawrence's more aesthetic photographs dealt with water and the reflection of light upon the rippling surfaces at different times. In the image at right, there is a double reflection of the sunlight on the horizon as well as a foreground reflection on the ripples, with the division being caused by the dark cloud cover in between. This is the only photograph in the albums cropped into a circular shape and numbered, showing it was probably an experiment of some kind. This image also features a sample of his mounting strips and calligraphic script on an album page. This view was most likely off the western walkway or perhaps from the fog-signal room roof, where several other images were taken. The below photograph shows another reflective view of the full moon breaking through a layer of dark clouds across the horizon off Tillamook Rock. (Both, BB.)

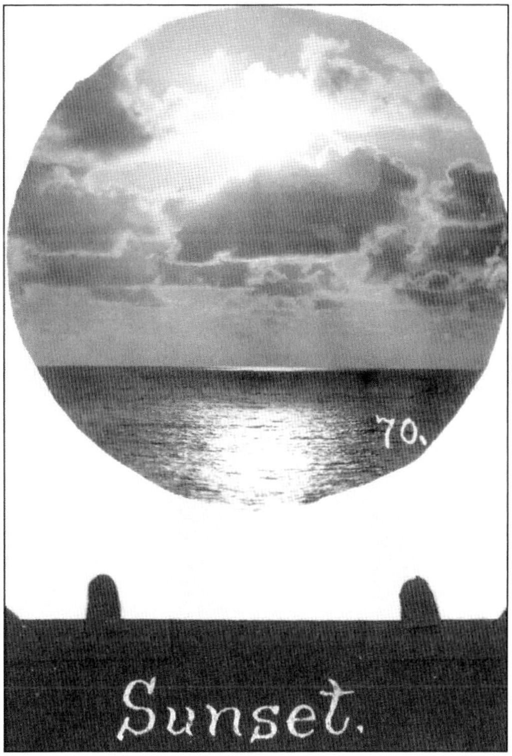

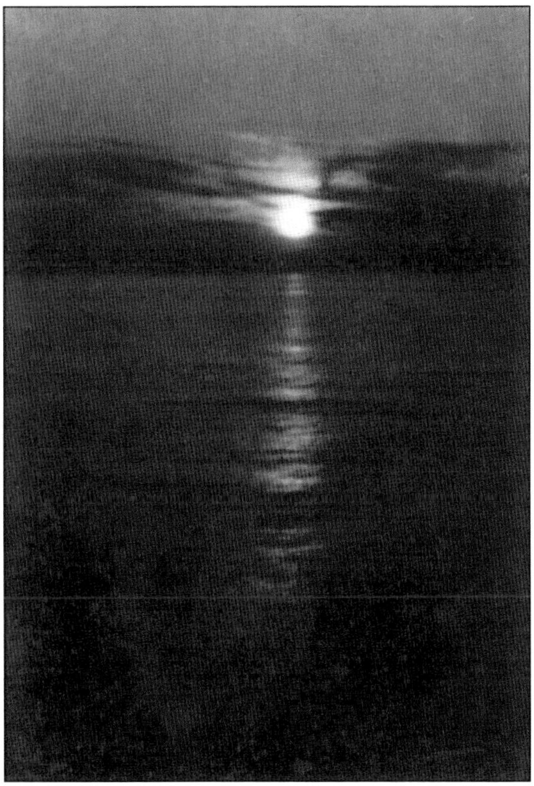

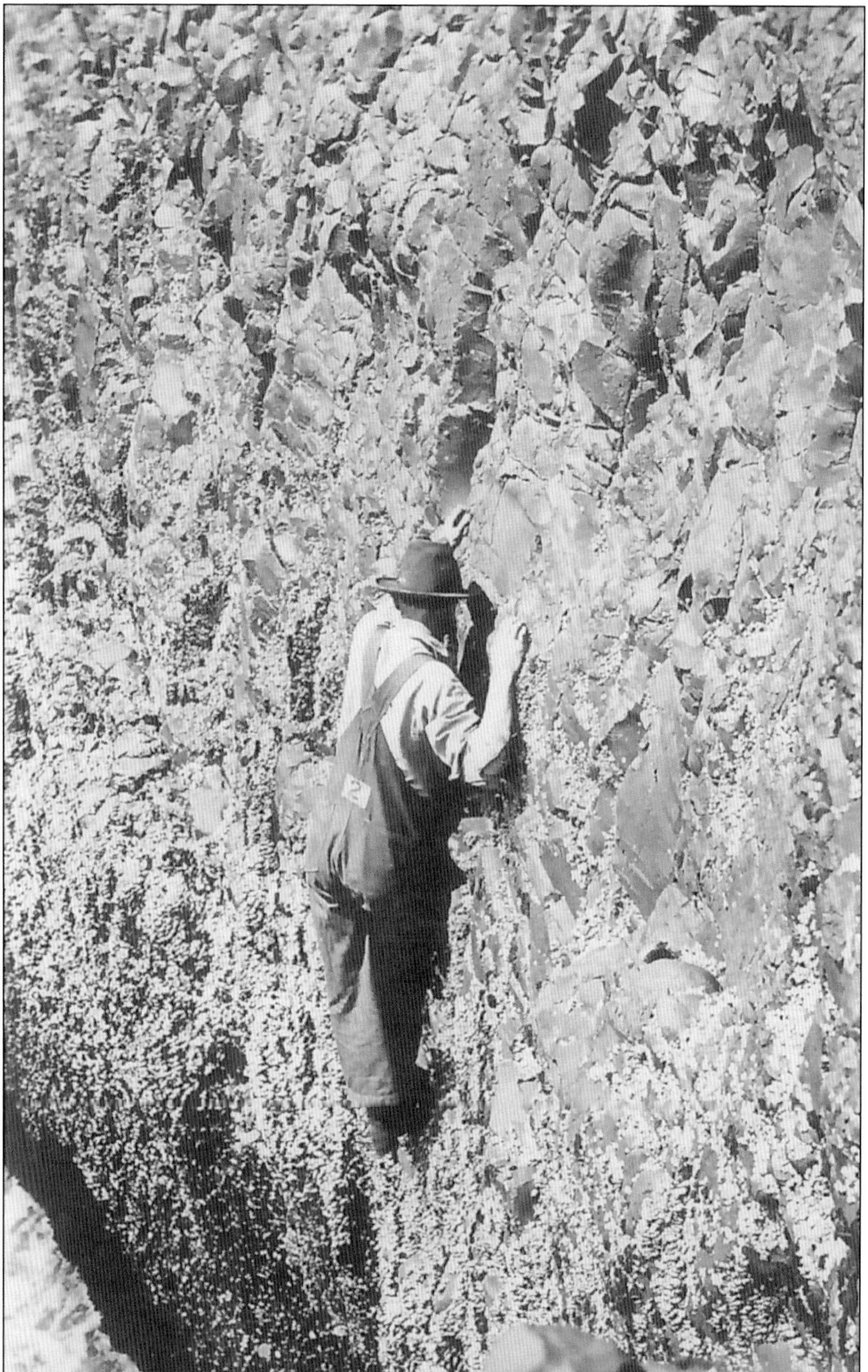

It appears Walter T. Lawrence did some "dodging and burning" of the image while creating this print of the crevice. The rocks gradually change in contrast and realism from the top of the photograph to the bottom near the water. Keeper Howard L. Hansen clings to the vertical rock face by his fingertips and toes as he moves across the crevice without any safety backups. (JHW.)

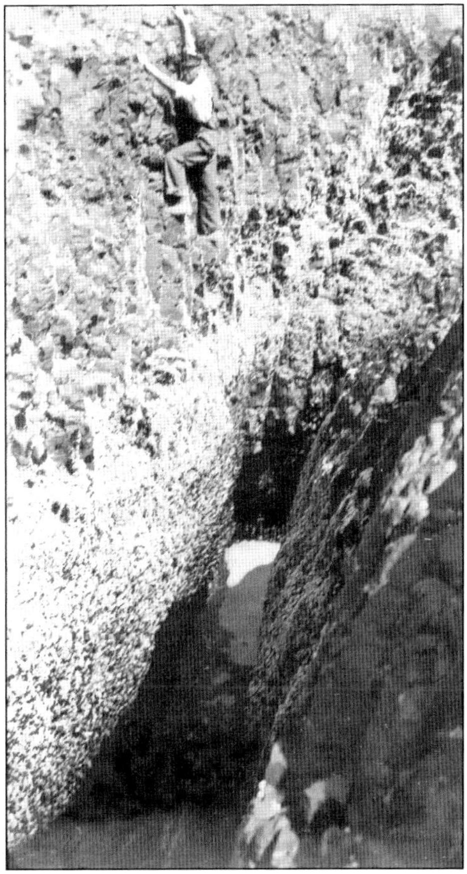

In these two photographs, Walter T. Lawrence takes a turn climbing through the crevice to the outer entrance. It is incredible that these keepers would climb such a sheer face of rock just for fun with no harnesses or safety devices, particularly when they knew how easily the smaller rocks could become dislodged. They seemed to take delight in one-upping each other in the dangerous locations they chose for their photographic essays, such as the very top of the derrick or the top of the lighthouse tower. It is almost miraculous that none of them ever had an accident through all their picture-taking adventures. (Both, BB.)

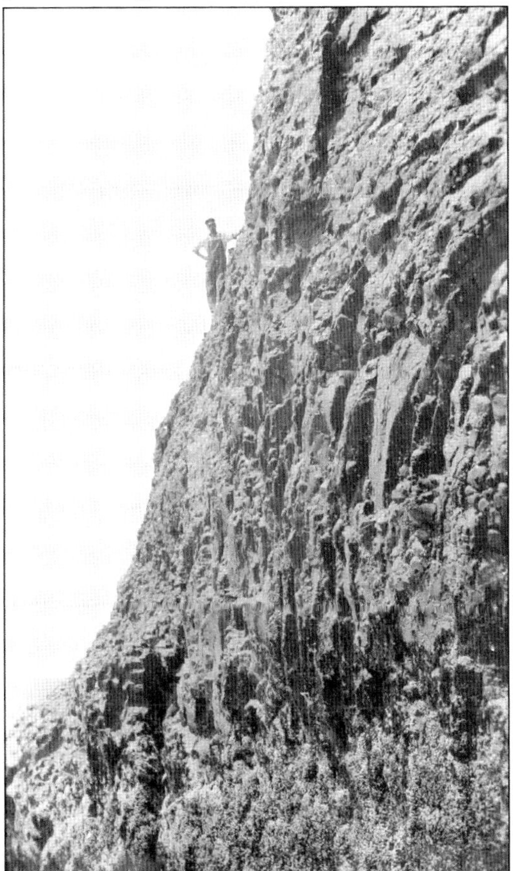

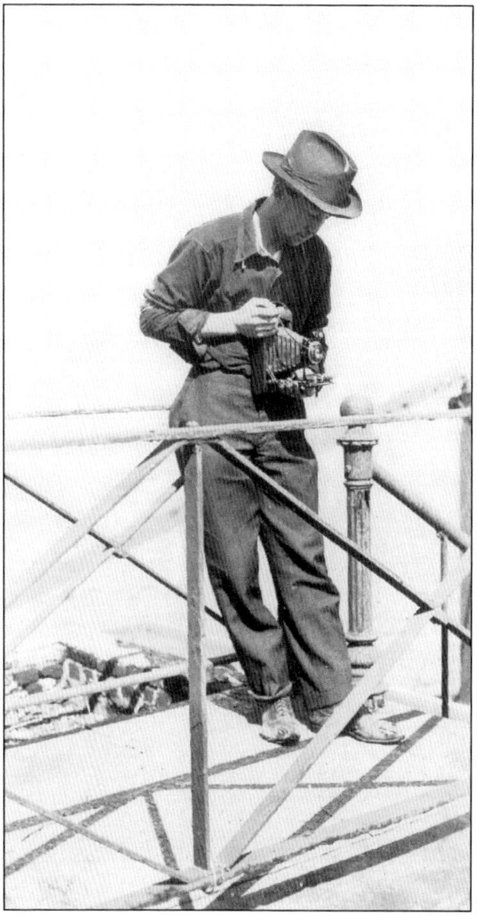

Keeper Howard L. Hansen is holding a slightly different model of the folding Kodak No. 2 Brownie camera than that of Walter T. Lawrence. Designed as a camera for the masses, the Brownie line was affordable and easy to operate, making photography a fun pastime for many people in the early 20th century. (BB.)

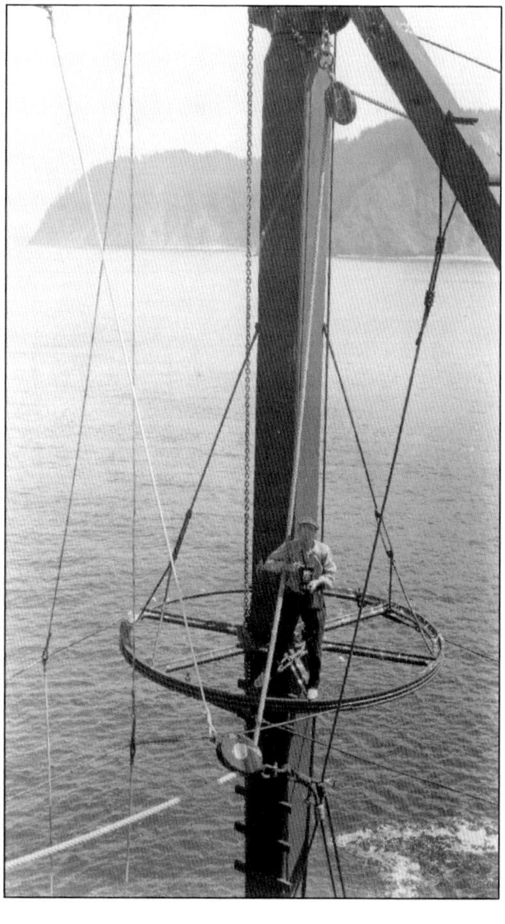

The derrick mast appeared to be a favorite spot for the keepers to take photographs. There are many images in the albums of them climbing, sitting, standing, dancing, and working on different parts of the derrick assembly. Here, keepers Hansen and Lawrence are probably taking photographs of each other, with Hansen on the mast wheel and Lawrence on the roof of the dwelling, judging by the angle of the view. Notice the detail and rigging of the derrick components that surround him on his perch. (CGNW.)

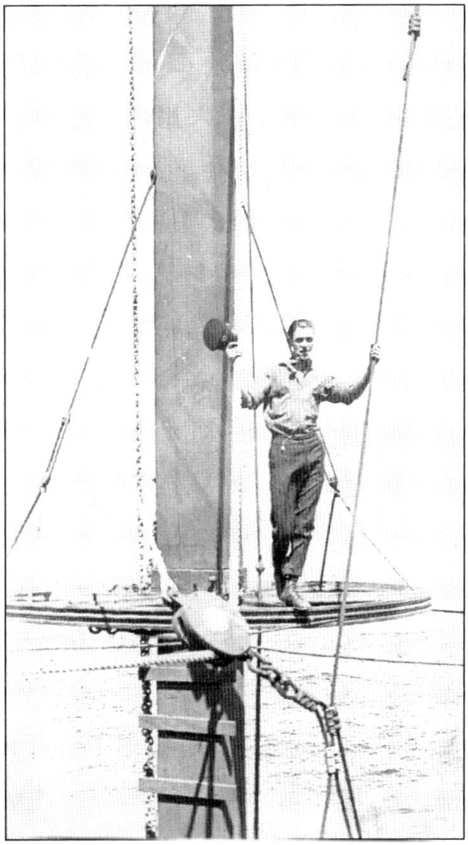

The next few photographs are part of a series in which Walter T. Lawrence goes derrick-climbing. The first one shows him in one of his classic poses with his hat off and smoking his pipe as he stands on the derrick wheel. The second image shows him at the very top, hat off again. He would have come across the stiff derrick leg that runs back toward the winch house rather than climbing up the post from the wheel. One misstep here would have meant the demise of the photographic subject and one less keeper for Tillamook Rock! (Both, BB.)

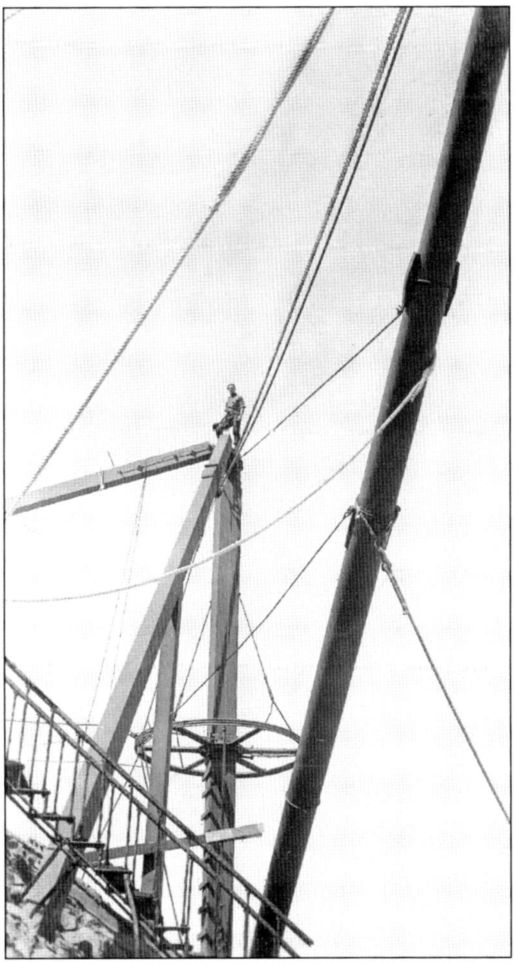

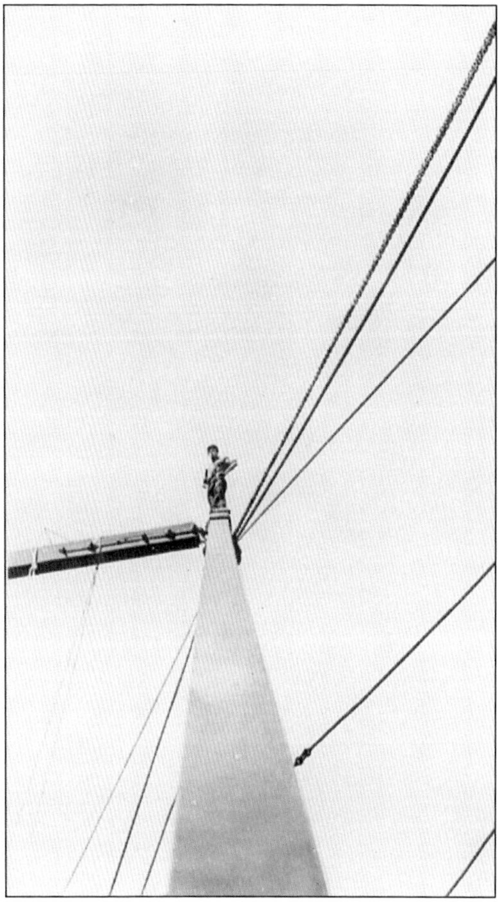

These two photographs utilize interesting perspective in showing the views from both ends of the derrick mast: Howard L. Hansen is shooting up to where Walter T. Lawrence is at the very top, and Lawrence is shooting down through the derrick wheel toward the ocean below. It was highly unlikely that head keeper Robert Gerlof was on the Rock the day these were taken. He certainly would have been concerned over safely issues. In fact, in all the hundreds of photographs that exist of the four young keepers, there is not one of Gerlof. He was known to avoid being photographed and once, when he thought a photographer visiting the Rock had taken his picture unawares, he purportedly dropped the basket onto the rocks in an effort to smash the camera. Since all four young keepers appear in multiple images taken on the same day, that would necessarily make Gerlof the fifth keeper on liberty in the work rotation. (Left, CRMM; below, BB.)

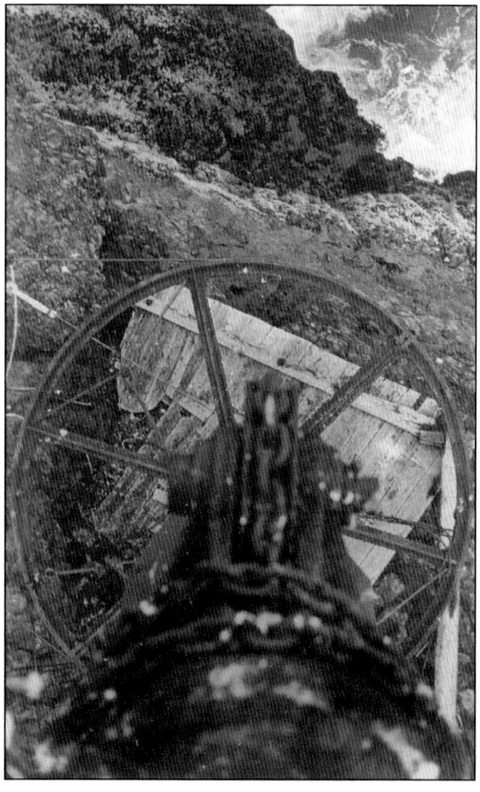

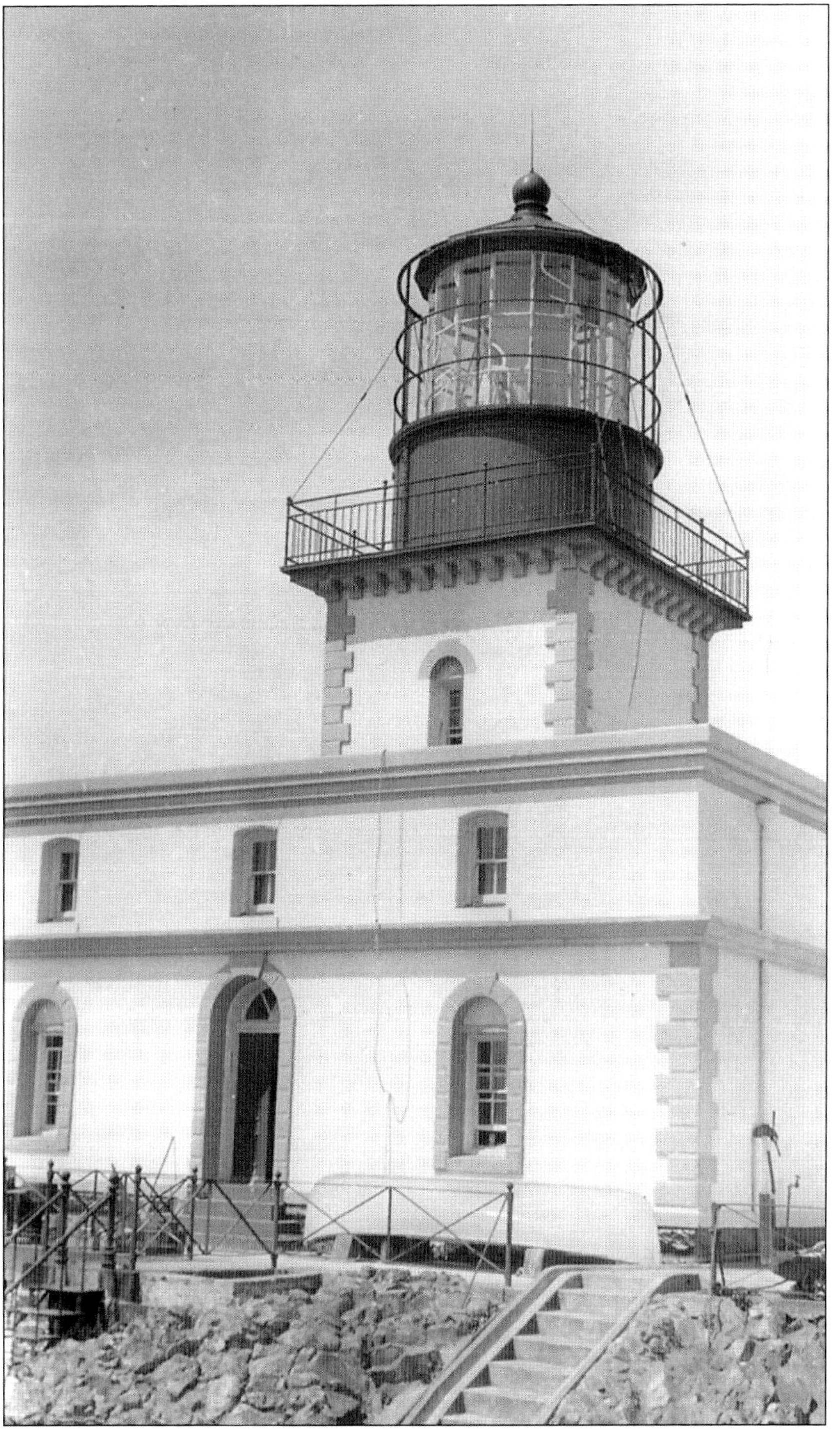

The one benefit of being at the very top of the 45-foot derrick mast was the eye-level view of the lighthouse. This image is the only one showing this close-up vantage point of the east main entrance to the lighthouse in a crisp, clear photograph. The interior astragals are even visible inside the lantern dome. (LHD.)

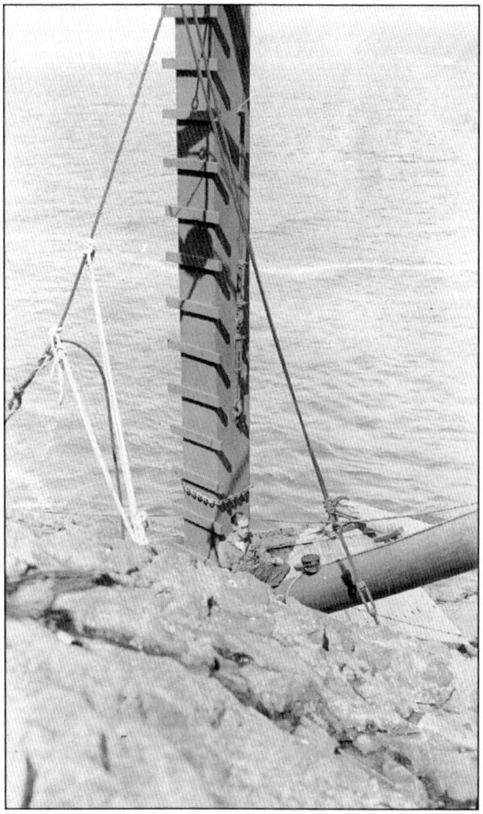

After completing his arduous climbing and photographing of this series, Walter T. Lawrence finally sits next to his hat, resting on the base of the derrick mast. Meanwhile, Orlo E. Hayward takes his turn on top to do some cleaning. Being fourth assistant and the youngest meant that he was probably given the odd jobs that no one else wanted to do, but maybe he thought that cleaning the derrick top was not altogether bad, since he is smiling in the photograph. After all, a good lighthouse keeper always wants to be ready for inspection wherever the inspector might look. (Left, BB; below, JHW.)

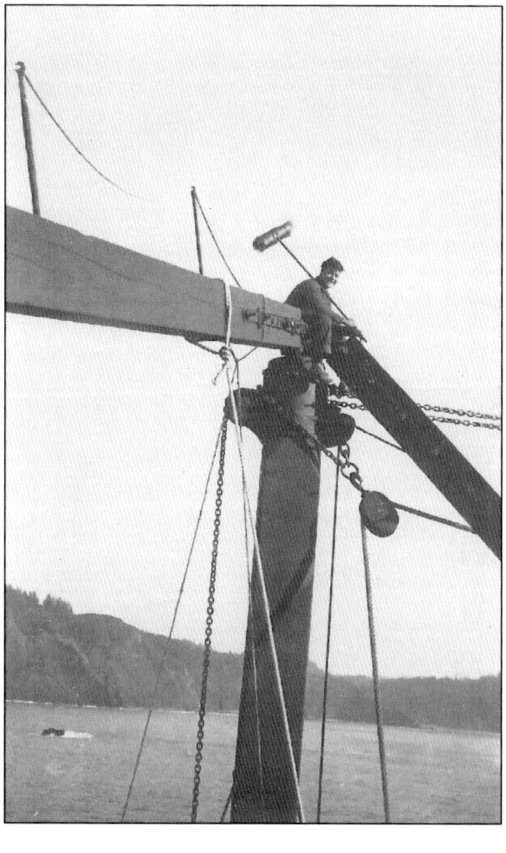

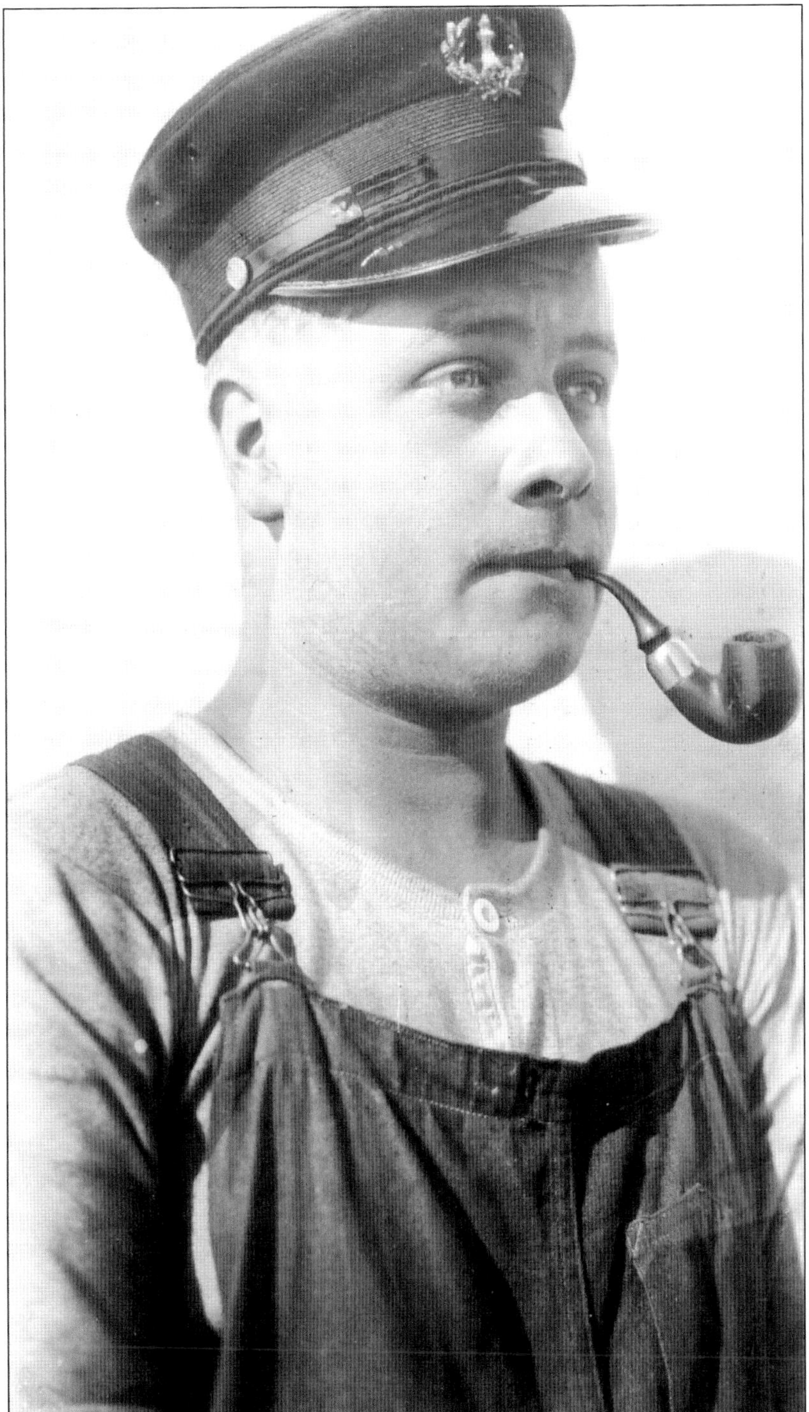

Keeper Orlo E. Hayward was only 17 years old when he started his lighthouse career on Tillamook Rock. He went on to serve at New Dungeness, Cape Flattery, Coquille River, Slip Point, Patos Island, Cape Blanco, Point No Point, and Lime Kiln lighthouses over the next 25 years, finally retiring in 1944. (CGNW.)

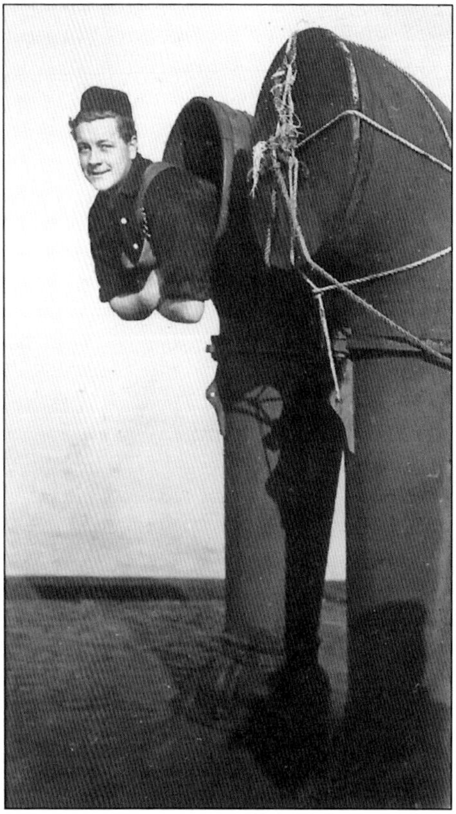

Robert Gerlof, who was from Germany, used to refer to the foghorns as "fog singers." Perhaps Orlo E. Hayward is preparing to sing along in this fun photograph. He was the largest of the four young keepers, being six feet tall and muscular, so this photograph gives a good sense of the size of the trumpet. (BB.)

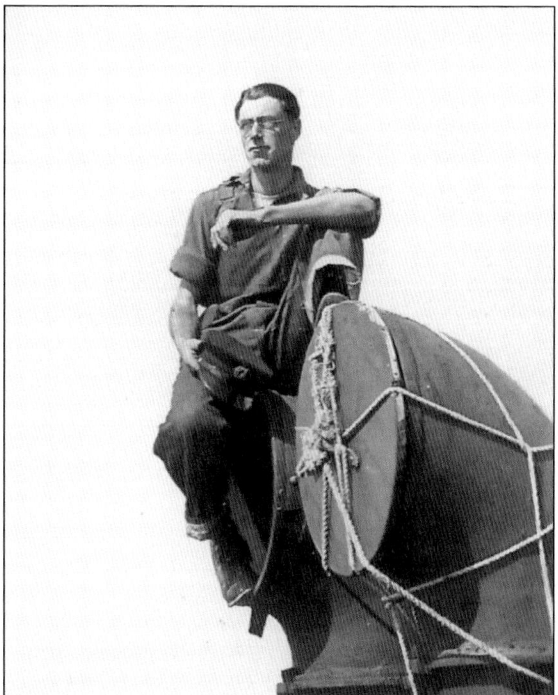

Walter T. Lawrence takes his turn in a reflective moment perched on top of one of the foghorns with his hat in hand. In every photograph where Lawrence appears, he is always either wearing or holding his hat, no matter the activity, dress, or place. Even in his photographs taken at Heceta Head Lighthouse when on liberty, riding a horse, or apple-picking up a tree on a ladder, he is wearing it. He must have identified with it strongly for the years he was a lighthouse keeper. (BB.)

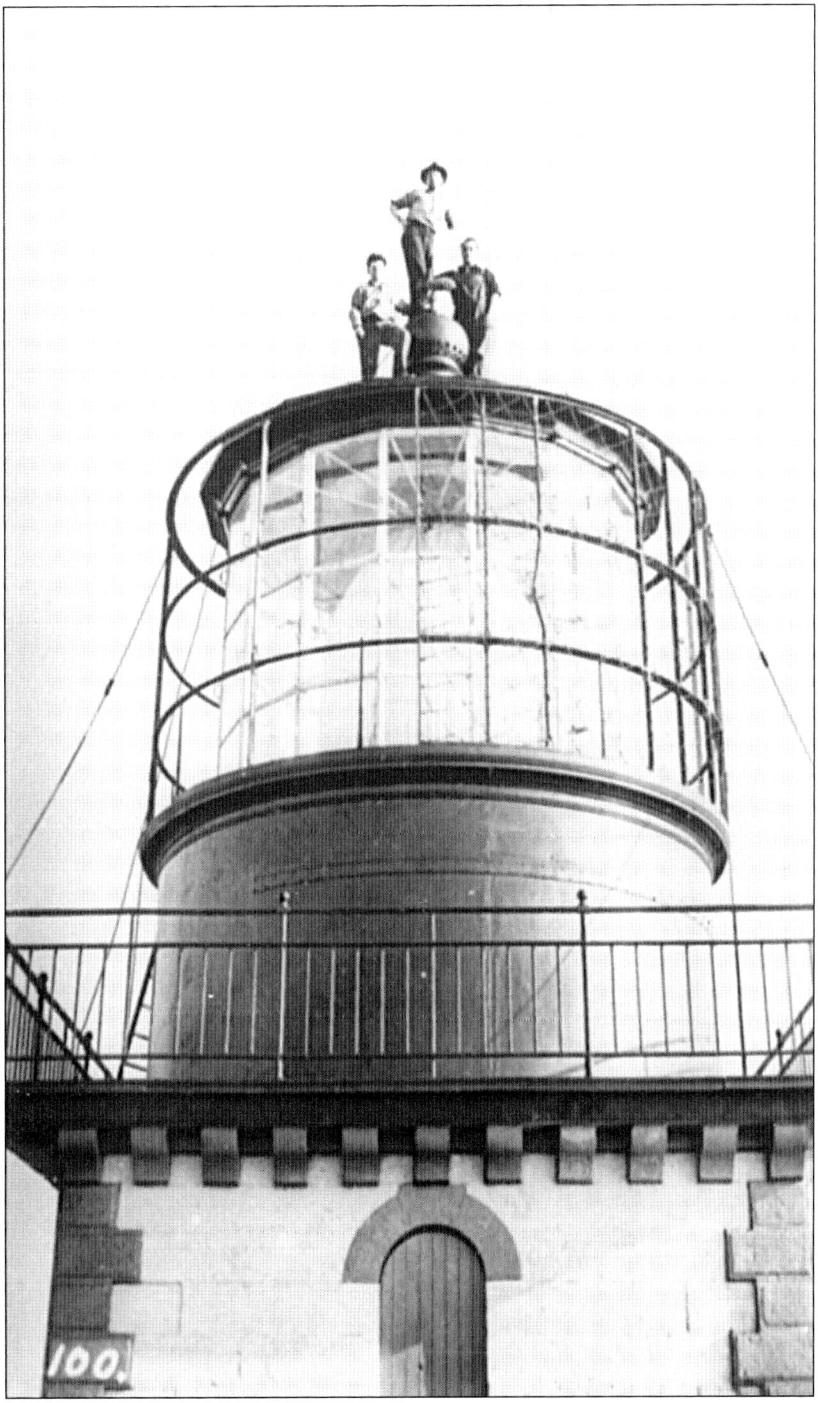

From left to right, keepers Raymond Bay, Howard L. Hansen, and Orlo E. Hayward stand at the highest possible point on the tower of Tillamook Rock Lighthouse while Walter T. Lawrence takes the photograph from below. The first order Fresnel lens inside the lantern is covered with a drape to protect it in the daylight hours, and the bent bar in the protective screen, caused by rock damage, is clearly visible. (CRMM.)

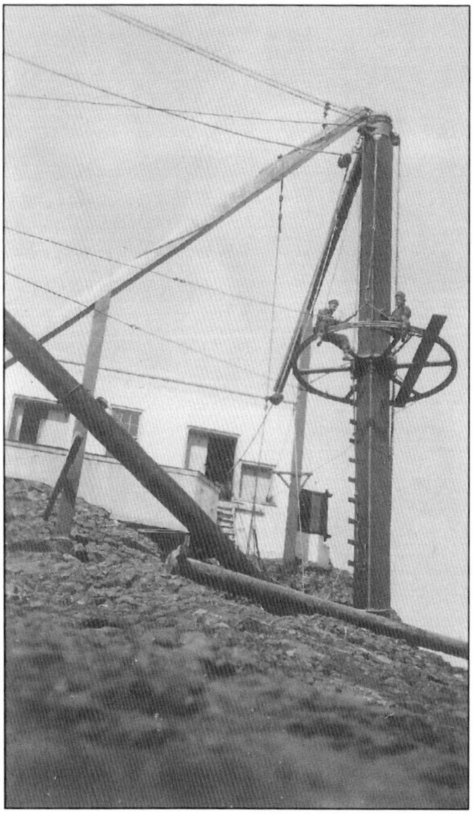

It appears that Walter T. Lawrence (left) and Orlo E. Hayward are doing some kind of maintenance or cleaning of the wheel on the derrick. All the outside equipment had to be continually cleaned, painted, or treated to keep it from being corroded by the continual exposure to salt water. (JHW.)

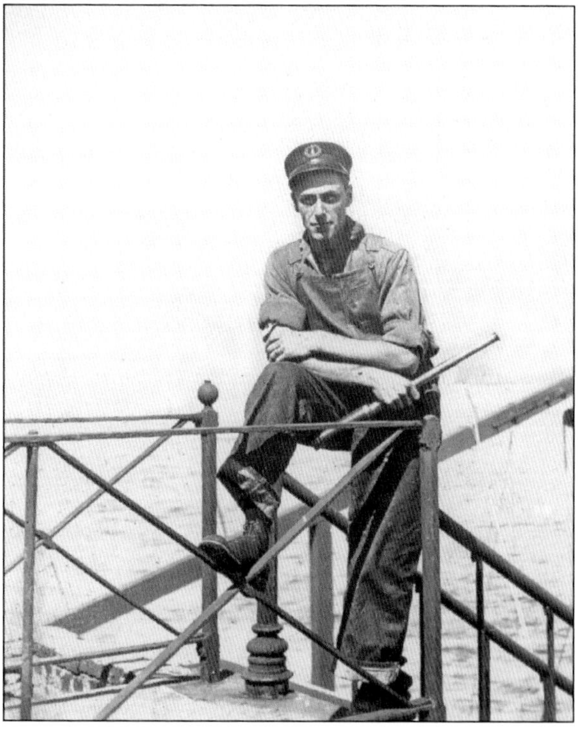

Walter T. Lawrence used the government-issued Lighthouse Service telescope to spot the incoming tender on its approach to Tillamook Rock. The tender's arrival was greatly anticipated because of the mail and fresh provisions it always brought and the opportunity for one of the keepers to go on shore leave. (BB.)

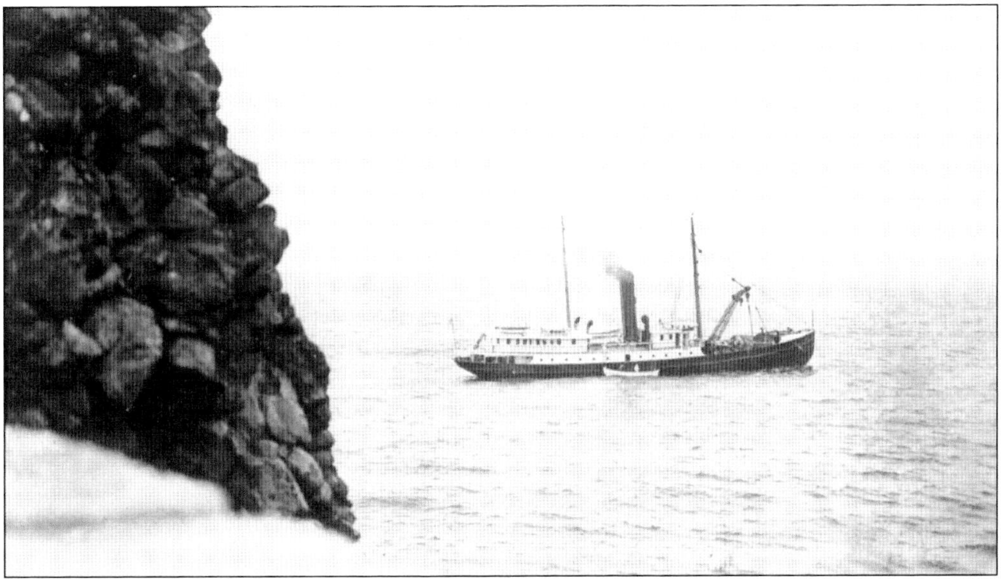

Walter T. Lawrence labeled this photograph "Our Tender," showing a sense of personal ownership the keepers felt because of their reliance on the tender for daily survival. In government documents, the *Manzanita* (1880), shown here, appears to be the tender that visited the Rock the most frequently and over the longest period of time during the lighthouse's 76-year history. (BB.)

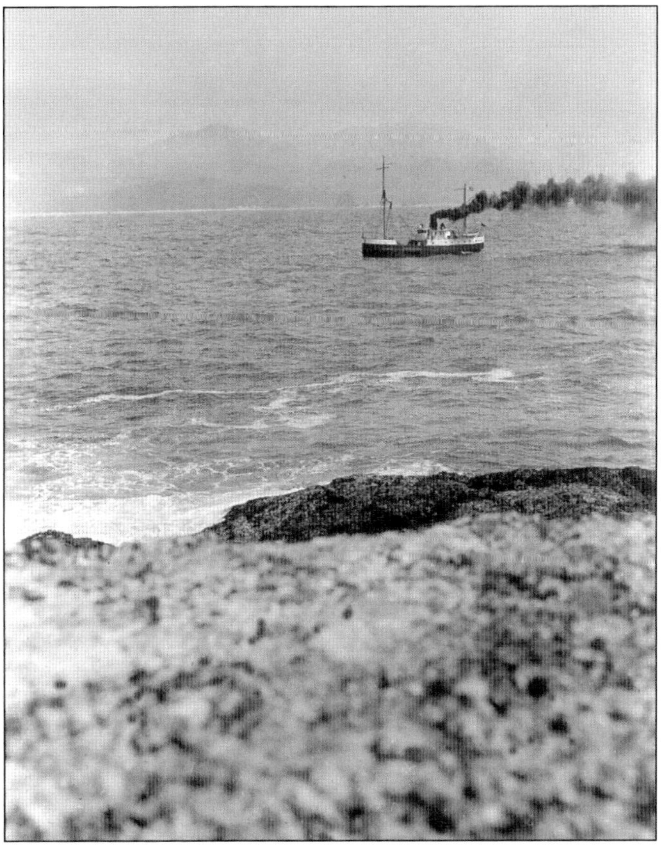

The lighthouse tender *Rose* (1916) also frequently supplied Tillamook Rock. It was a smaller tender but was still able to provide all the required services. Unfortunately, there were times when the seas were too rough for any tender to unload provisions. Orlo E. Hayward reported that they were once down to some beef jerky, a can of salmon, and some crackers before the tender could resupply them. (BB.)

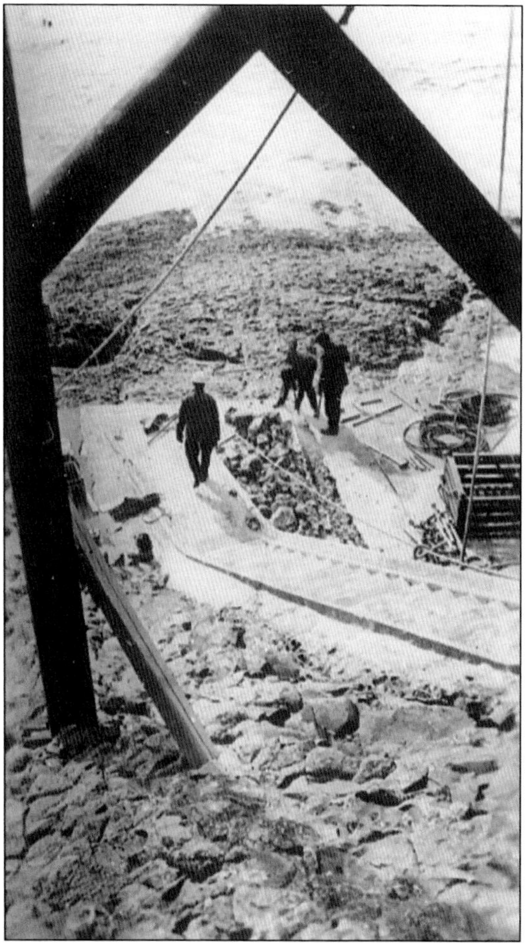

When the tender finally did arrive, all the cargo had to be hoisted up to the landing platform by the derrick boom, then loaded onto the service cart and hoisted again up the tramway to the top of the rock to be brought into the lighthouse or, in the case of the kerosene, to be stored outside in the "oil house." Texaco was awarded the government contract to provide "lighthouse oil," which was especially formulated for use in kerosene vapor lamps. The Texaco star emblem is clearly shown stamped on each crate. (Both, CRMM.)

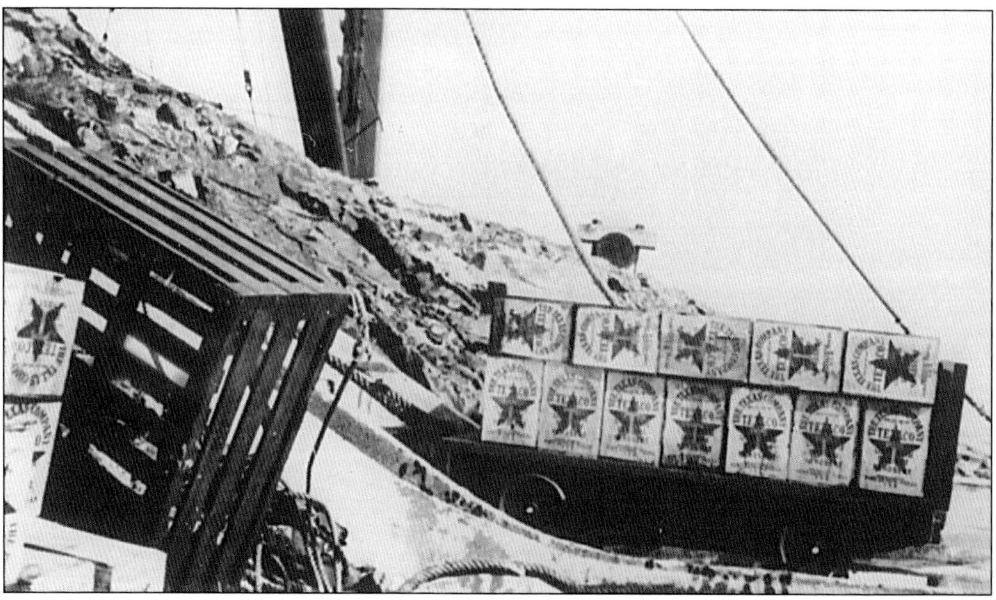

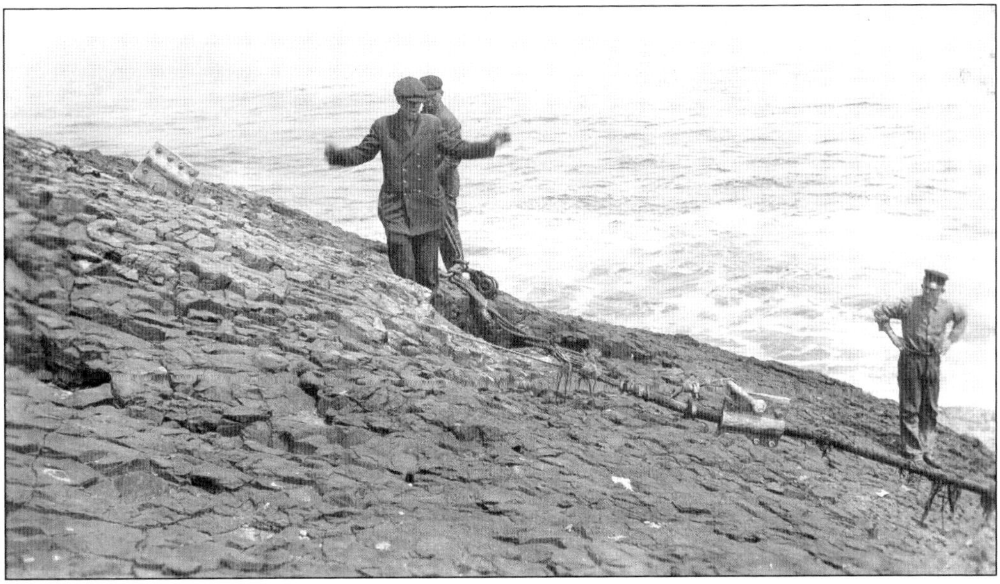

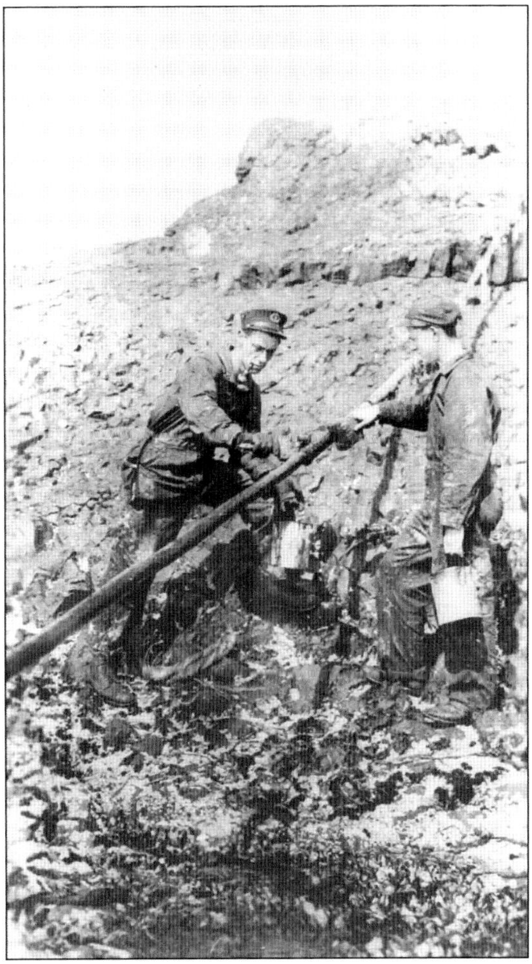

One of the biggest concerns of living on the Rock was the isolation and lack of communication with anyone on shore. It took several years for a telegraph cable to be laid to the lighthouse. When the cable was destroyed in a storm, it then took several more years for a telephone line to be laid in 1920. The above photograph shows the new telephone cable being brought up on the Rock, ready to be attached and anchored. On the far right, keeper Raymond Bay observes it all happening. After it was connected, keepers Walter T. Lawrence (left) and Bay applied some dark protective substance to it, as shown in the photograph at right. They must have been very excited on the day that they made their first phone calls from Tillamook Rock. (Above, BB; right, CRMM.)

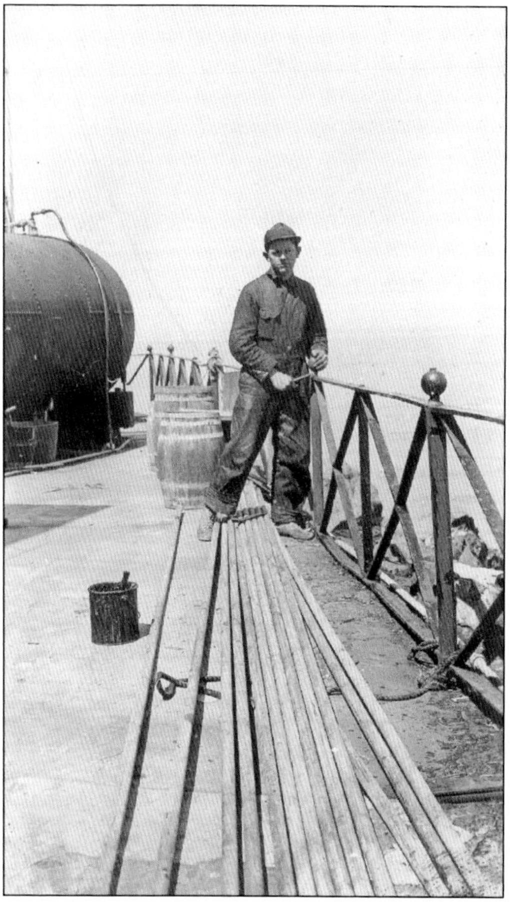

These two photographs show the expected lighthouse keeper work ethic mixed with some Walter T. Lawrence humor. In the album where they are mounted, the pictured at left is entitled "Raymond Bay chipping fence with the boss around," while the below photograph is captioned "Raymond Bay chipping fence with the boss gone." It is doubtful that head keeper Robert Gerlof had gone anywhere, since Bay is working so diligently. After all, what better way to get to the very bottom railing to chip paint off of it than by lying down next to it? (Both, BB.)

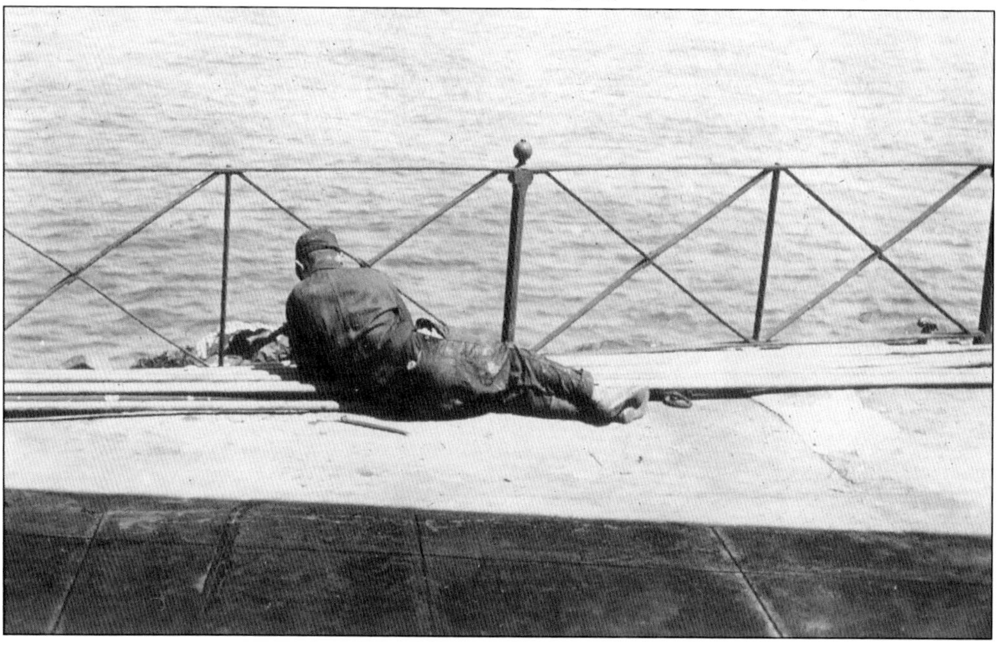

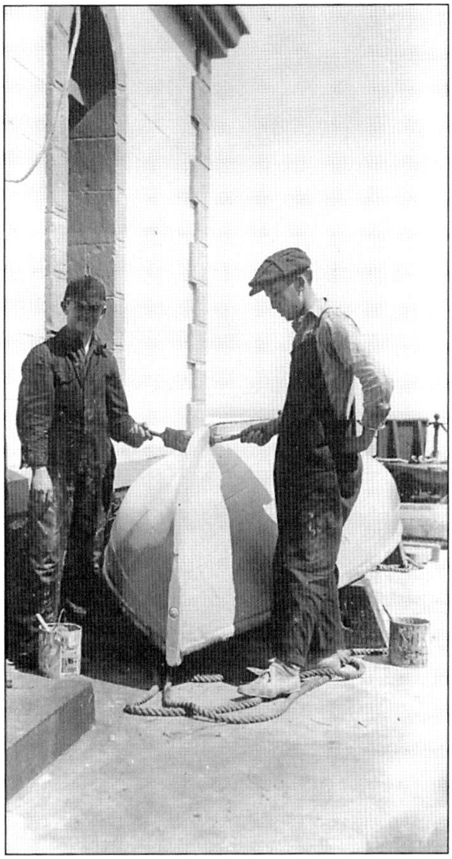

Chipping and painting were major occupations at most lighthouses, and Tillamook Rock was no exception. In the image at right, keepers Raymond Bay (left) and Howard Hansen give the station's whaleboat a coat of paint. It is doubtful that the boat was used much, as it was extremely difficult—if not dangerous—to try to launch it from the Rock. In the below photograph, Walter T. Lawrence (left) and Orlo E. Hayward take their turns painting the trim of the original roof level. In 1898, a five-foot attic space was added with a new roof built on steel I-beams in an effort to provide more protection to the dwelling during storms. Even if the rocks pierced the top roof, they would likely not have enough remaining force to go through the second one. (Right, JHW; below, BB.)

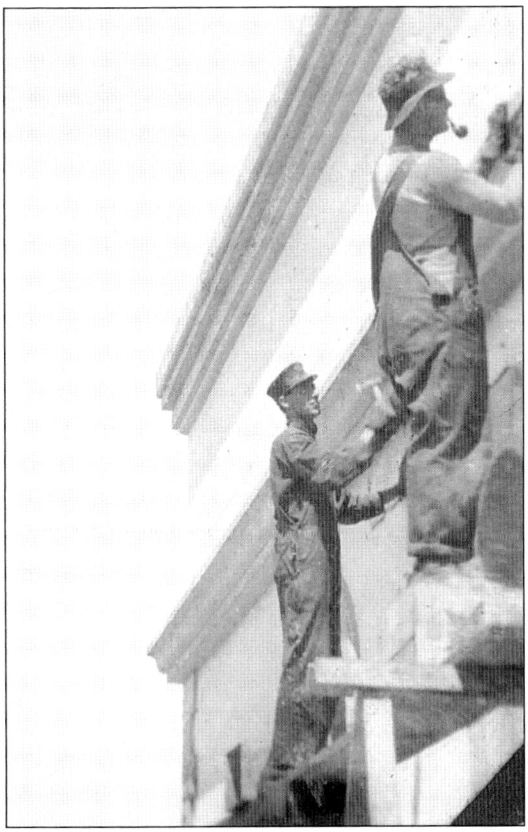

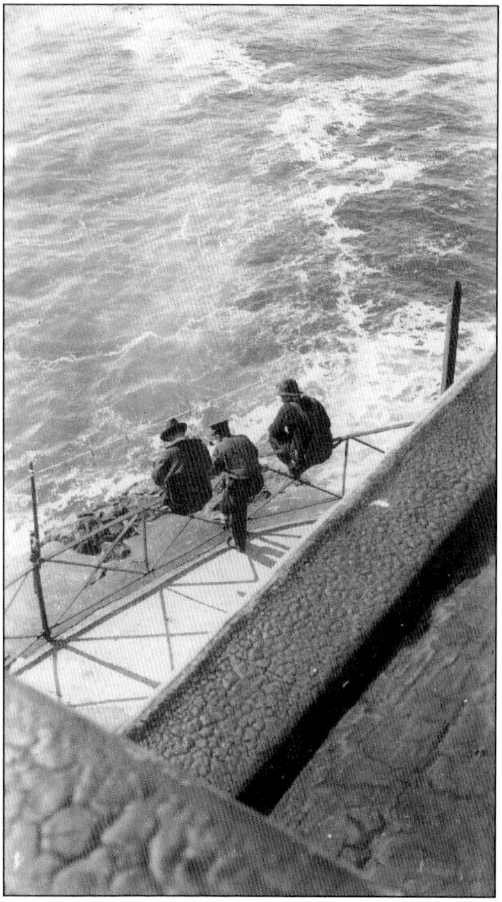

From left to right, keepers Howard L Hansen, Walter T. Lawrence, and Orlo E. Hayward relax while perched on the narrow guardrail that surrounds the lighthouse. Lawrence titled this photograph "Dreams." Raymond Bay must have taken it from the lighthouse roof. (BB.)

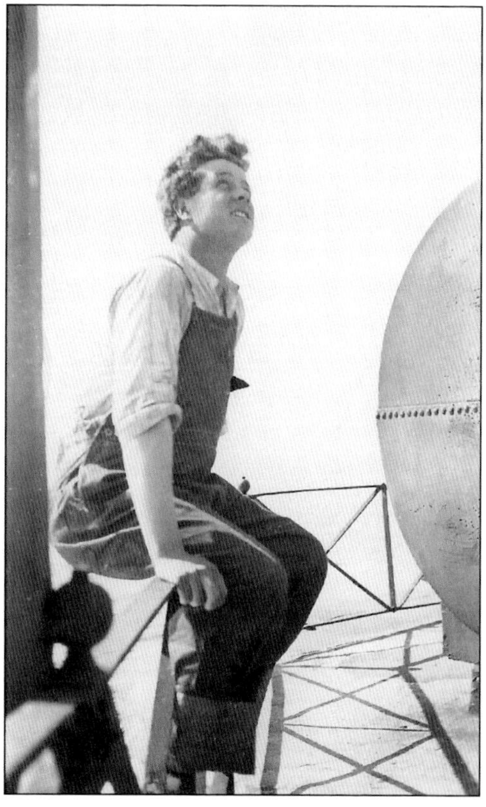

Orlo E. Hayward does some daylight stargazing in this photograph, similarly perched on the guardrail. It is evident these keepers had very little fear of heights or losing their balance. They regularly chose to perch in narrow places with huge drops below them. (JHW.)

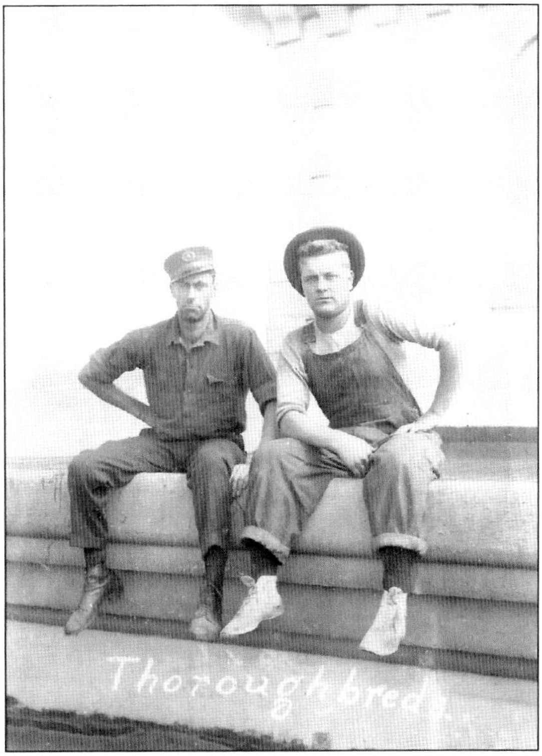

Walter T. Lawrence (left) and Orlo E. Hayward are first pictured in a photograph that Lawrence captioned "Thoroughbreds" in which they try to portray serious expressions indicative of seasoned, hard-working lighthouse keepers. They give the seriousness another attempt in the photograph below. It is almost believable, but not quite, given their boyish antics displayed in many of the other photographs. (Right, JHW; below, CRMM.)

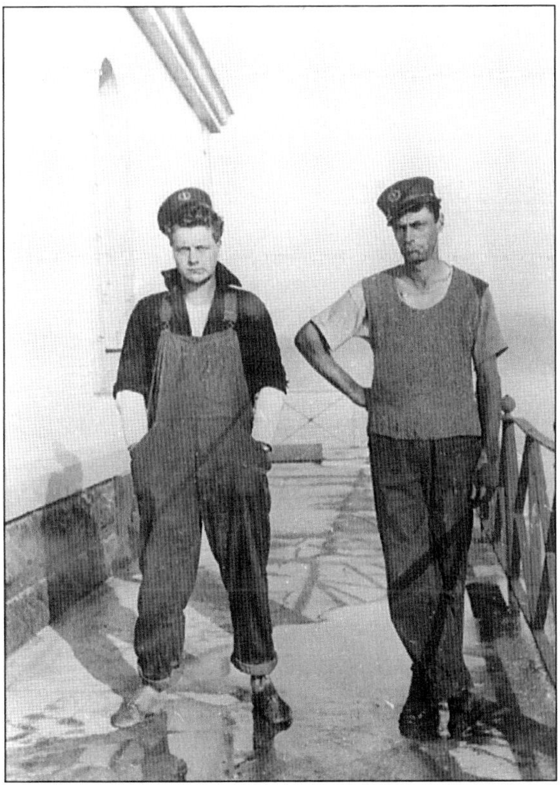

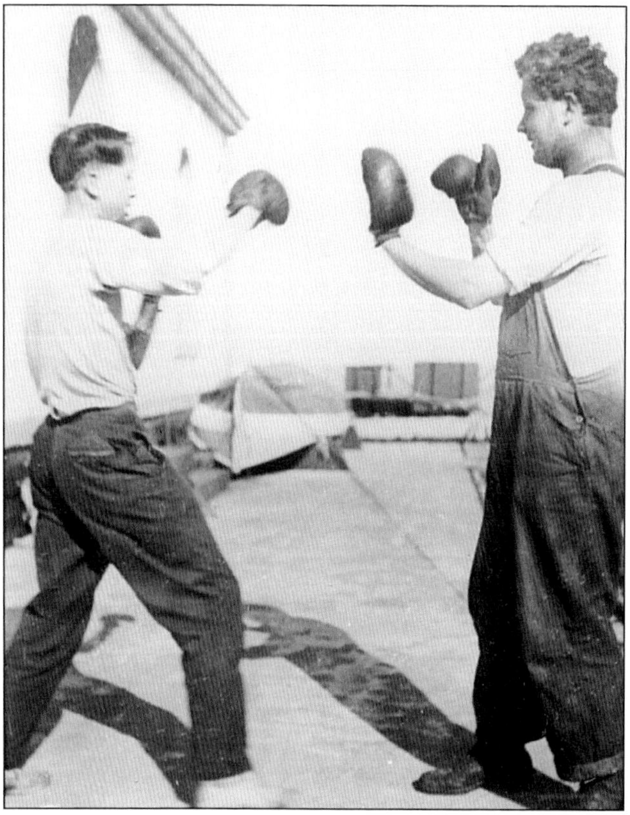

Keepers Howard L. Hansen (left) and Orlo E. Hayward give boxing a try in these two photographs. Over the years, there were many ways keepers entertained themselves in their off-duty hours: reading, cards, fishing, music, photography, boxing, baking, golfing, and climbing—whether it be on the derrick, crevice, or lighthouse. Considering the limited space they had both inside and outside the lighthouse, they had to be somewhat inventive with how to make the most of their free time. As shown in the photographs in this chapter, these four young men appear to have succeeded very well at that. (Both, CRMM.)

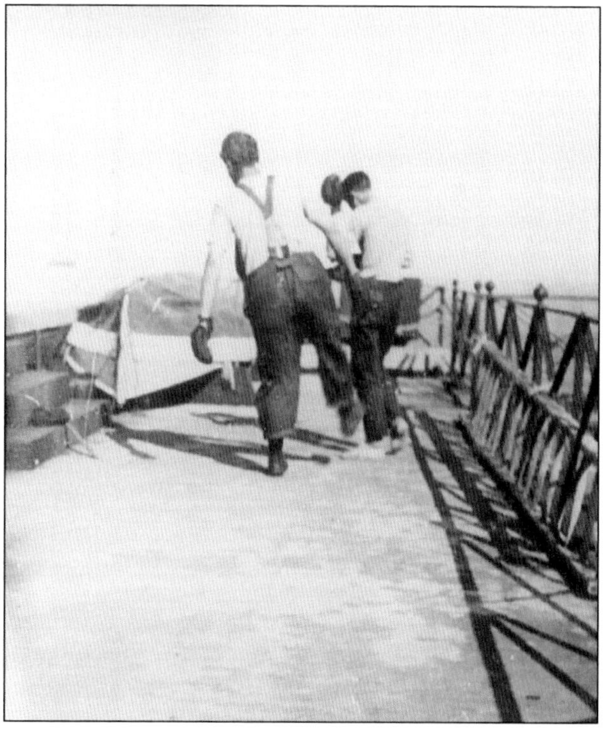

The young keepers must have had fun trying to think of different poses and places to take photographs on the top of a rock out in the Pacific. In the photograph at right, Orlo E. Hayward (bottom), Howard L. Hansen (middle), and Raymond Bay form a sort of pyramid, while the below image shows Hayward (left) and Bay with Walter T. Lawrence acting as a wheelbarrow. This photograph was taken on top of the lighthouse roof, where the texture and cracks in the asphalt layer are visible. Many different methods were tried over the years to protect the roof from the recurring damage caused by intense storms. In December 1894, a 135-pound boulder hurled up by a severe storm broke a 20-foot-square hole through the roof of the dwelling and took out the kitchen stove. The boulder was saved by the district superintendent and kept in his office to show visitors until at least 1933. (Right, JHW; below, CRMM.)

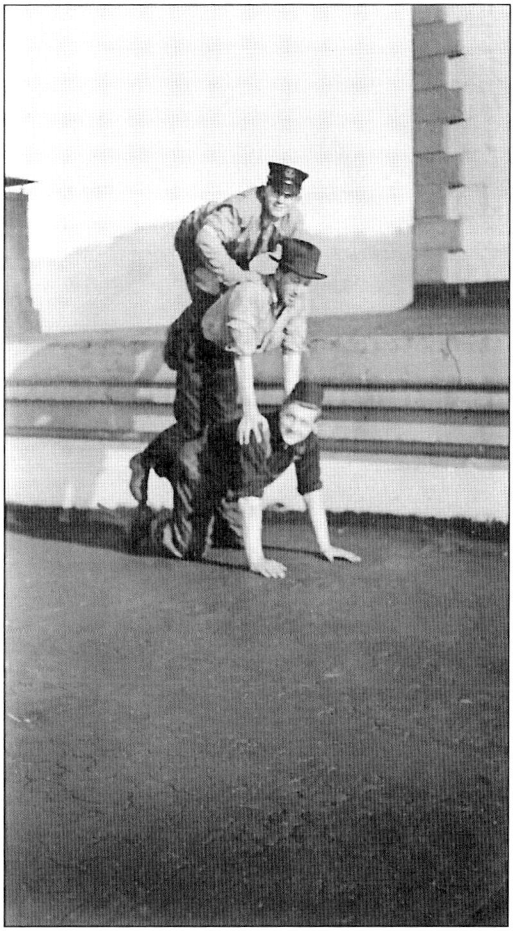

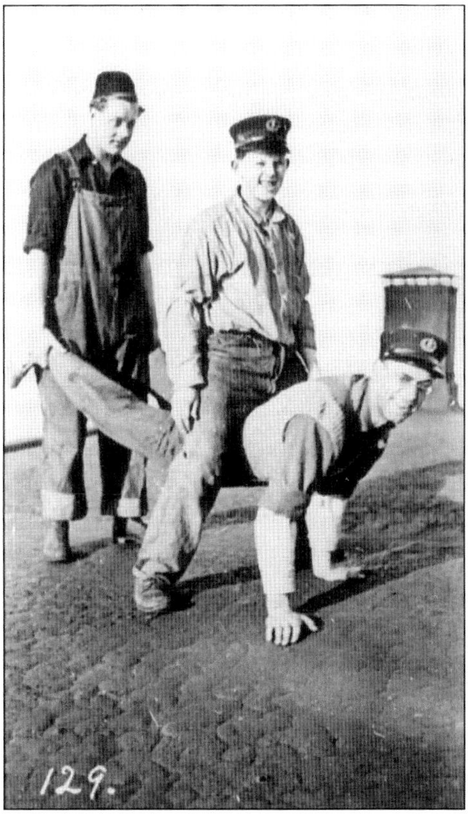

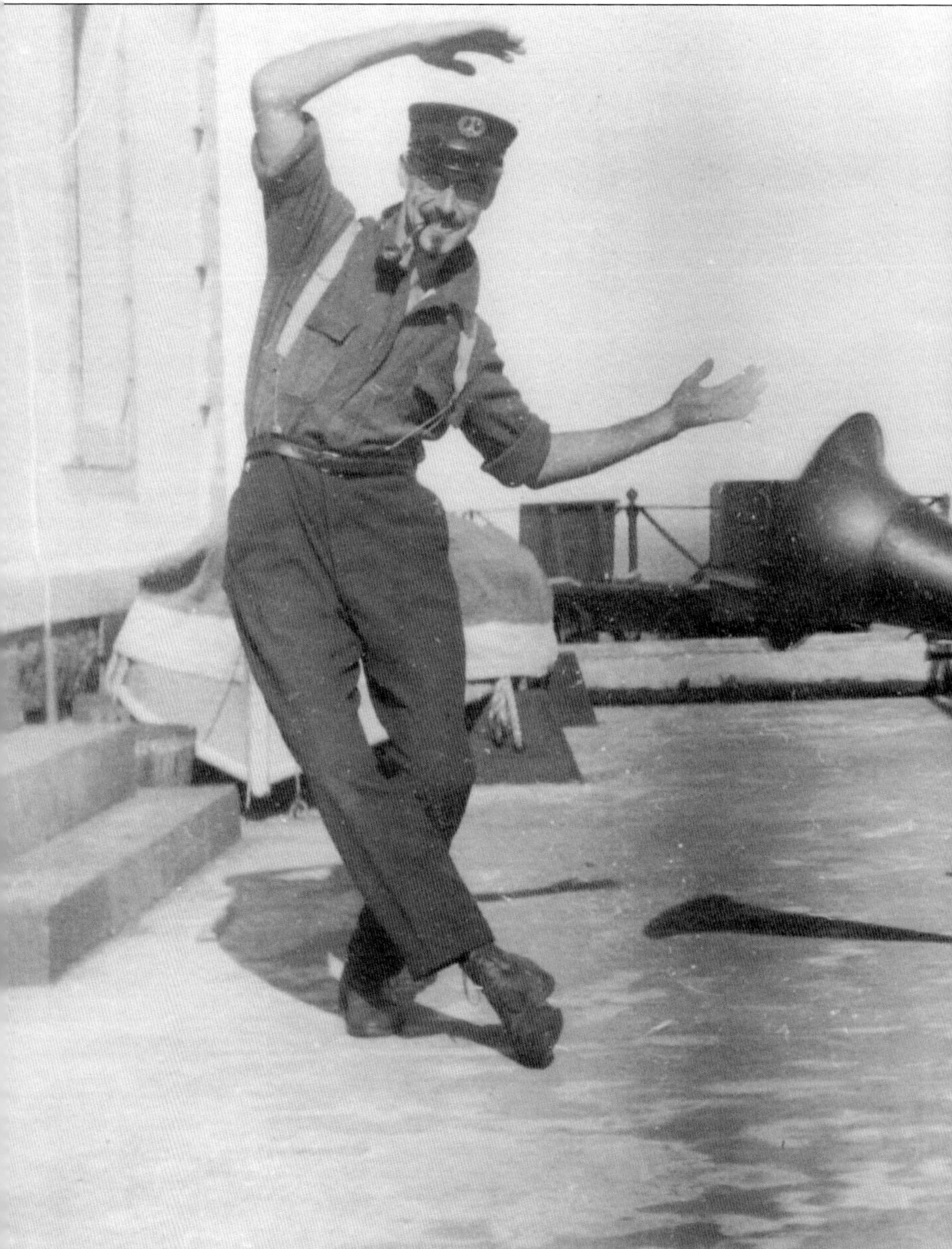

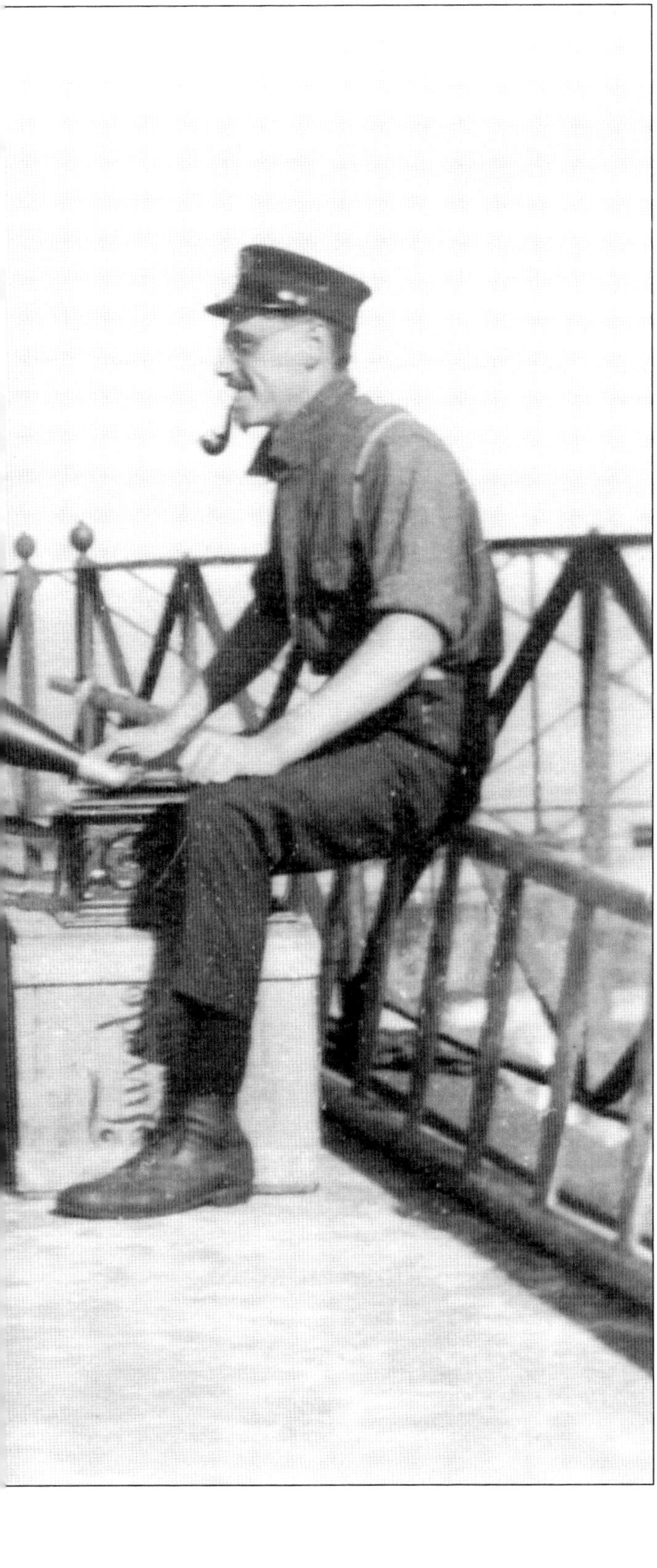

This famous "dancing keeper" image is one of a series that shows Walter T. Lawrence experimenting with the technique of creating a double exposure photograph. Here, he sits behind the phonograph while watching himself dance in front of it. On the back of this photograph, he wrote "How's this for dancing to your own music?" In 1945, keeper Jim Gibbs found the old wind-up phonograph upstairs in a small storage room near the tower landing and used it to listen to records while on the Rock. (LHD.)

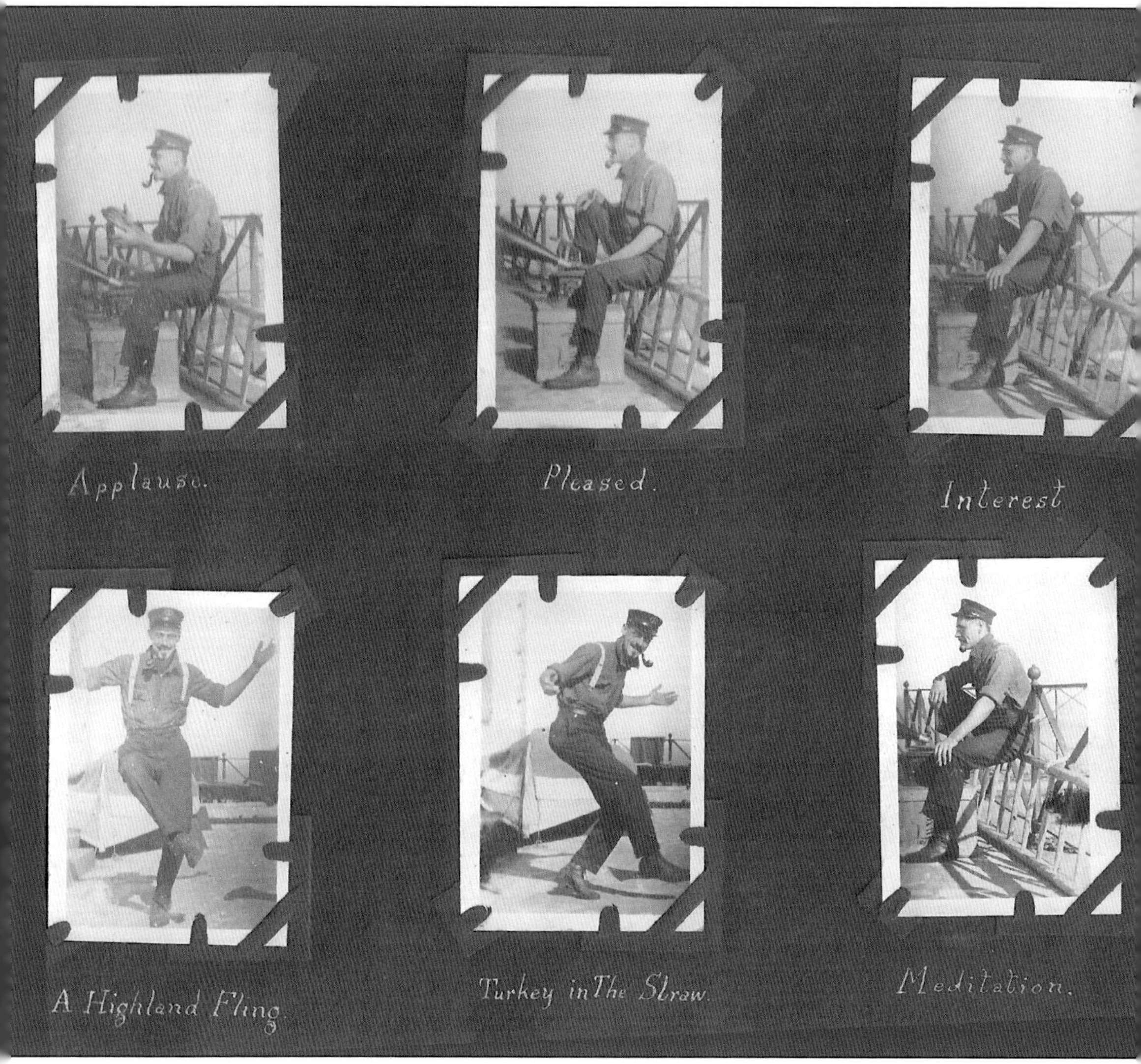

This full page from one of Walter T. Lawrence's albums contains several poses of him doing different dance moves and sitting behind the phonograph; then, using two photographs he joined together, he created his double exposure prints. At least he was dancing in a safe place on the deck rather than some hazardous location, as shown in other photographs. His labeling of emotions is also fun to note. (BB.)

Dancing and playing music of all types seemed to be another favorite pastime. Here, Orlo E. Hayward shows his hula steps while Raymond Bay beats a homemade drum and Howard L. Hansen sits atop the foghorn while playing a violin. There reportedly was a piano at the lighthouse at one point. To take this photograph, Walter T. Lawrence must have been on the lantern deck of the lighthouse tower, as the three keepers are on top of the fog-signal room roof quite a distance below, directly behind the tower. (BB.)

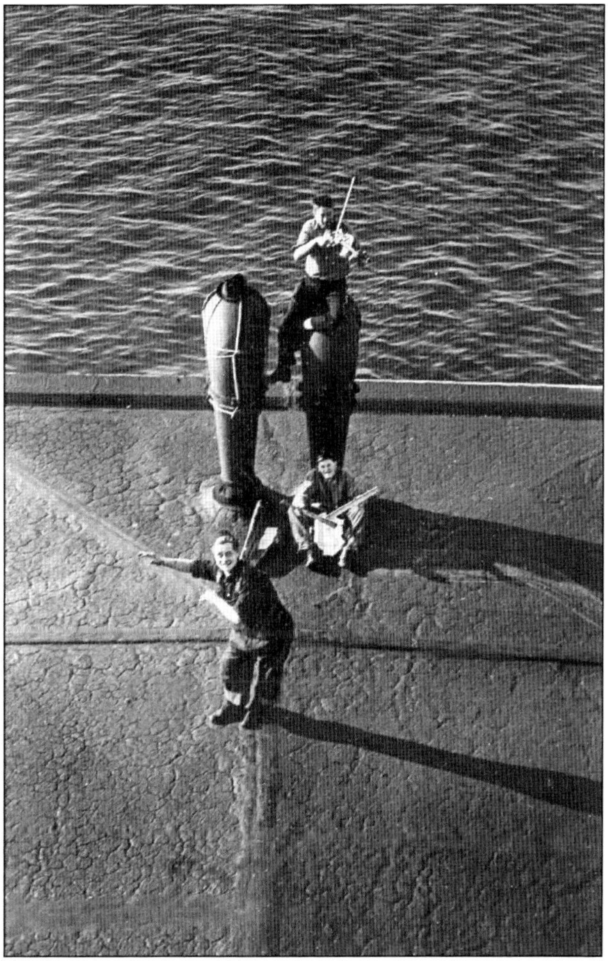

From left to right, keepers Hayward, Bay, and Hansen enjoy what appears to be beer on Tillamook Rock in 1920. Beer was forbidden at lighthouses, but many keepers still drank it, and Hayward later admitted to making it and then hiding it when the inspector came. (JHW.)

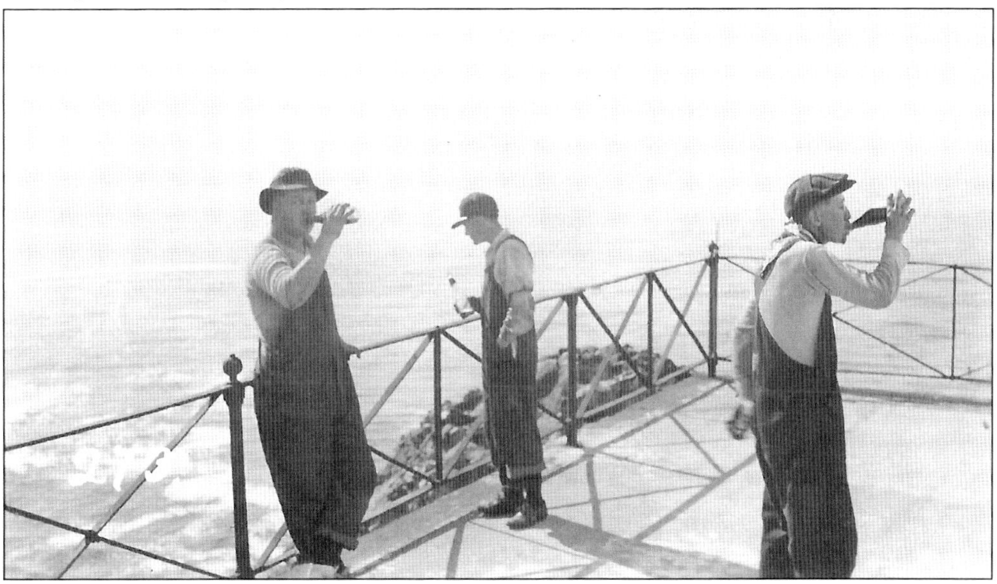

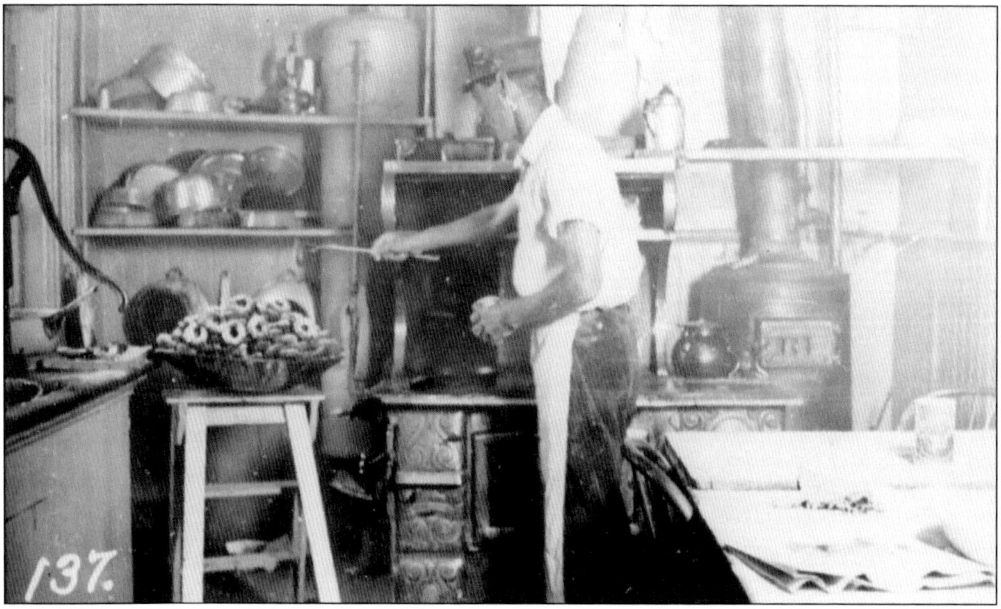

With apron on, Howard L. Hansen stands at the kitchen stove making a huge bowl of donuts, while on another day, Walter T. Lawrence (left) and Orlo E. Hayward relax with feet up at the kitchen table in these rare photographs of the lighthouse interior. Keepers were expected to rotate cooking duties like all other chores at the lighthouse. In a letter to Hayward some years later, head keeper Robert Gerlof fondly reminisced about making donuts in the kitchen. With four hungry young men, the donuts probably did not last long. This was the same kitchen stove that was pushed off its foundations and cracked by flooding seawater during the great 1935 cyclone. (Above, CRMM; below, USLHS.)

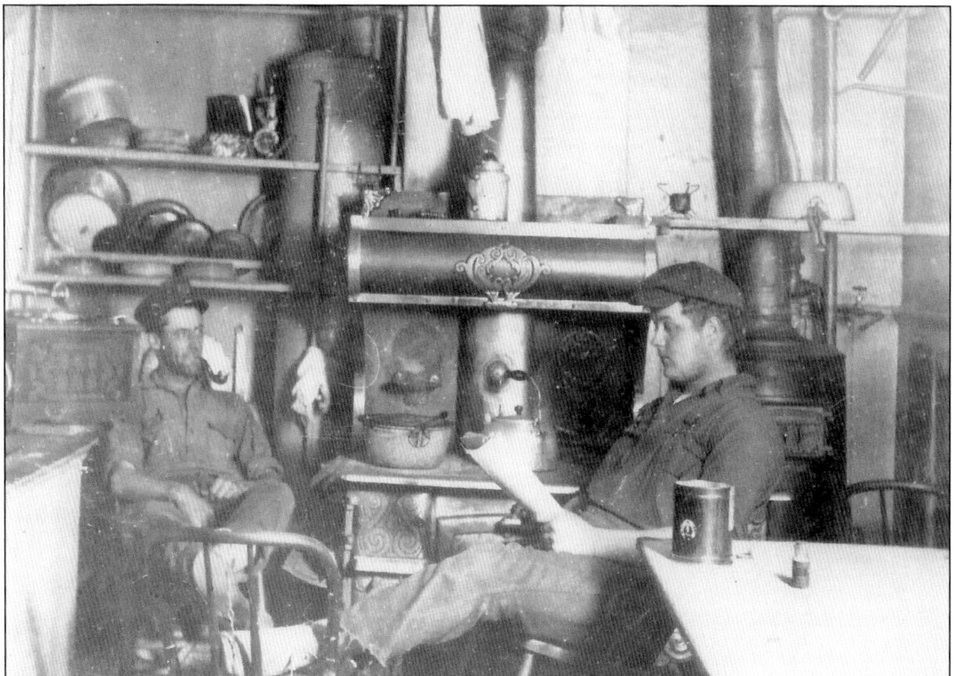

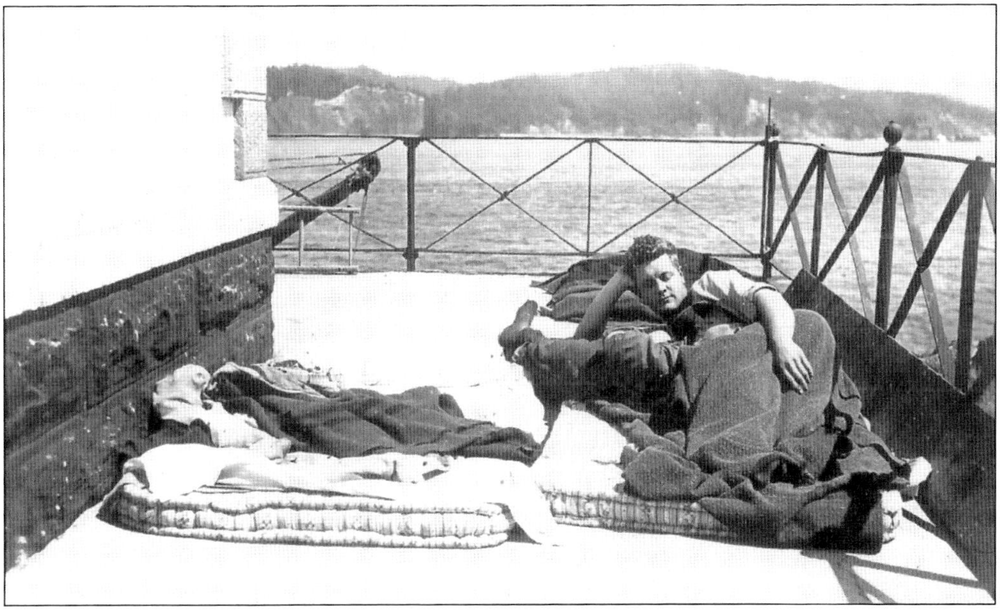

Orlo E. Hayward cradles Raymond Bay in his lap out on the deck at Tillamook while "camping out." Jim Gibbs tried to sleep on the deck one night during his 1945 tenure, but without much success, as he was first attacked by mosquitoes and then seabirds that used him for target practice. This photograph of these two looks like they met with some success and are enjoying the next morning's lazy feeling. (JHW.)

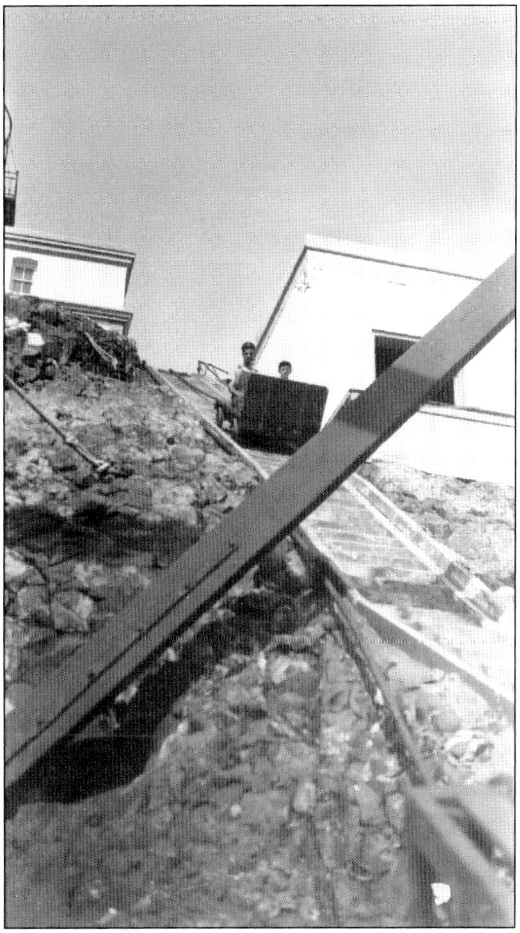

Walter T. Lawrence and Raymond Bay enjoy a ride in the service cart down the tramway stairs to the loading dock at Tillamook Rock. The cart was normally used to hoist provisions and supplies up to the lighthouse from the landing platform below the derrick where the cargo was offloaded from the lighthouse tender. (CGNW.)

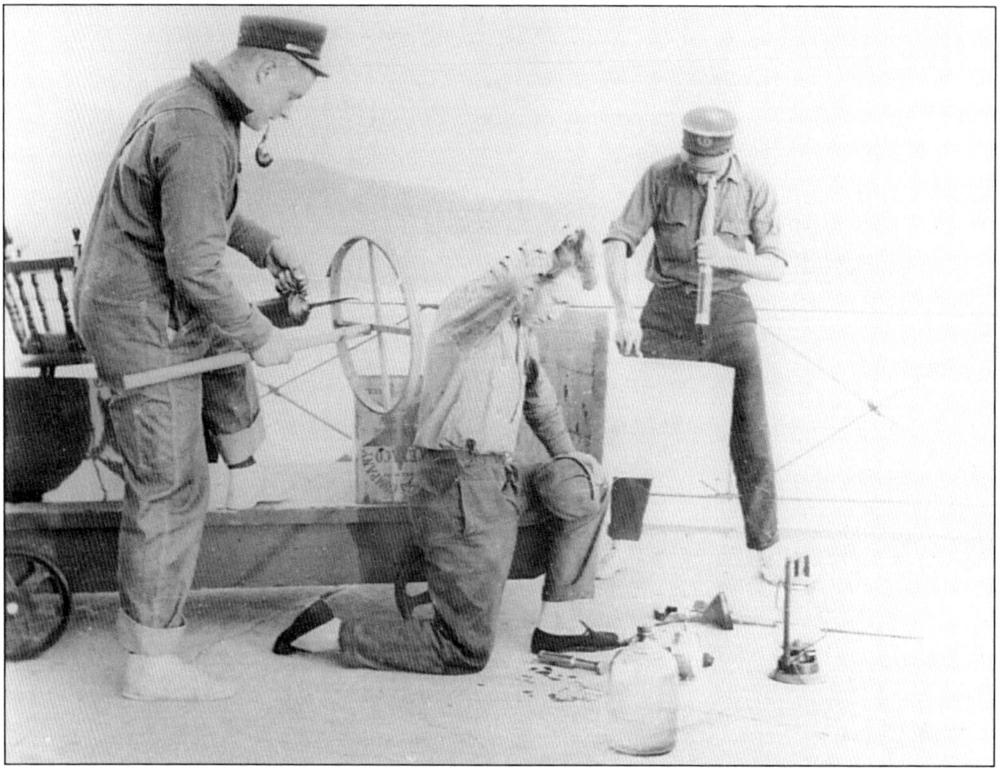

In this two-part "pit-stop" vignette, the keepers work on their "car" before Orlo E. Hayward climbs back into the driver's seat ready to ride again. Walter T. Lawrence uses the lighthouse telescope to spot the problem, while Hayward oils the steering wheel. Note the kitchen chair he sits on, the kerosene crate holding up the steering wheel, a bottle of kerosene representing gas, a lantern for the headlight, a clock for the speedometer, and Howard L. Hansen working on the supposed engine with a large hand tool in front. Robert Gerlof, in a letter sent to Hayward seven years later, mentioned the fun they had racing the car on "Broadway" at Tillamook Rock. (Above, CRMM; below, JWH.)

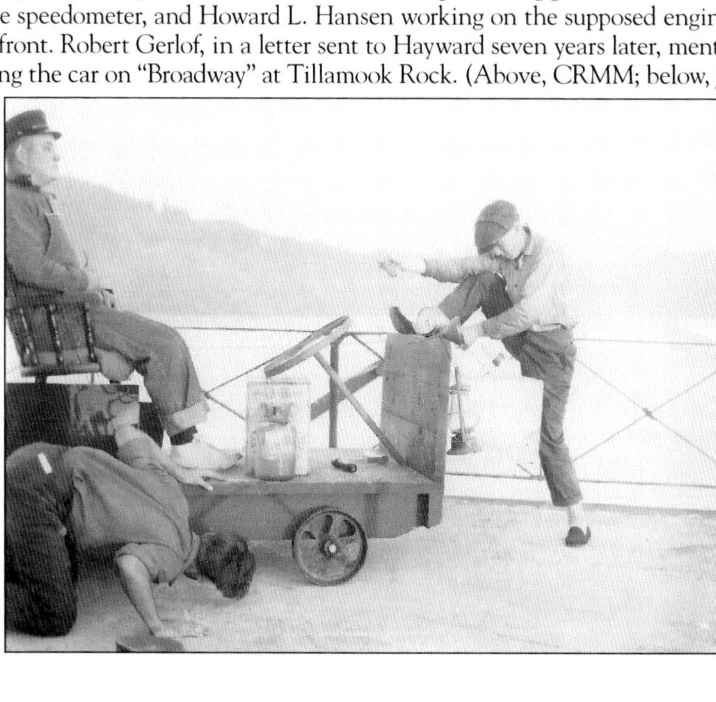

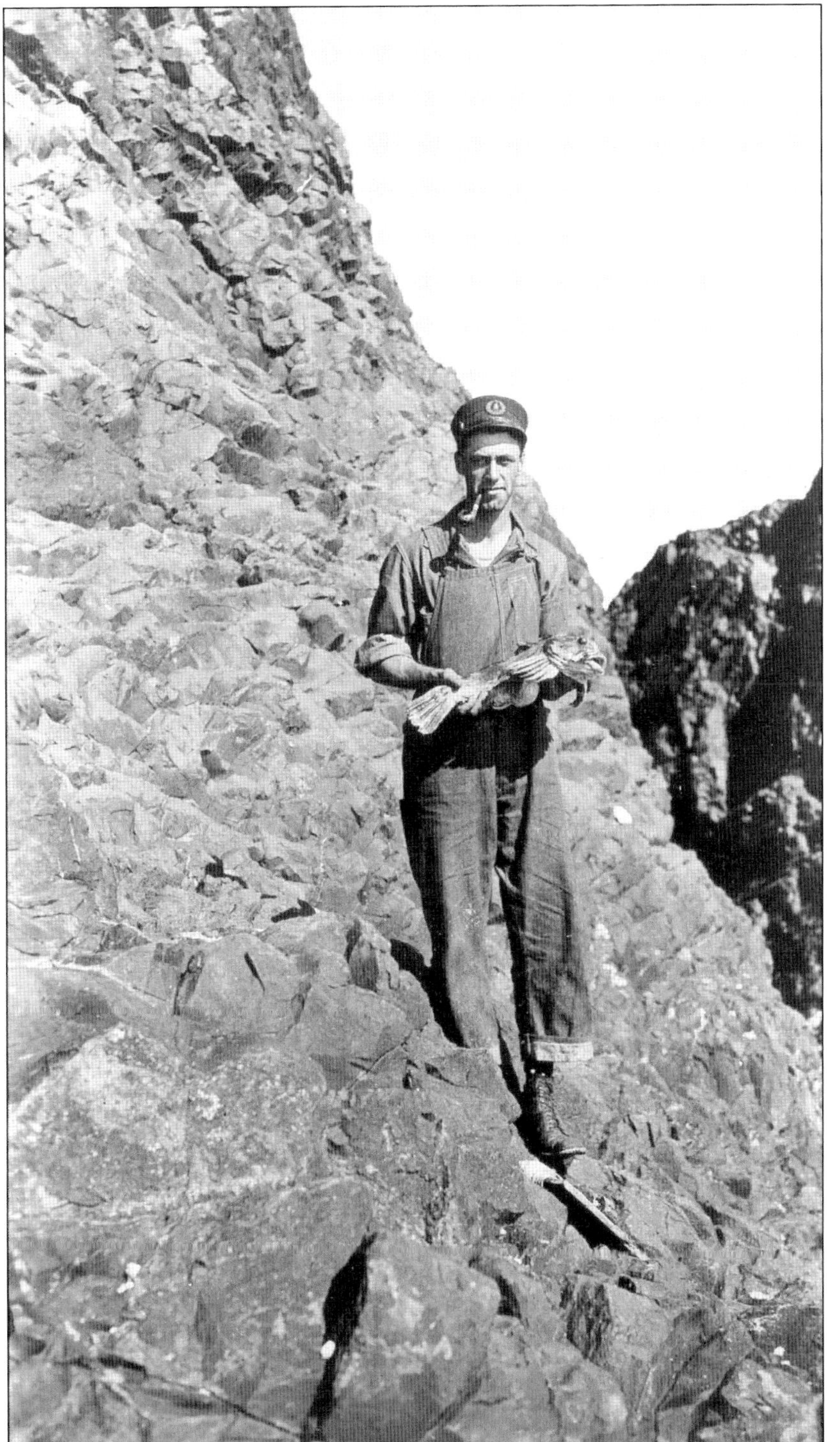

The crevice provided great fishing on calmer days. Here, Walter T. Lawrence proudly shows off a lingcod he caught. Many keepers used to rely on catching fish to supplement their meager pantries. It was the one thing they could always have that was fresh. (BB.)

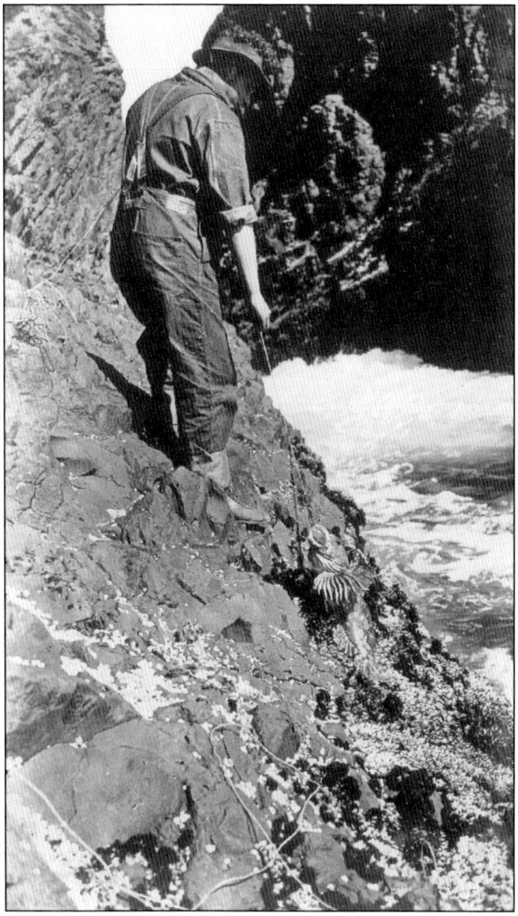

Orlo E. Hayward shows off his fishing skills and successful result in this series that Walter T. Lawrence titled "Catching the Big Ones." While considered a rather ugly fish, the lingcod were "good eating," according to 1950s keeper Lon Haynes, who said they tried to catch them multiple times from the crevice but did not have much luck. Perhaps because these young men had familiarity with Oregon coastal fishing from being raised at Heceta Head Lighthouse, they knew how to attract them. (Both, BB.)

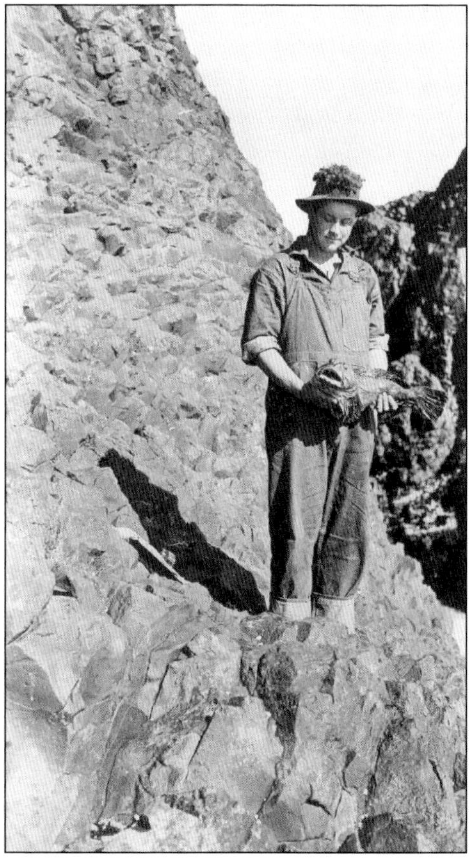

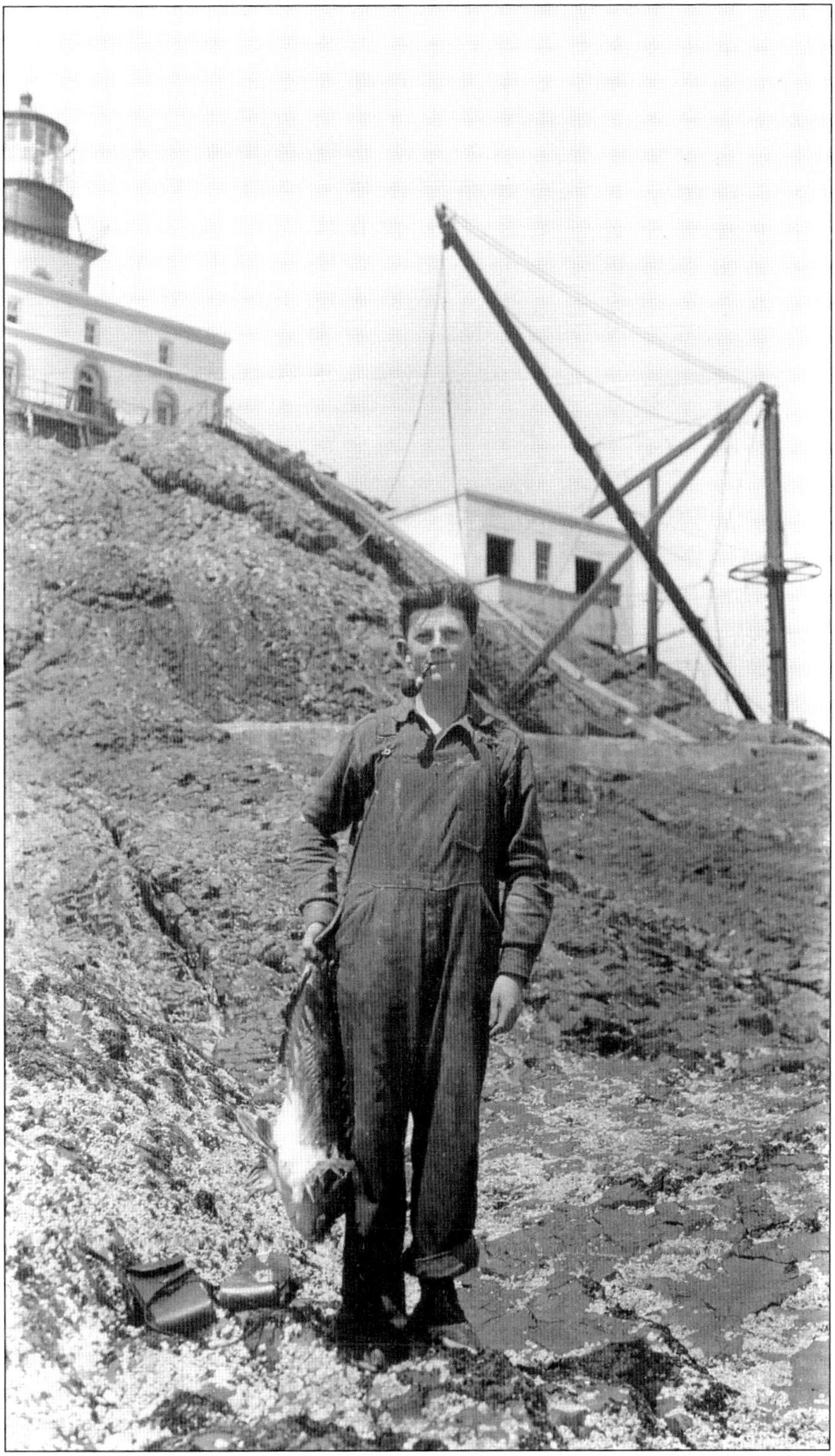

With pipe in mouth, and apparently enjoying his obvious success, Raymond Bay shows off a huge lingcod he caught. It is interesting that both Bay and Howard L. Hansen went into the fishing industry after they left lighthouse service a few short years later. (CGNW.)

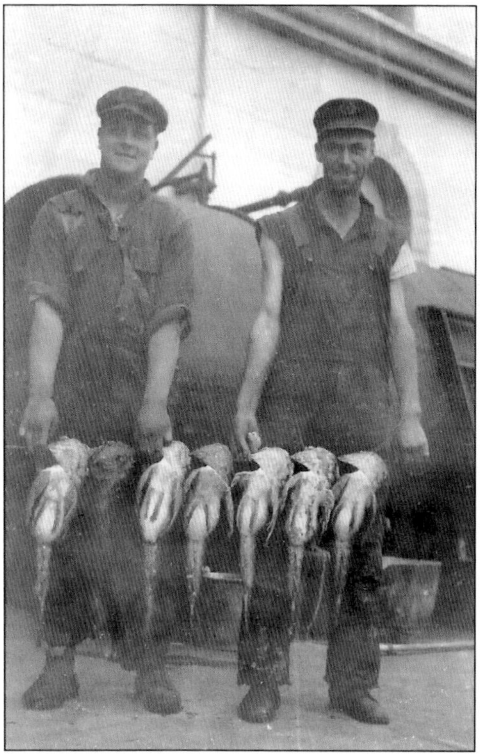

In the image at left, Orlo E. Hayward (left) and Walter T. Lawrence proudly display their big haul of lingcod skewered on a rod. Shown below, not to be outdone, Howard L. Hansen (left), with camera slung over his shoulder and a large mess of fish in his right hand, and Raymond Bay, holding a huge lingcod in either hand, trudge back up from the crevice toward the landing platform stairs. After all the fun, relaxation, antics, and picture-taking sessions shown in this chapter were finally finished, the ever-constant lighthouse duty beckoned for all keepers on Tillamook Rock. (Both, JHW.)

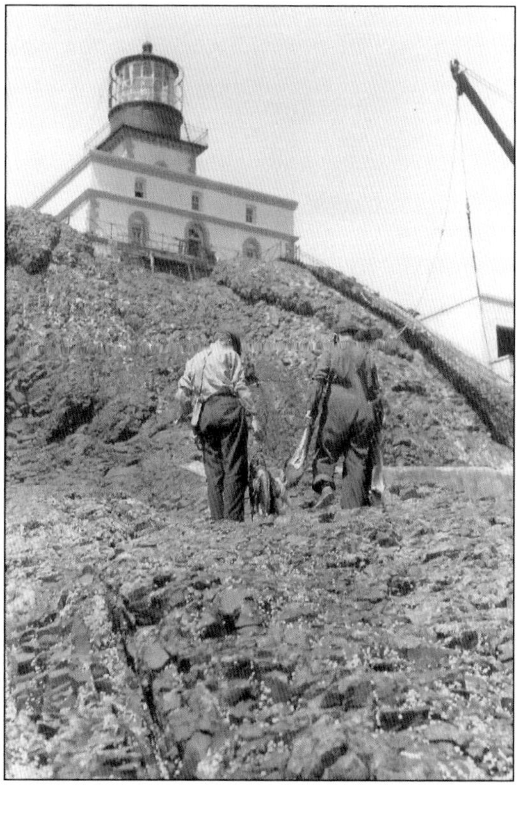

Three

Tilly's Wrath

While it appears that the nickname Terrible Tilly was first coined about 50 years ago, it certainly could have been applied from the very beginning to aptly describe what happened on Tillamook Rock during the horrific winter storms that occurred almost every year. From 1880 onward, the United States Lighthouse Board's annual reports are filled with descriptions of the incredible damage caused as a result of massive waves and boulders being flung at the lighthouse on these occasions.

The lighthouse roof was continually being crushed in or pierced through, letting in seawater that decimated the living quarters below while almost drowning the keepers. The glass windowpanes in the lantern were frequently broken by the monster waves that washed over the top of the lighthouse 134 feet above sea level, and sea debris mixed with rocks would chip and crack prisms of the delicate glass Fresnel lens. Specially designed iron storm shutters and wire screens were put up around the lantern to try to keep the sea and rocks at bay, but severe damage still occurred.

The derrick and boom assembly were broken and washed away on at least two occasions, and the outbuildings and iron tanks regularly sustained heavy damage. There were even several documented instances when large chunks of the Rock that weighed many tons broke off and plunged into the churning seas.

Keepers reported feeling vibrations as waves hit the sides of the Rock with great force. In an 1886 newspaper article, a member of the construction crew who was there during the intense 1879 storm recounted, "No words of mine can begin to convey any idea of the horrible shriek and roar and gurgling! But it was the jar of the ledges that startled us the most, when with an explosive shock, like the report of a heavy gun, the enormous waves struck." It was miraculous that none of them perished in that particular storm, considering their tenuous living quarters.

But of all the storms ever recorded on Tillamook Rock, the most horrendous was that of October 21, 1934. It truly was "Terrible Tilly's Perfect Storm," the details of which are described in this chapter.

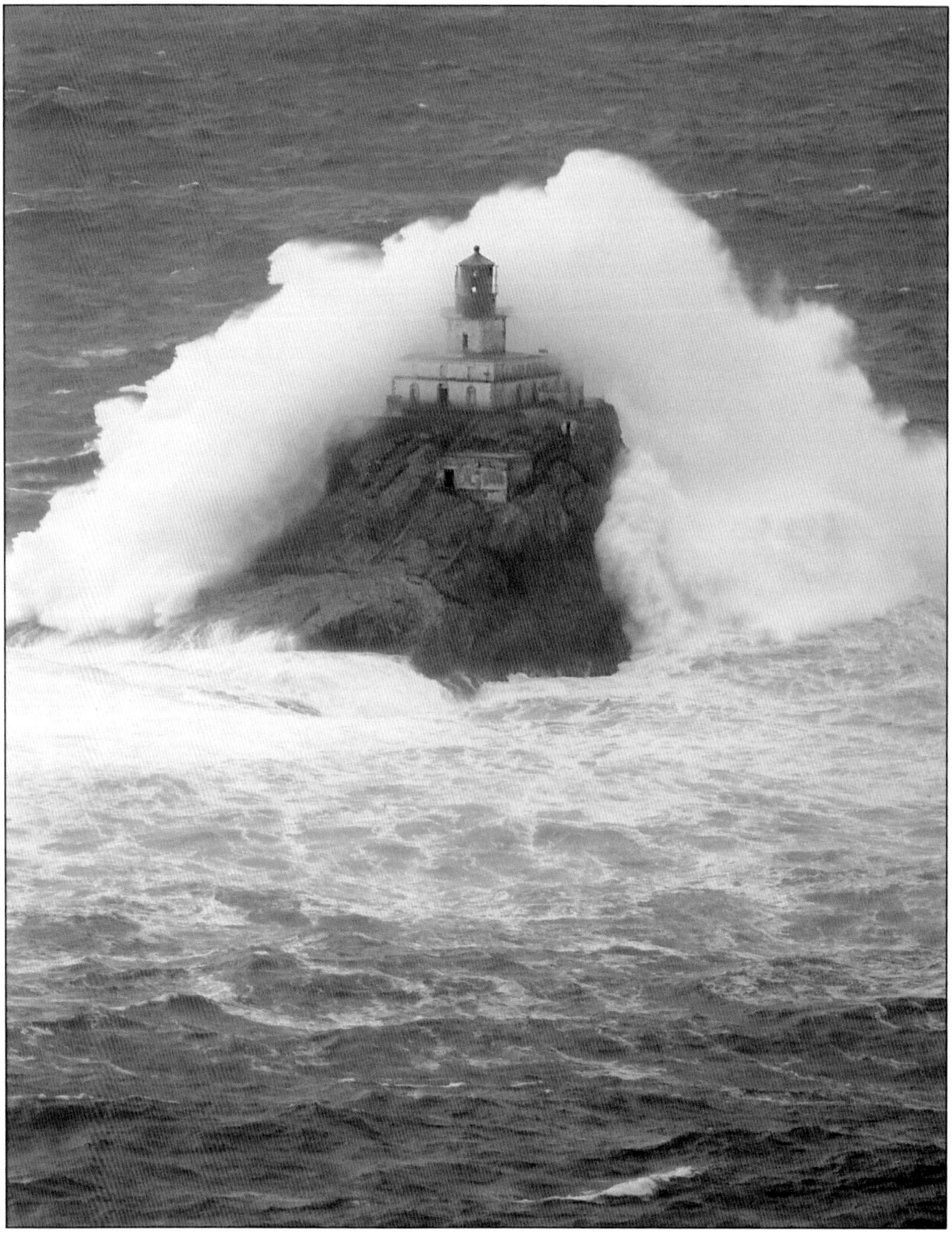

This 2010 photograph shows the kind of huge waves that can crest over the 134-foot top of the tower and entirely submerge the lighthouse during storms. It is easy to see how these waves, when mixed with broken-off boulders from the Rock, could do such severe damage to the lantern and dwelling. This image was taken from the Tillamook Head Trail that leads from Indian Beach at Ecola State Park to Seaside, Oregon. (Gary Loveless.)

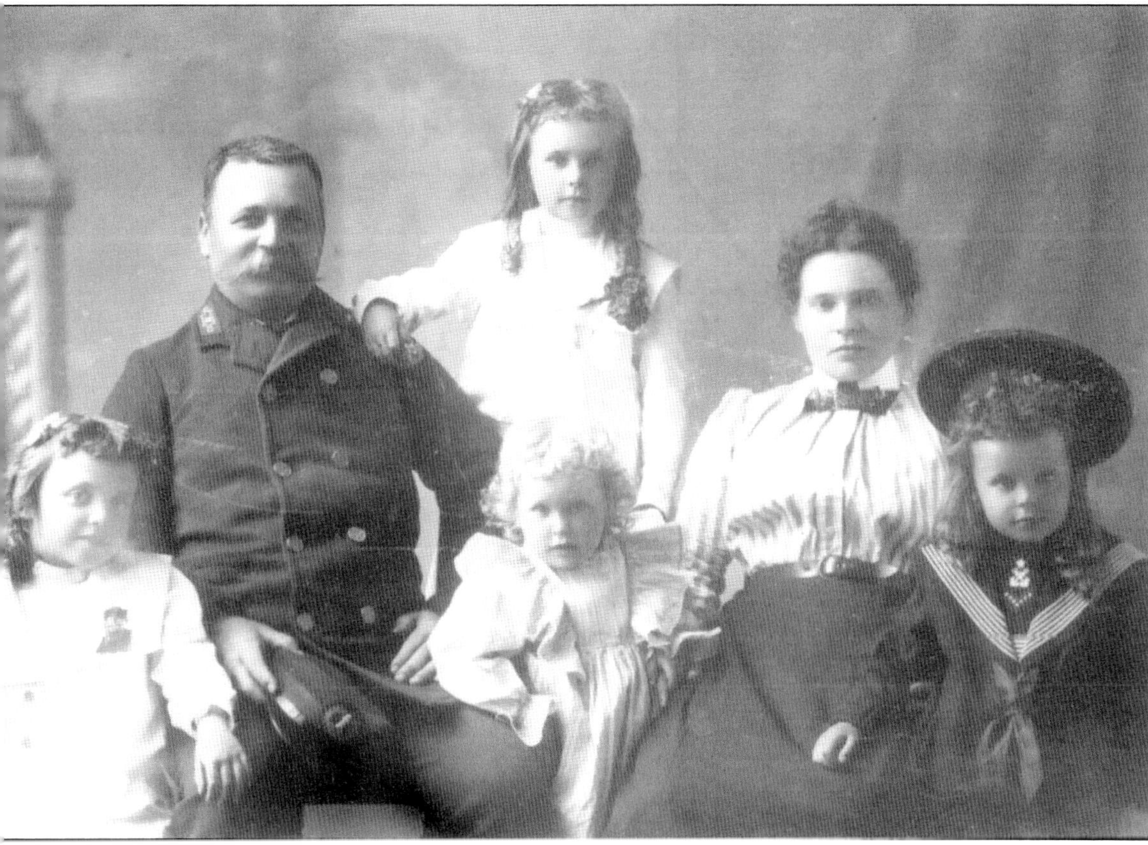

Julius William Dahlgen (b. 1858) served at Tillamook Rock Lighthouse from 1901 to 1919, spending the last 10 years as head keeper. Dahlgren's daughter Shirley Cole recalled that she and her mother "prayed for the men out there" during a cataclysmic storm in October 1912 that did considerable damage to the light station. The commendation Dahlgren received stated "the Bureau is grateful to learn that it has in its service men who perform their duty under such adverse conditions." In 1913, head keeper Dahlgren and assistant Daniel W. Clark almost did not make it the mile to shore and were shipwrecked at Elk Creek when the lighthouse boat was carried south by the current. It took 24 hours for them to be rescued. Pictured in this c. 1901 photograph are, from left to right, (first row) Julia, Florence, and Harold; (second row) William, Helen, and Sophia (William's wife). (Nancy Brooks Tynkila.)

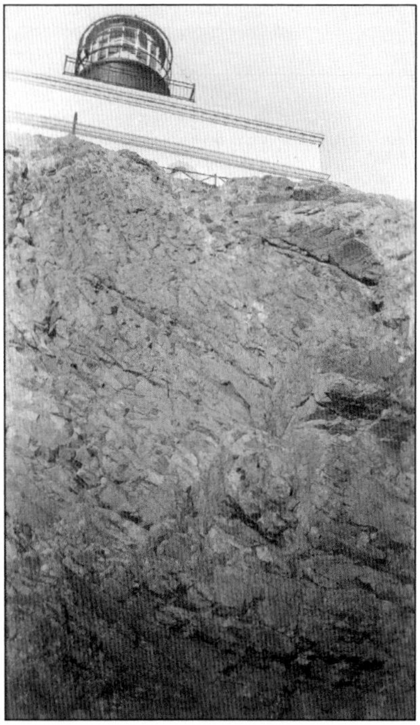

This photograph, taken by Walter T. Lawrence in 1920, shows an interesting but dangerous view of the lighthouse and texture of rock strata from inside the crevice looking up the side to the tower. During storms, broken-off boulders were cast upward by the waves and into the lantern room, as it was a straight shot from the crevice to the windowpanes. (BB.)

This June 2017 aerial view shows the exact location and funnel-like shape of the crevice on the south side of the lighthouse. The pressure that built up at the closed east end acted as a catapult for any debris or broken rock that was carried into the fissure during a storm. Even on relatively calm days, it could be a dangerous place, though the fishing was said to be good there. (USFWS.)

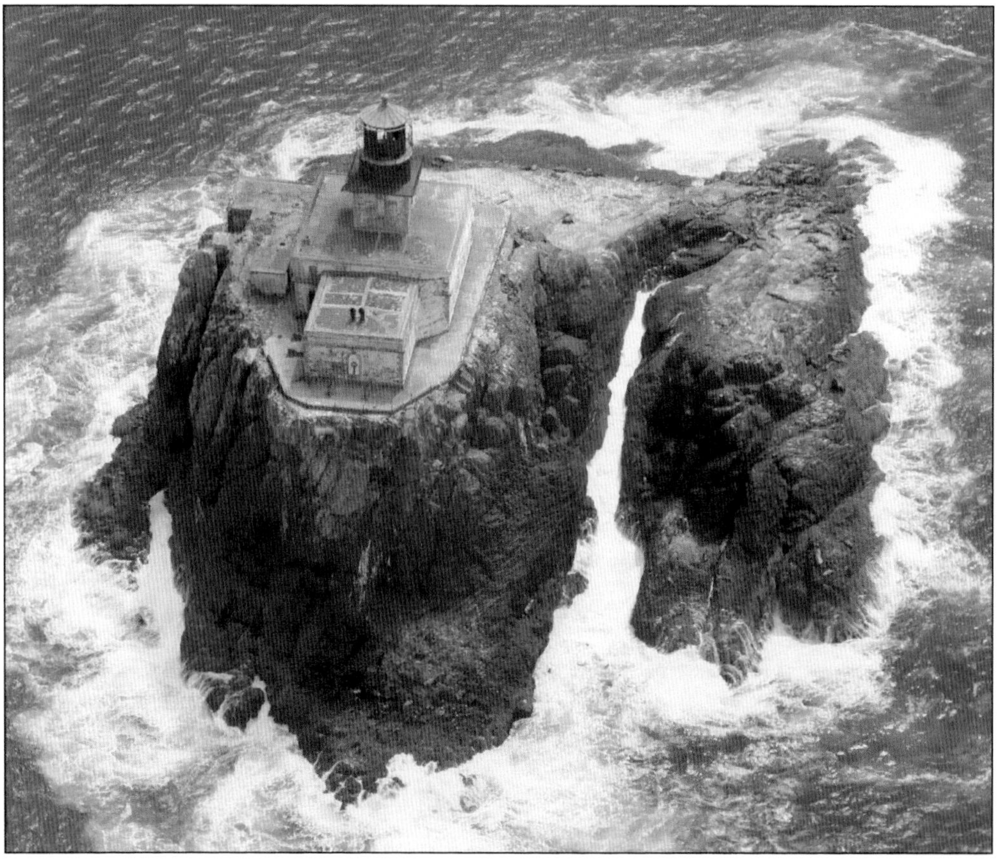

During the horrendous October 21, 1934 storm, wave-catapulted rocks broke 16 panes of the lantern glass, which let huge amounts of seawater wash debris down the tower stairs. The keepers were swept off their feet in swirling water up to their necks as they struggled to bolt the emergency wood shutter panels over the openings. With waves completely submerging them every three minutes, they felt they were in real danger of either drowning or being washed out into the ocean through the empty three-foot pane openings before they could accomplish their task. (LHC.)

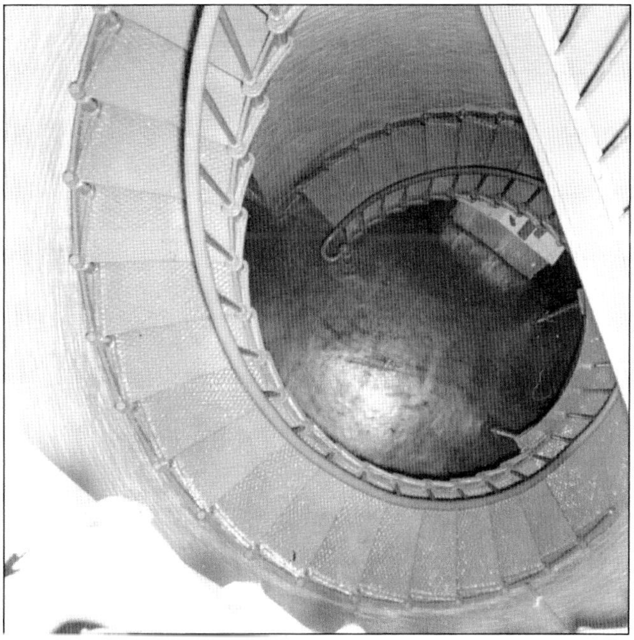

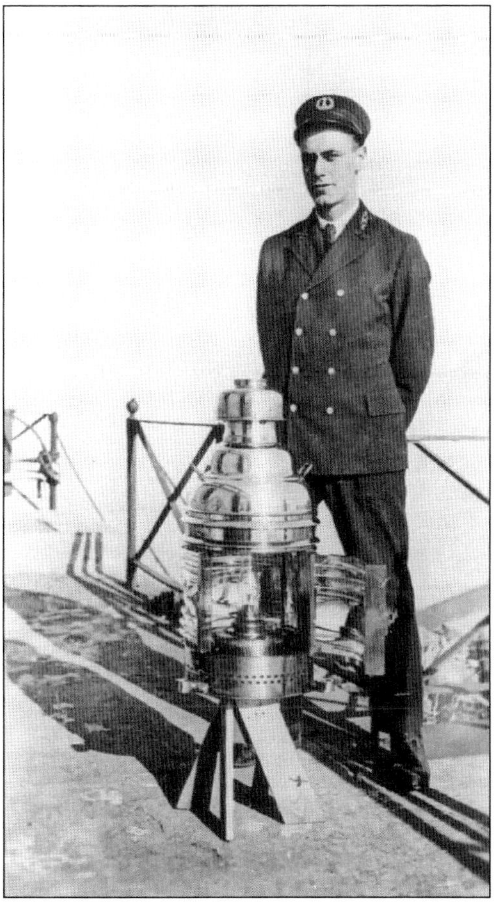

Walter T. Lawrence stands next to an emergency lens lantern in this 1920 photograph. In 1934, when the storm left the first order Fresnel lens inoperable, a five-day emergency lens lantern, similar to this one, was used until the regular light could be repaired and reestablished six days later. (CRMM.)

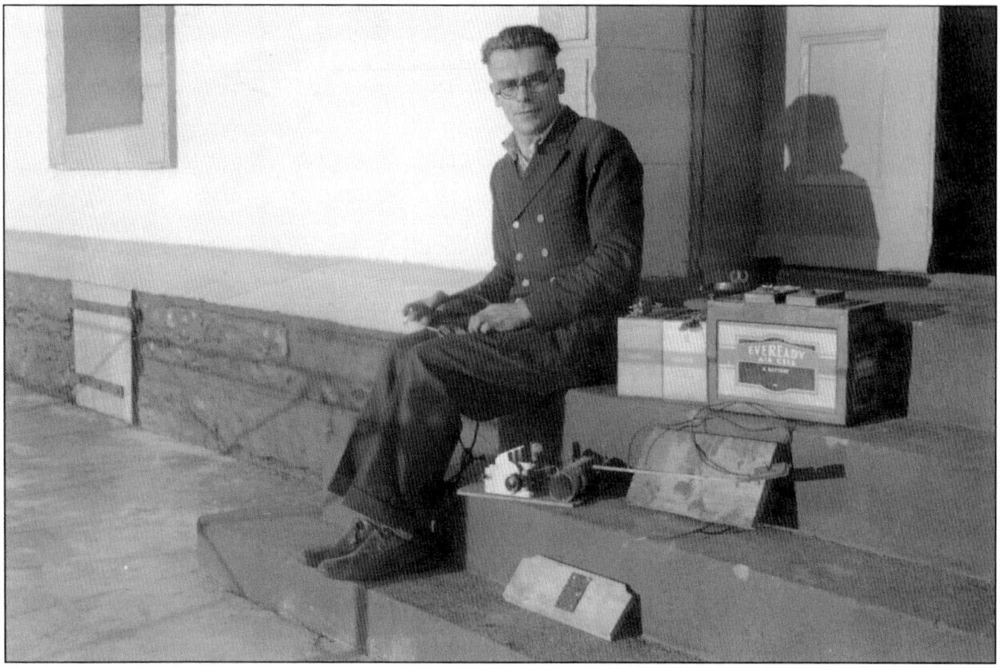

First assistant keeper Henry Jenkins sits on the front steps of Tillamook Rock Lighthouse amidst the salvaged scrap equipment he used to assemble his shortwave radio, shown on the second step, which provided the only communication during the 1934 storm. It took him an hour to make contact with mainland ham radio operators, who relayed messages back and forth to the 17th Lighthouse District office in Portland. The telegram notifying the office of the situation is shown below. Jenkins constructed the radio using parts from a standard broadcast receiving set, telephone receiver, dry batteries, and odds and ends of wire, tinfoil, brass, wax paper, and other fittings. Jenkins, along with head keeper William Hill, fourth assistant Hugo Hansen, and substitute keeper Werner Storm, all received commendations for their "conduct and attention to duty and resourcefulness" during this stressful event. (Above, CGHO; below, NARA.)

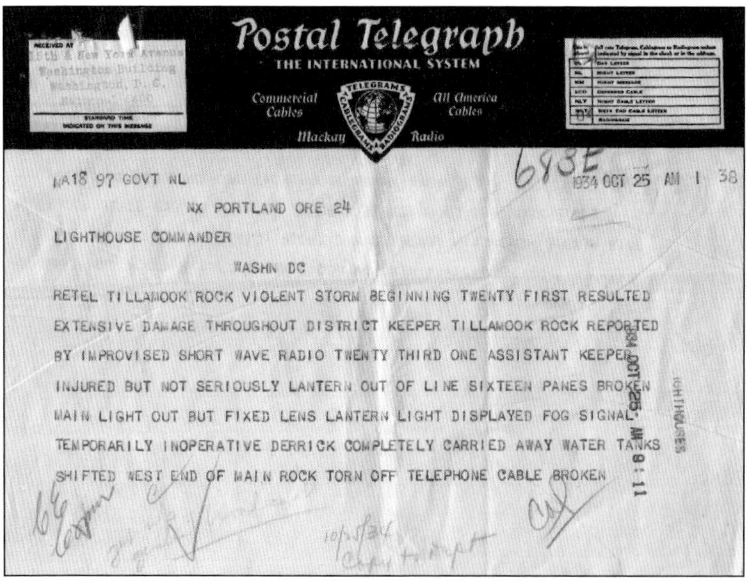

Postal Telegraph
THE INTERNATIONAL SYSTEM
Commercial Cables — All America Cables — Mackay Radio

RECEIVED AT 15th & New York Avenue, Washington Building, Washington, D. C.
STANDARD TIME INDICATED ON THIS MESSAGE

NA18 97 GOVT NL — 1934 OCT 25 AM 1 38

NX PORTLAND ORE 24

LIGHTHOUSE COMMANDER

WASHN DC

RETEL TILLAMOOK ROCK VIOLENT STORM BEGINNING TWENTY FIRST RESULTED EXTENSIVE DAMAGE THROUGHOUT DISTRICT KEEPER TILLAMOOK ROCK REPORTED BY IMPROVISED SHORT WAVE RADIO TWENTY THIRD ONE ASSISTANT KEEPER INJURED BUT NOT SERIOUSLY LANTERN OUT OF LINE SIXTEEN PANES BROKEN MAIN LIGHT OUT BUT FIXED LENS LANTERN LIGHT DISPLAYED FOG SIGNAL TEMPORARILY INOPERATIVE DERRICK COMPLETELY CARRIED AWAY WATER TANKS SHIFTED WEST END OF MAIN ROCK TORN OFF TELEPHONE CABLE BROKEN

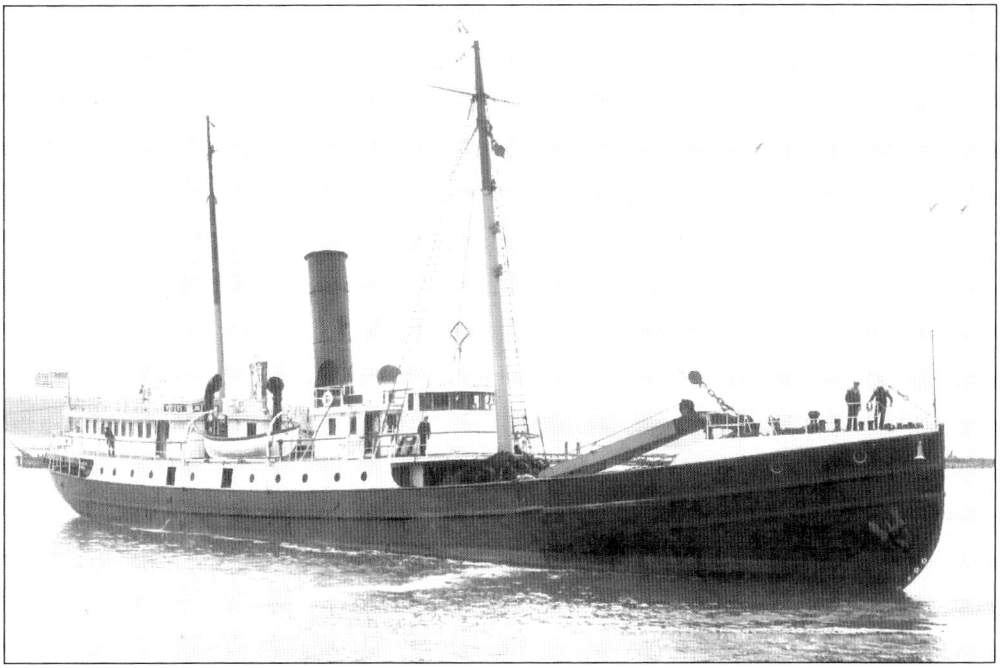

When the storm subsided, the keepers busied themselves in making what repairs they could until early on the morning of October 27, when the lighthouse tender *Manzanita* arrived, carrying the necessary items to get the station operational once again. Two days later, the original flash signature was once again exhibited at Tillamook Rock Lighthouse. These two photographs, both taken in 1929, show the *Manzanita* (above) and its crew (below), from left to right, Chief Eng. H.C. Binder, Radio Op. R.F. Dibbs, Second Officer J.B. Martin, Capt. Charles A.A. Modeer, Second Eng. R.A. Burns, First Officer Claude Asquith, and Second Eng. P. Clark. First Officer Asquith was in command of the tender during the urgent trip out to the Rock following the storm, since Capt. Modeer was on leave. It was dangerous and difficult to brave the rough seas while the storm was winding down but still very active. (Both, CGNW.)

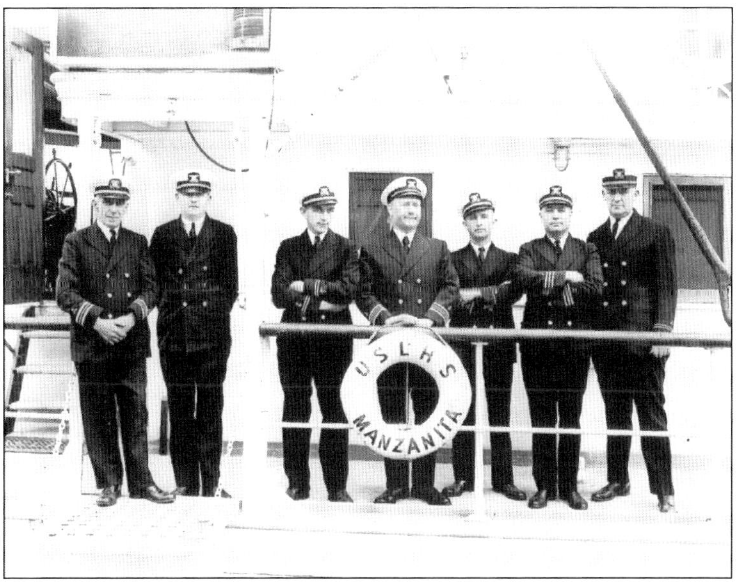

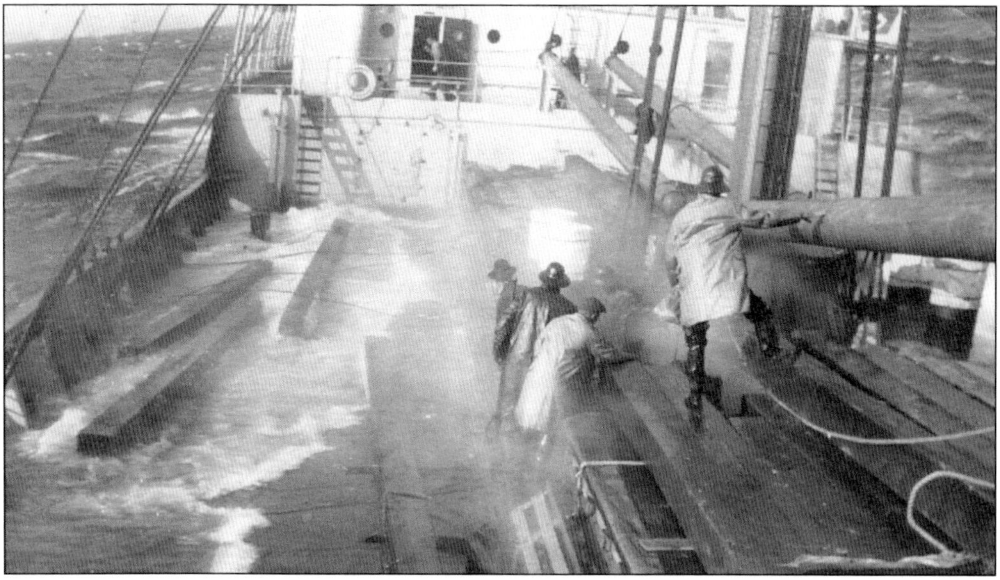

This 1930s photograph of the *Manzanita* in stormy seas, with its cargo of lumber washing across the deck, shows what it might have looked like as it rushed to the aid of the crippled lighthouse on Tillamook Rock following the October 1934 cyclone. (CRMM.)

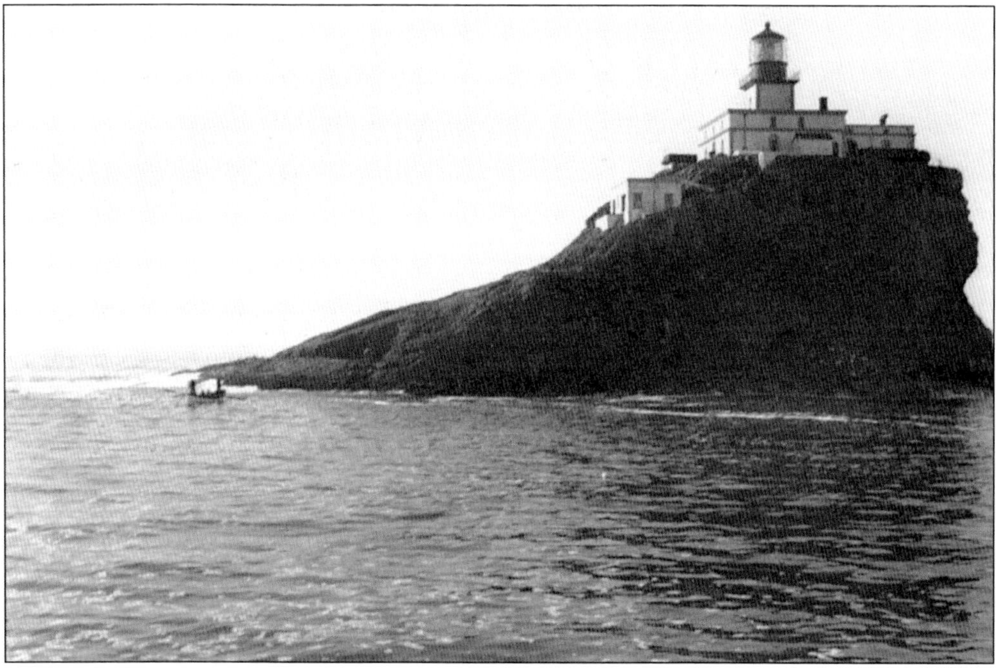

Appearing like an impregnable fortress upon the rocky top with no visible means of access, this very rare view of a derrick-less Tillamook Rock Lighthouse was taken only six days after the horrific 1934 October storm that swept the entire derrick and boom assembly into the sea. The photograph was taken by 17th District Assistant Superintendent E.C. Merrill, who arrived on the tender *Manzanita* for an inspection visit to assess the storm damage and debrief the keepers about their experiences during the storm. His subsequent report was used for the write-up of the storm that was recounted in the November 1934 issue of the *Lighthouse Service Bulletin*. (JGC.)

Assistant Superintendent Edward C. Merrill is shown with stopwatch in hand as he checks the precision of the timed flashes from the Tillamook Rock lighting unit in 1937. When he came to inspect the lighthouse a few days after the storm of 1934, he was appalled at the damage that had taken place in a matter of just a few hours. The storm has since been classified as an extratropical cyclone with peak wind gusts of 109 miles per hour. (LHD.)

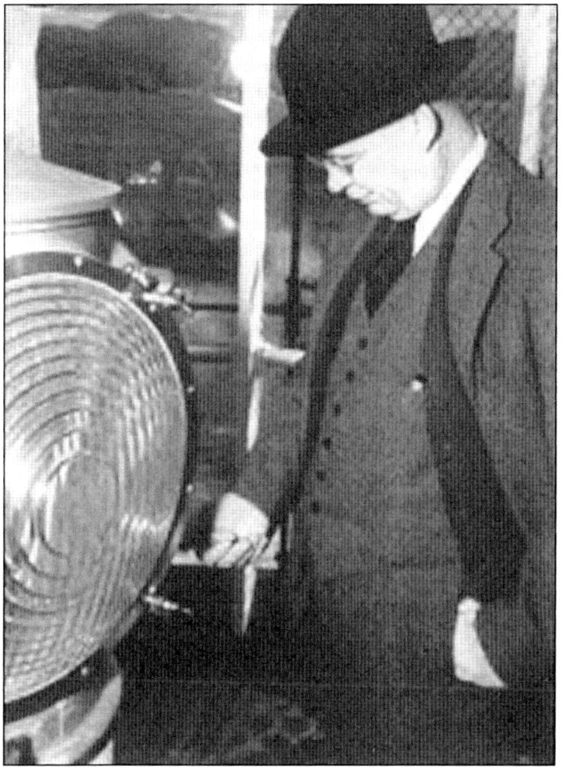

A sobering view shows the destroyed cast-iron railing that looked like it was ready to topple over the cliff edge to join the missing sections that had already succumbed. One of the 60-pound boulders that did the damage sits nearby, while a lone pulley from the derrick assembly is a reminder of what forces were unleashed at the height of the cyclone on the night of October 21, 1934. (CGHO.)

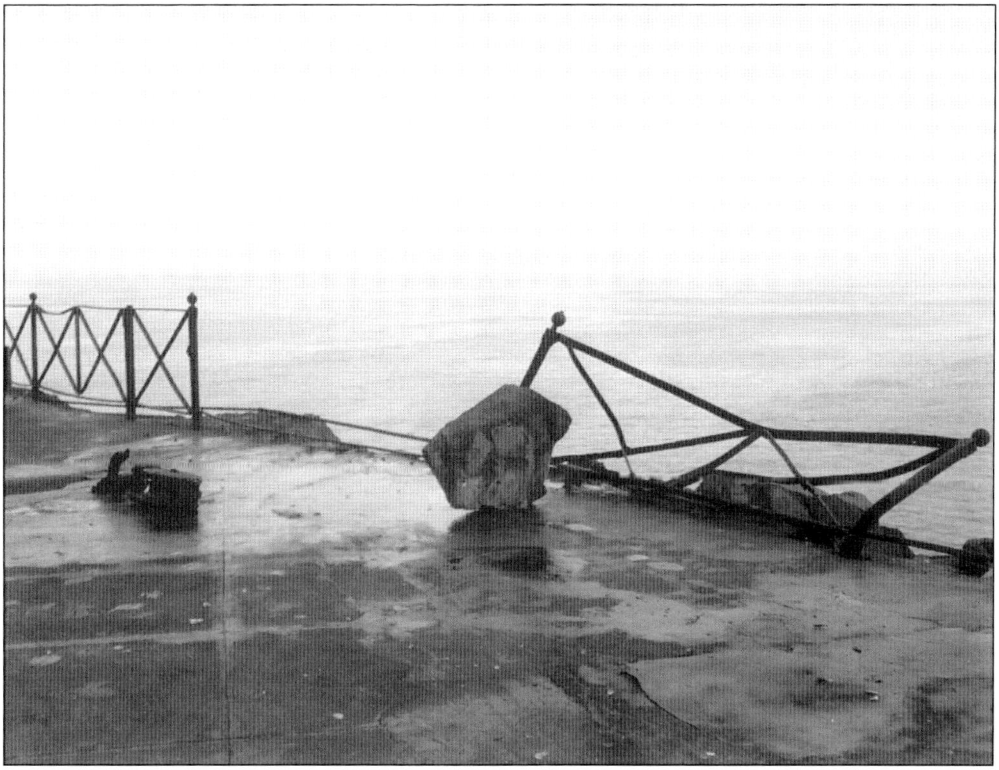

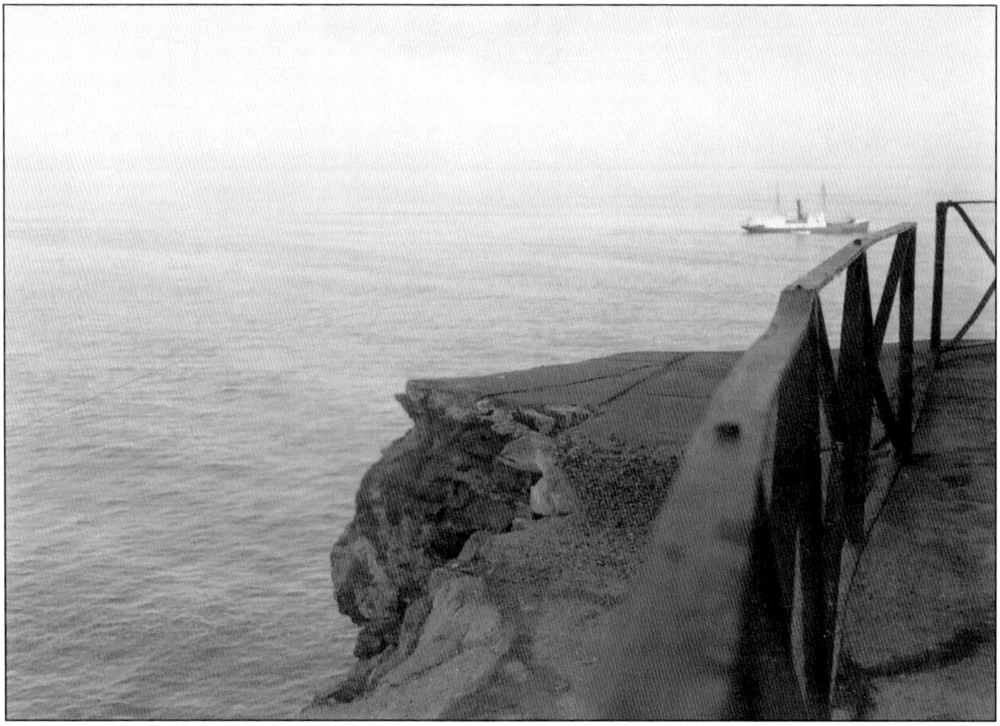

Six feet of the west end rock overhang broke off during the October 1934 storm and plummeted into the sea. Assistant keeper Henry Jenkins believed the resulting cataclysmic waves, which threw up boulder fragments from the fractured rock, were what contributed to the shattering of 16 storm glass panes in the lantern and swept the derrick away. What is left of the overhang shows a stress crack in the protective cement cap that had been applied more than three decades earlier. In the distance, the lighthouse tender *Manzanita* awaits the return of the inspection team. (CGHO.)

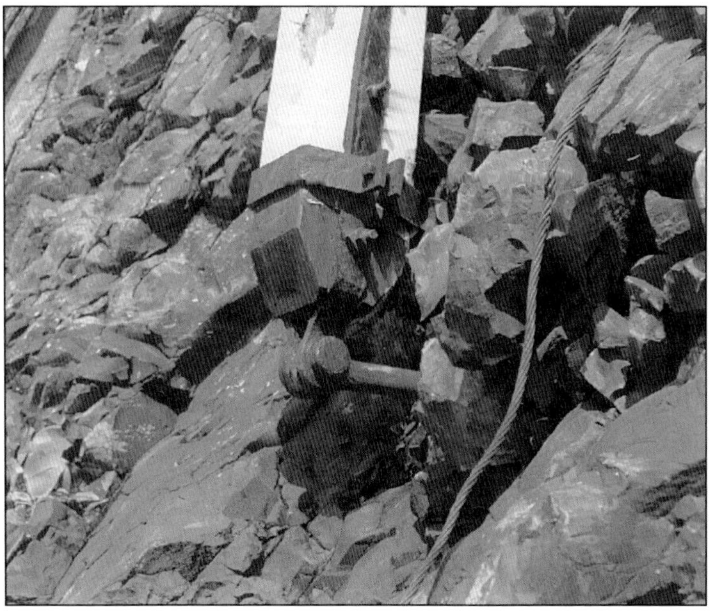

According to Assistant Superintendent E.C. Merrill's written report, "All that remained of the derrick was the bottom end of the two stiff legs which were anchored into the solid rock. One of the anchorages, 3 [inches] in diameter eyebolts, and three feet long pulled loose, crumbling the rock around the anchor bolt." (CGHO.)

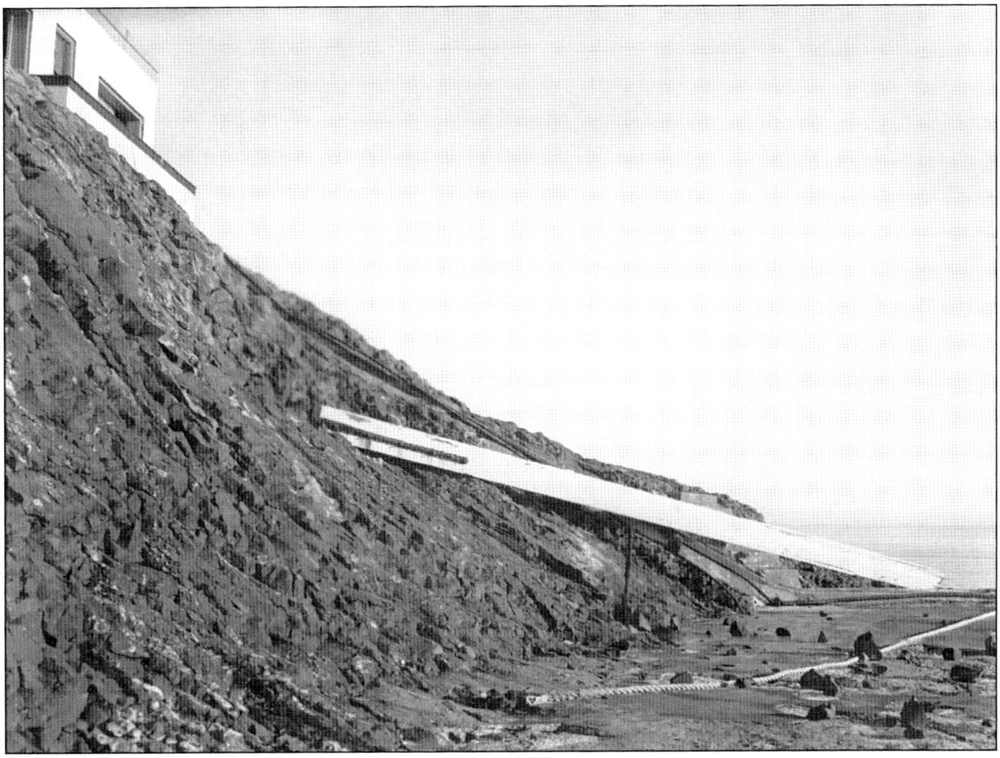

These two photographs show what remained of one of the two derrick legs that were destroyed in the storm. In service from the very beginning in 1881, the wood stiff leg derrick was built on the gentler-sloping eastern side of the Rock, opposite of the western overhang, yet close enough to the southern crevice that it was still subjected to being hit by rocks and debris during storms. Note the remains of the hoisting gear that rest amid the wrecked debris and are shown below the tanks on the cliff side. (Both, CGHO.)

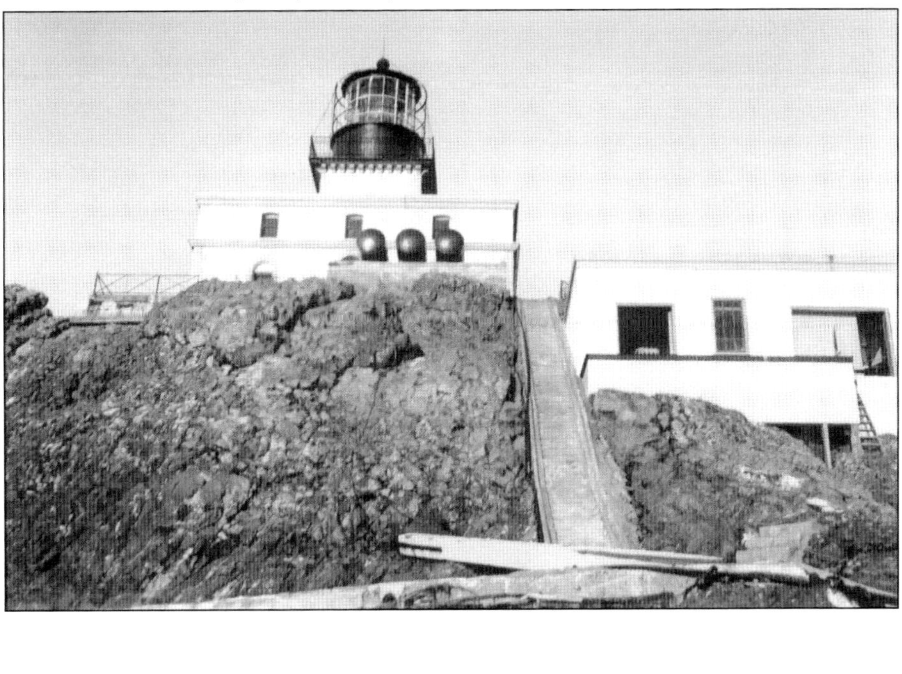

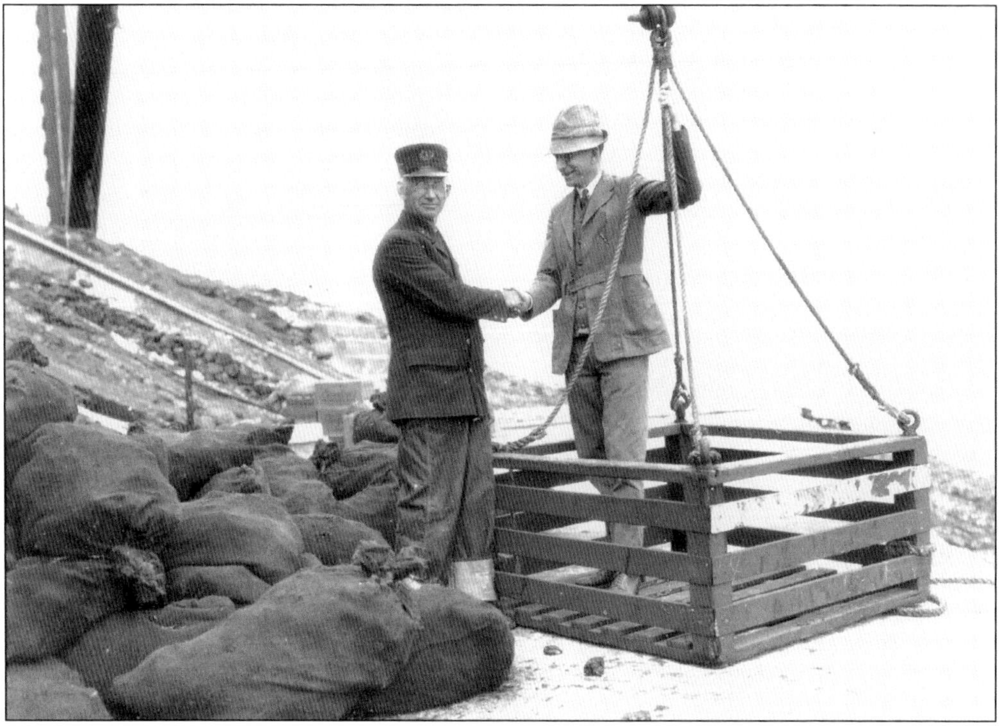

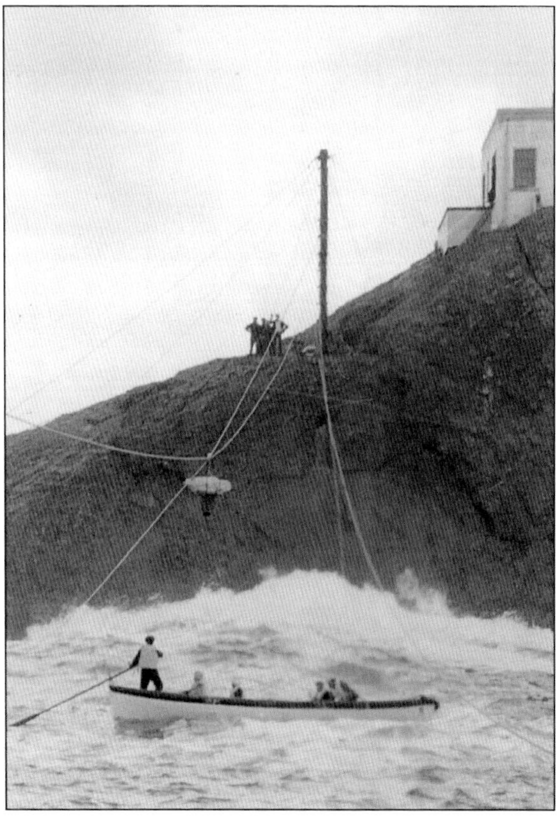

Head keeper William Hill (left) receives a congratulatory handshake from 17th Lighthouse District superintendent Ralph R. Tinkham during an inspection visit sometime following the storm. Hill was head keeper from at least 1930 to 1936 and was one of the "storm crew" on the Rock during the October 1934 cyclone. The following year, Ralph Tinkham was promoted to chief engineer of the US Lighthouse Service after having served in an administrative capacity in six different lighthouse districts since 1911. (CRMM.)

By the end of November 1934, three of the keepers and repair crew members had come down with bad colds that required them to be removed from the Rock. Since the derrick had not yet been replaced, a breeches buoy was rigged to take them off. The tender *Rose* was sent to get them, but due to another major storm, the seas were too rough, and it was several days before the successful rescue was accomplished. (CGHO.)

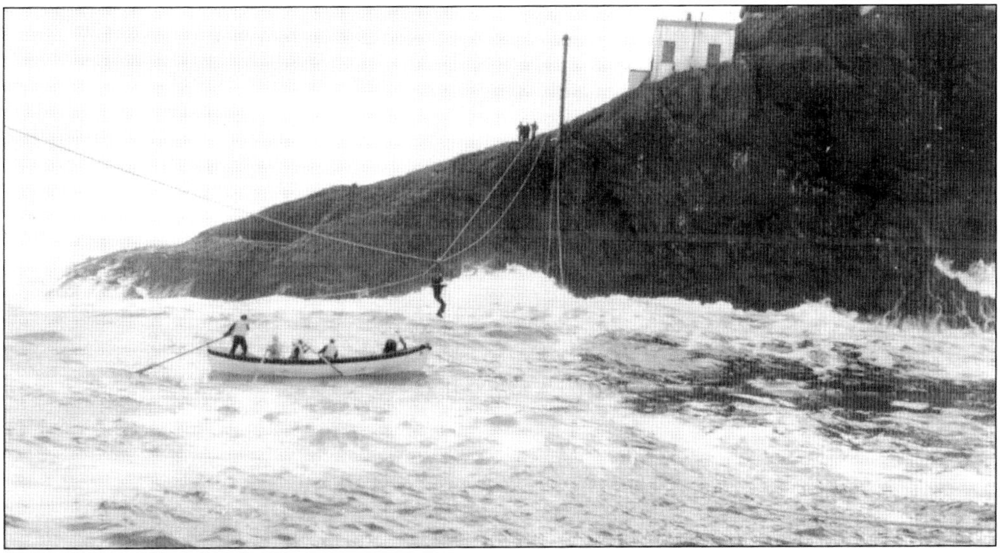

Crew foreman Harry Ratty is shown being brought off the Rock in a breeches buoy on December 1, 1934. In an article written for *National Geographic*, which published the photograph, Lighthouse Commissioner George Putnam wrote that the story of the 1934 storm at Tillamook Rock had been translated and distributed to all lighthouse keepers in Mexico as an example of courageous performance of duty. (CGHO.)

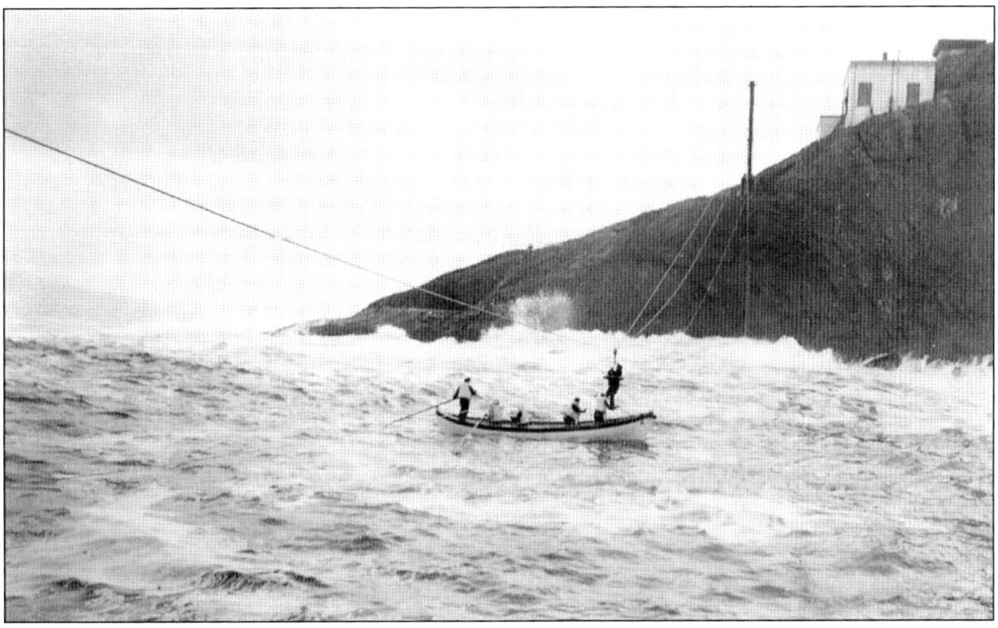

First assistant keeper Henry Jenkins is shown clutching the outgoing mail sack as he takes his turn riding down the breeches buoy to the cargo boat. In 1932, when keeper Henry Hill was bringing the mail off the Rock while riding in the derrick basket, it missed the cargo boat and sank 20 feet under the surface. Hill's later nonchalant comment was that he "seemed a long time coming up." (CGHO.)

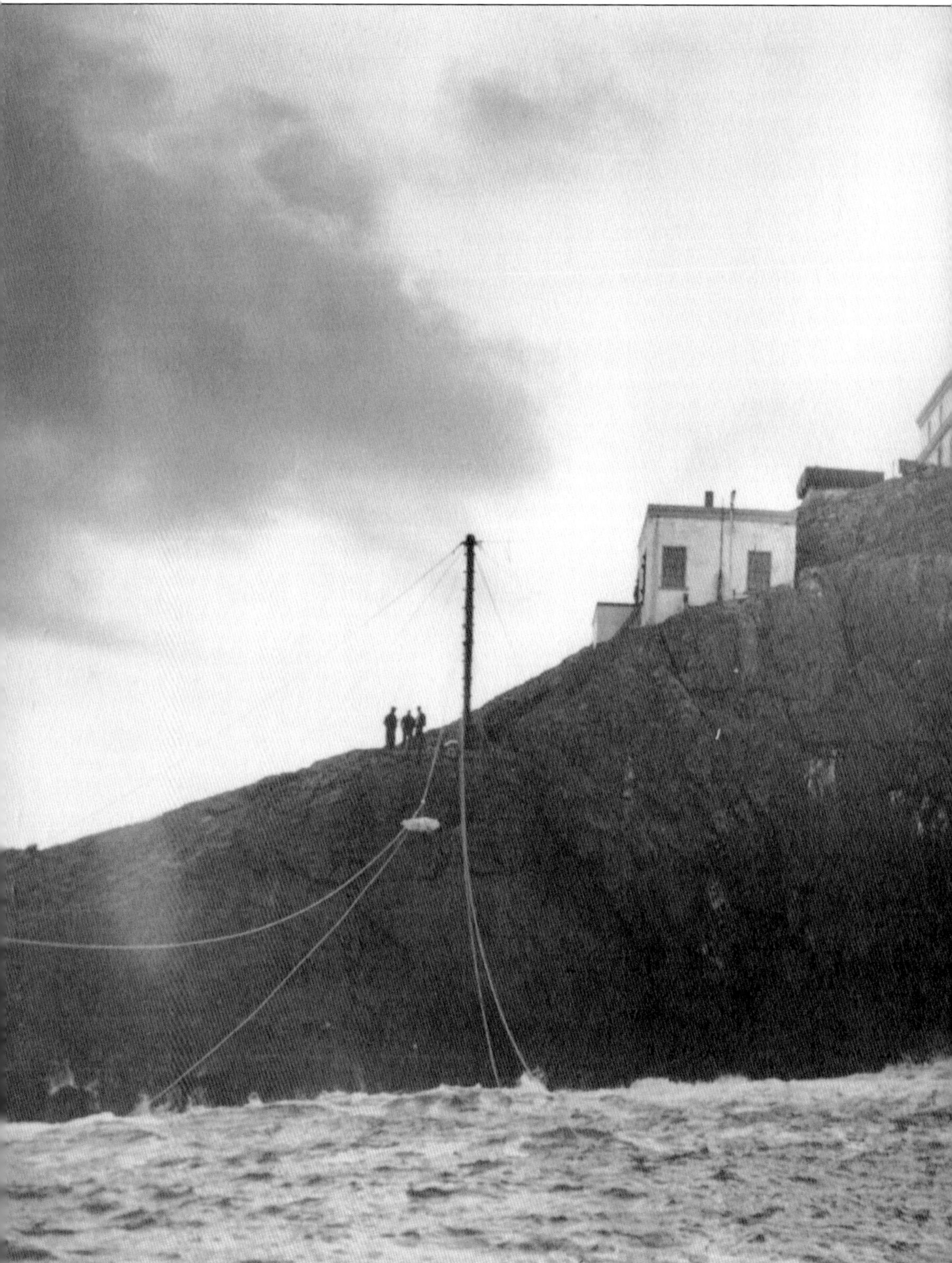

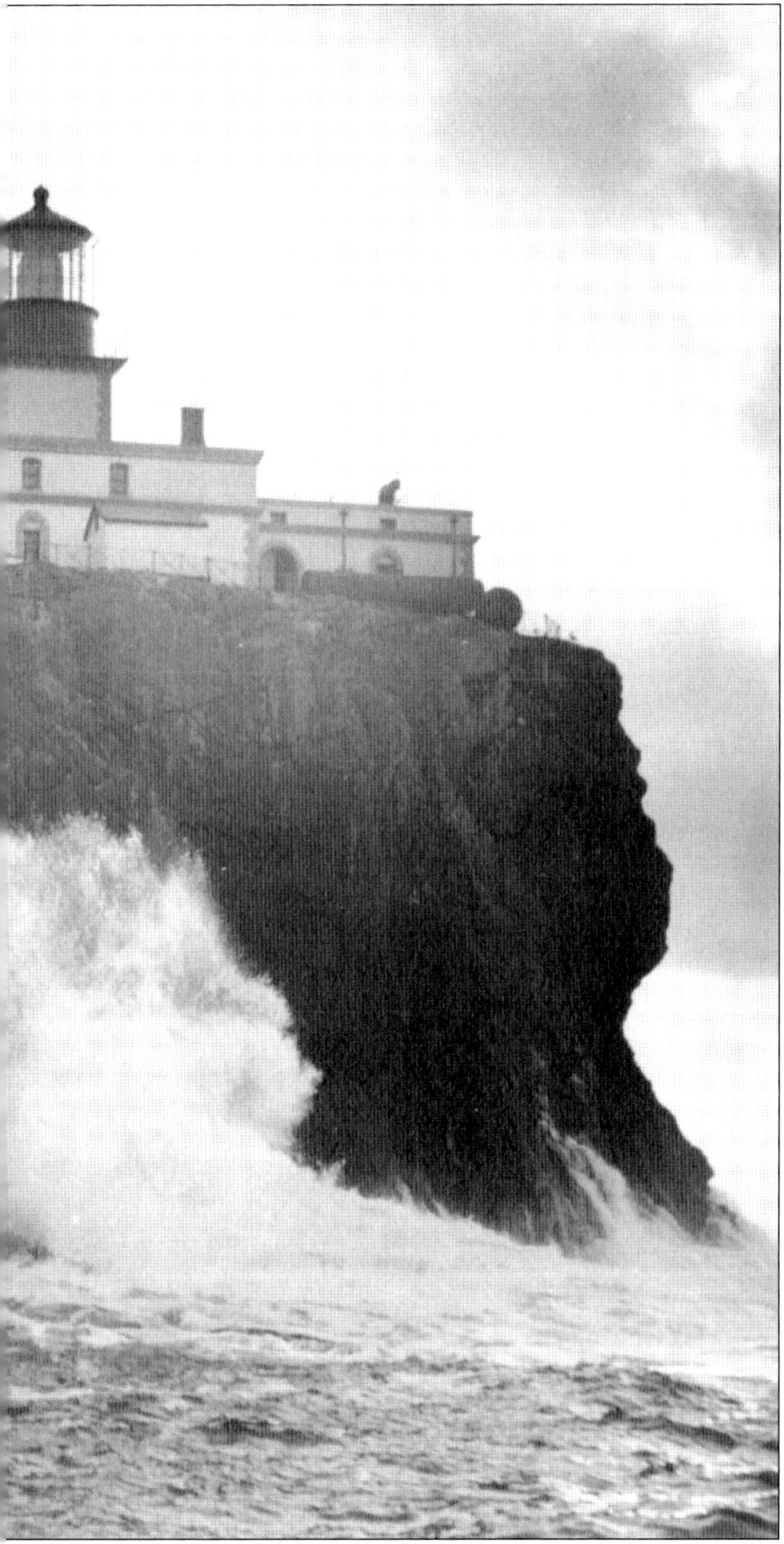

This dramatic photograph—taken from the lighthouse tender *Rose* on December 1, 1934—shows the intensity of the seas breaking against the Rock the day the rescue was made. The December rescue was said to have been among the most daring performed at sea, and commendations were given to Capt. J.H. Jensen and First Officer E.C. Davis of the tender *Rose* for their "skill and excellent judgment" in successfully removing five men and landing two others during severe conditions. (CGHO.)

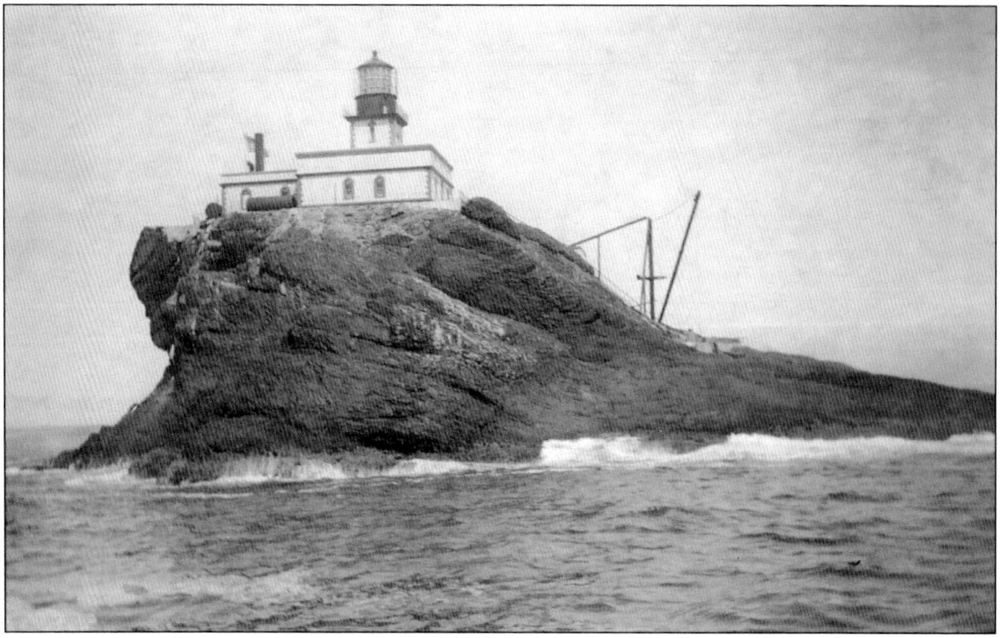

The next three photographs show exactly how much of the west end of the Rock was broken off during intense storms over the years. The above photograph, which was taken sometime before the severe storm of October 18, 1912, shows the "nose" of the west end still intact at far left. According to head keeper William Dahlgren, as reported in the January 1913 *Lighthouse Bulletin*, "I regret to state that on the evening of the 18th, or morning of the 19th, we lost a portion of the west end of the Rock, water and rocks coming over with so much noise, we could not tell, and did not know it had departed until next morning, when the sea went down, that we could go outside." The 1920 photograph below, taken by T.W. Otto, shows the stark result. (Both, CGHO.)

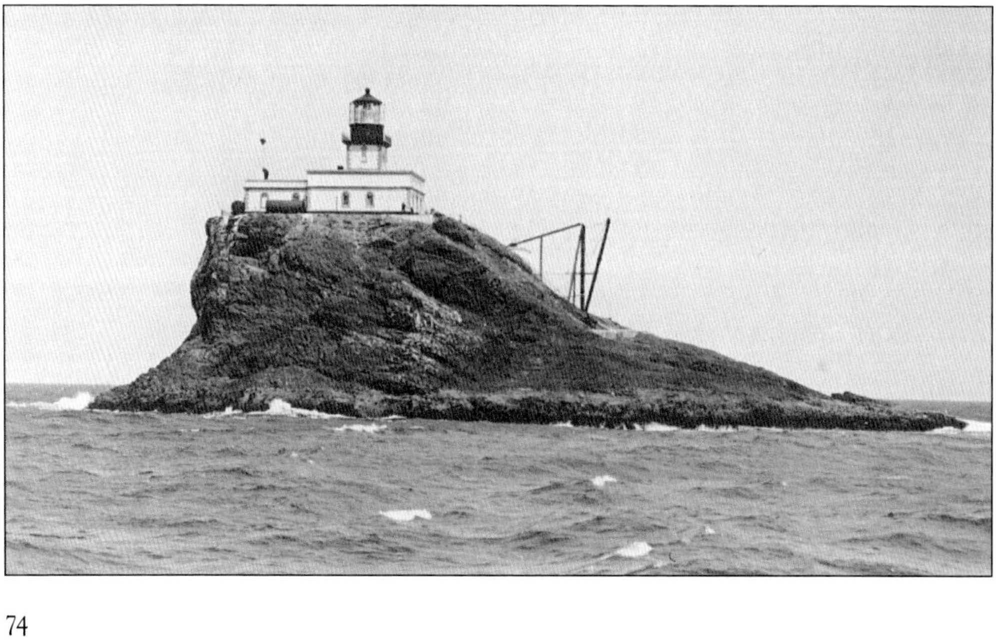

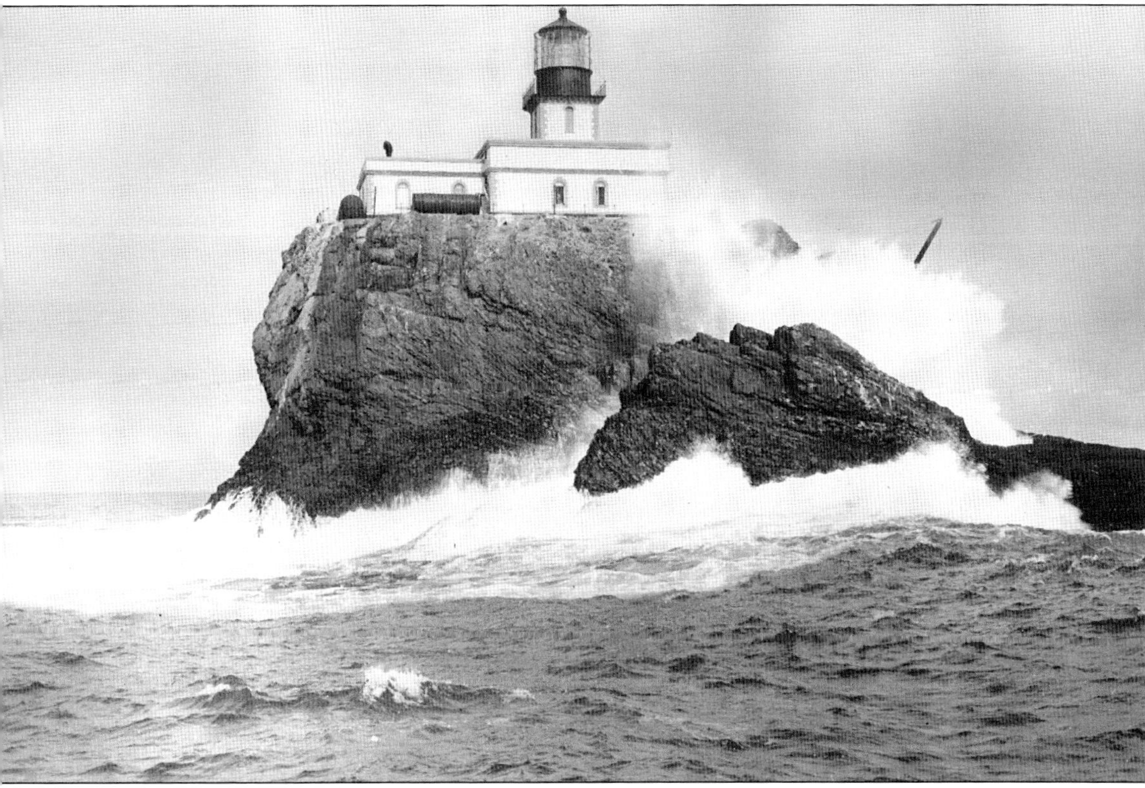

The last of the three comparison photographs featured on this page and the previous one was taken in early 1935 by *Manzanita* captain Charles A.A. Modeer. It clearly shows the missing six-foot lip on the top of the west end that broke off during the October 1934 cyclone. The derrick had been rebuilt by the time of this photograph, but the first order Fresnel lens had not yet been replaced. Note the intense wave action out of the east end of the crevice. Between the rock breakage on the west end and the crevice slingshot on the south side, the lighthouse was constantly facing a barrage of flying boulders during its entire operational life. Newspaper accounts reported on the many visible repairs on the inside of the lantern glass where keepers were continually having to replace broken panes. (CGHO.)

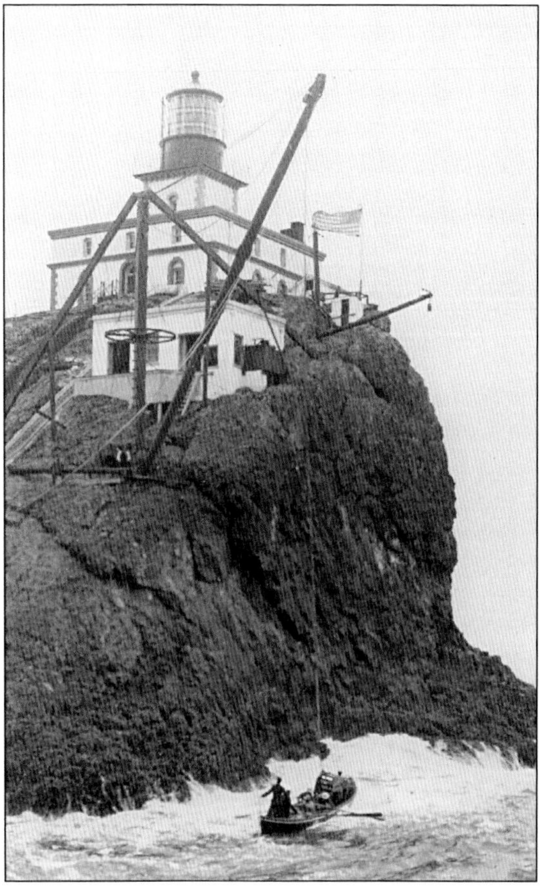

Communication was another area of concern raised by the 1934 storm. Over the years, there had not been much success keeping any type of cable from the lighthouse to the mainland in workable order. The first telegraph cable was suspended out from the Rock by means of a boom from a second small derrick. The small derrick, shown in the c. 1898 photograph at left, was built in 1893, but the cable only lasted three years before a severe storm broke it. Eventually, the derrick idea was abandoned, and a cable was laid off the northeast end of the rock, passing over a cable stand to keep it from chafing, as shown below. A white line painted on the rock surface under the cable to mark its trajectory served as a warning to ship captains of where not to drop an anchor. (Left, USLHS; below, CGHO.)

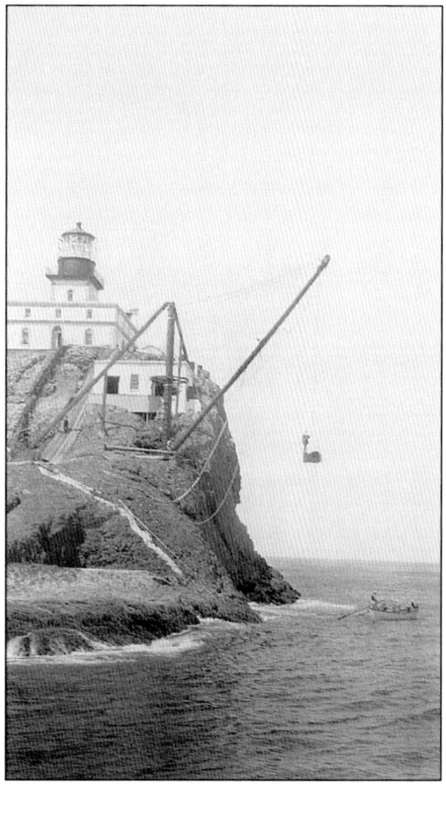

The submarine telephone cable to the mainland that perished in the 1934 storm was only three years old. This photograph shows workmen aboard the lighthouse tender *Rose* splicing the cable together while laying it in June 1931. At least two telephone cables were laid and then destroyed due to storm damage between 1920 to 1934, so after this point, rather than spend money to replace it yet again, a radiotelephone was utilized, making Tillamook Rock one of the first lighthouses to be so equipped. (CCHS.)

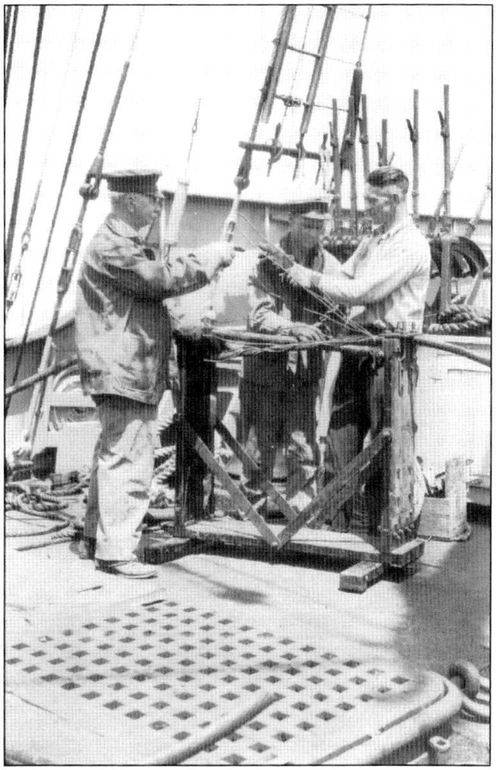

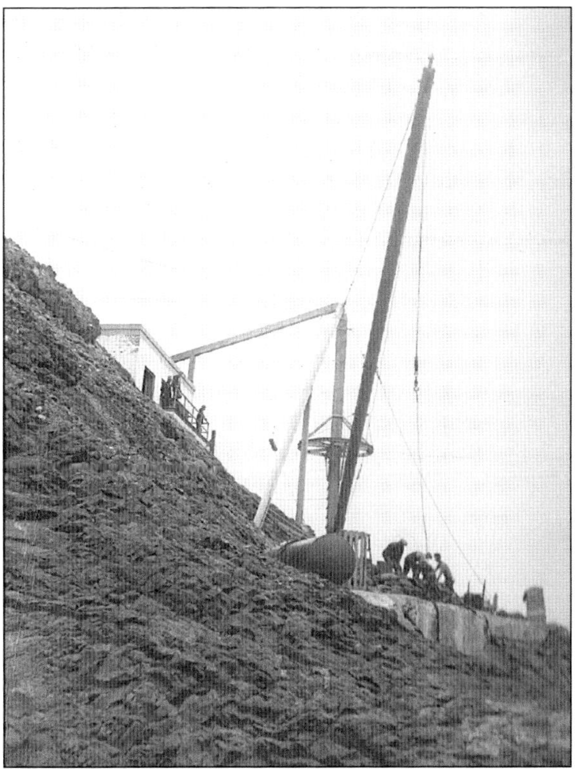

In May 1935, equipment was still being replaced from the storm seven months earlier. Note the large steel cylinder tank on the derrick landing platform that awaits hoisting and placement on top of the Rock. The storm reports mentioned how water and oil tanks had shifted on their foundations, loosening their saddles and anchorage rods. (JGC.)

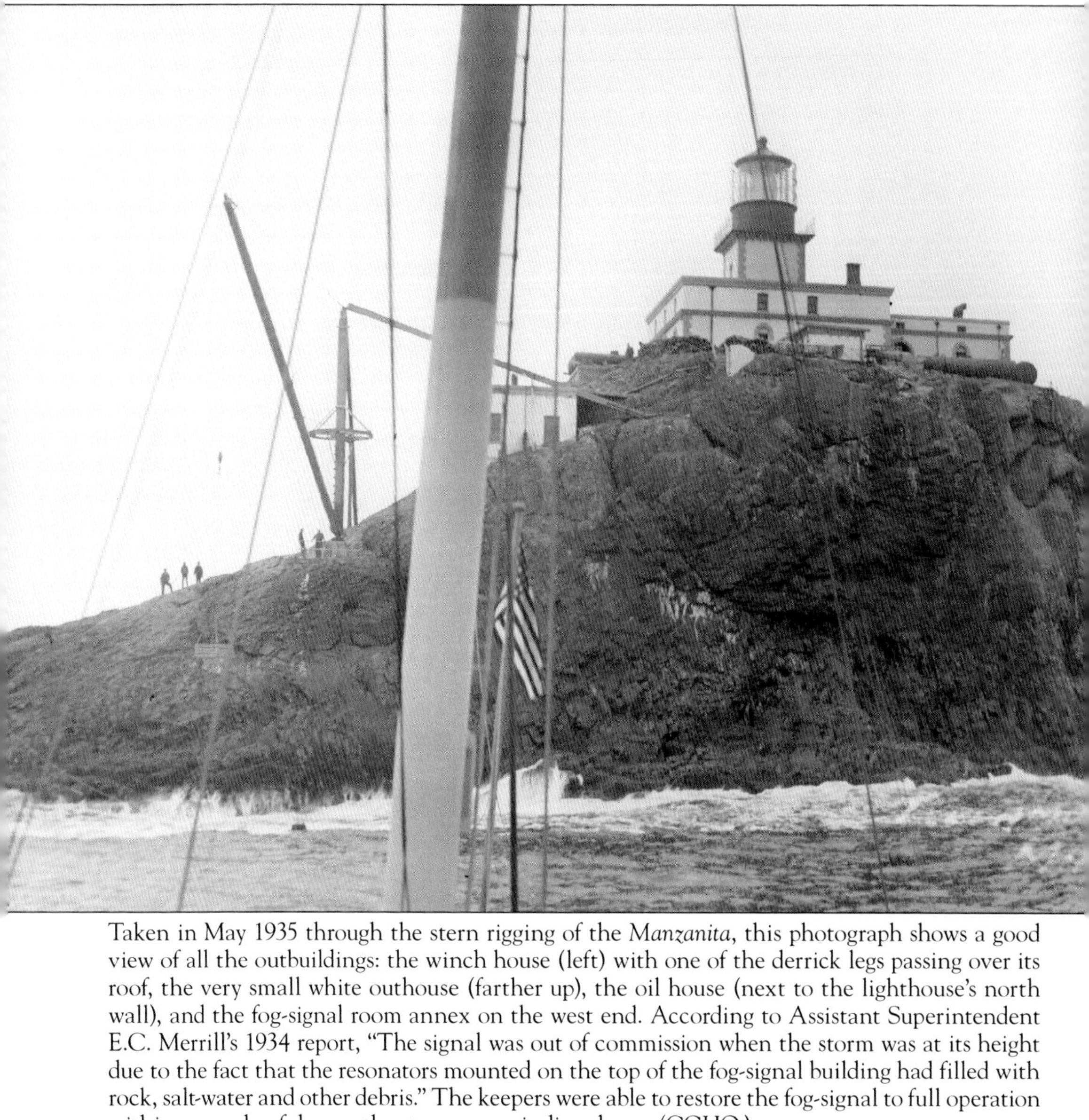

Taken in May 1935 through the stern rigging of the *Manzanita*, this photograph shows a good view of all the outbuildings: the winch house (left) with one of the derrick legs passing over its roof, the very small white outhouse (farther up), the oil house (next to the lighthouse's north wall), and the fog-signal room annex on the west end. According to Assistant Superintendent E.C. Merrill's 1934 report, "The signal was out of commission when the storm was at its height due to the fact that the resonators mounted on the top of the fog-signal building had filled with rock, salt-water and other debris." The keepers were able to restore the fog-signal to full operation within a couple of days as the storm was winding down. (CGHO.)

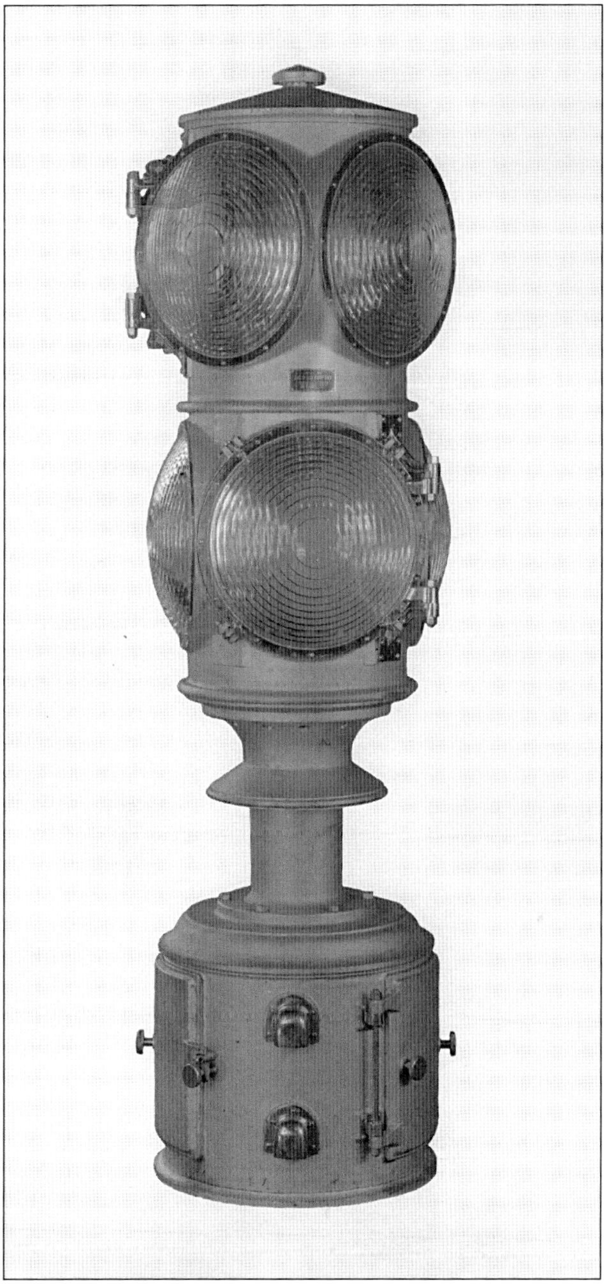

Assistant Superintendent E.C. Merrill's report recommended that the first order Fresnel lens be replaced with a third or fourth order lens so that the upper and lower part of the lantern could be closed off with steel plates instead of glass, which would "reduce the hazard and difficulty of maintaining the light in severe storms." He added that the prisms of the first order lens were all chipped to a considerable extent, and the damage from the storm had reduced the effectiveness and efficiency of the lens. As a result, in June 1935, the 1880 first order Fresnel lens was disassembled and removed from Tillamook Rock Lighthouse after 55 years of sterling service. It was replaced with this Type B Revolving-Duplex Composite Lighting Unit of 75,000 candlepower. The upper belt of lantern storm panes was permanently plated from this point forward. (CGHO.)

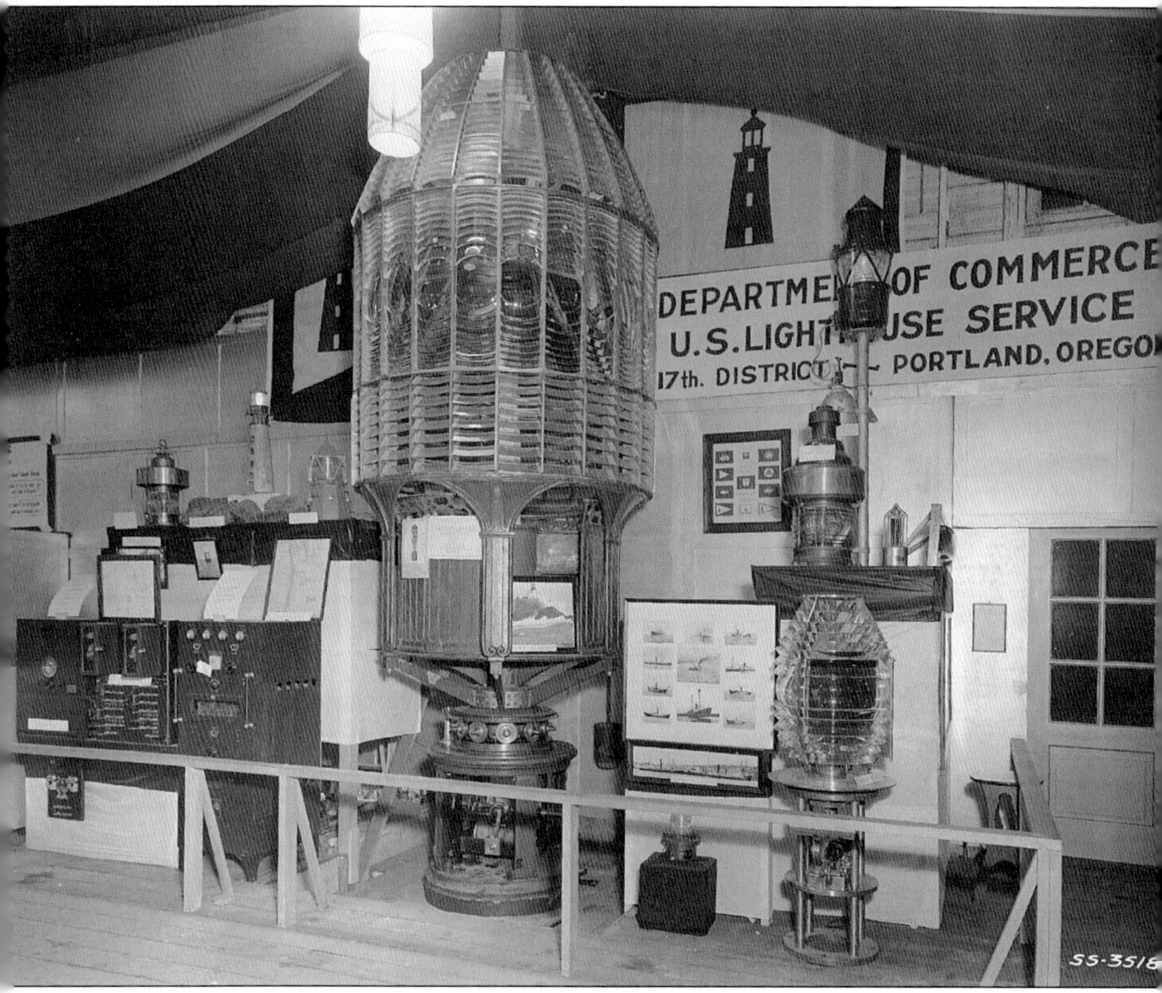

In October 1935, the retired first order Fresnel lens from Tillamook Rock Lighthouse was proudly displayed at the Pacific International Livestock Exhibition in Portland. In a 1940 article in the *Eugene Guard*, it was announced that the lens was to be on permanent loan to the University of Oregon, where it would be "a showpiece of the University where waves of faces instead of salty spray will surround it." But that never happened. It appears that World War II intervened, and the lens was left in storage in a campus warehouse. In 1947, a University of Oregon warehouse was destroyed by fire, its full contents unknown. Sometime later, a single prism donated to the Tillamook County Pioneer Museum was said to have been pulled from the ashes of a fire. Sadly, it is currently assumed that the lens was completely destroyed in that 1947 fire. (CRMM.)

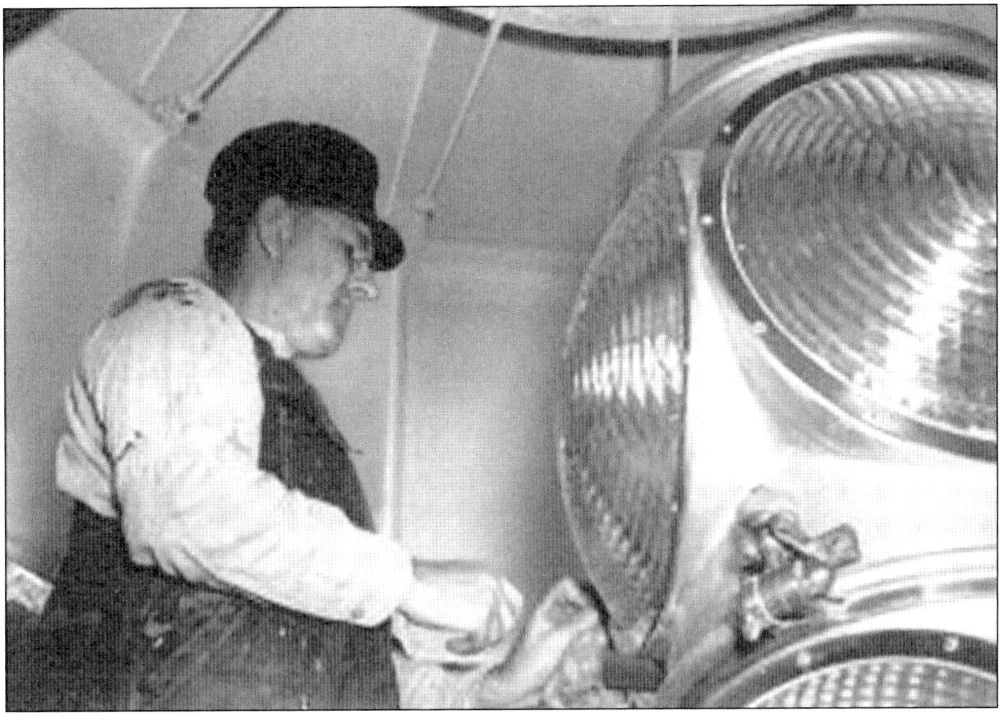

Head keeper Ed Laschinger tends to the lighting unit in the 1937 photograph above. Almost 20 years later, the unit still looked to be in excellent condition, as shown in the 1955 picture below. In each of the two tiers, there was a 500-watt T-20 lamp and four 18-inch pressed glass bullseye lenses with vertical fluting designed to give a six-degree beam spread. The light still fully rotated, keeping the characteristic white flash pattern once every five seconds, but it only took forty seconds for it to make a complete revolution instead of the two minutes the old Fresnel lens required. The one great benefit, according to an engineering report, was that since it was so tightly enclosed and well protected, there would be little chance for damage in storms. (Above, LHD; below, LHC.)

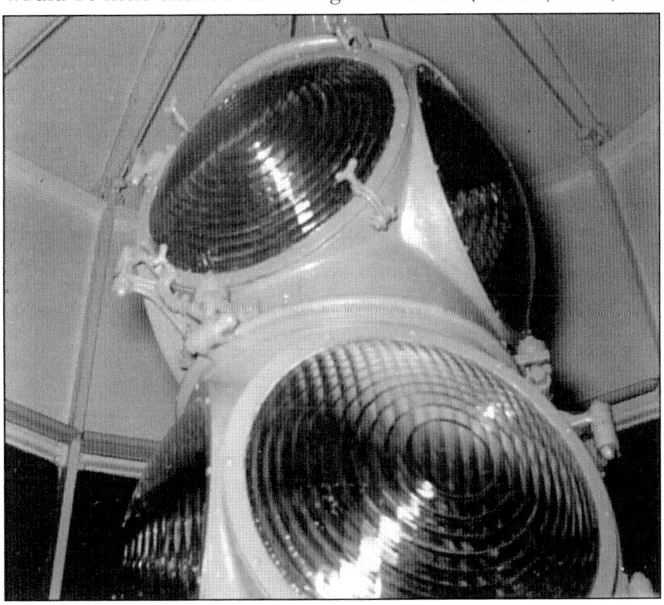

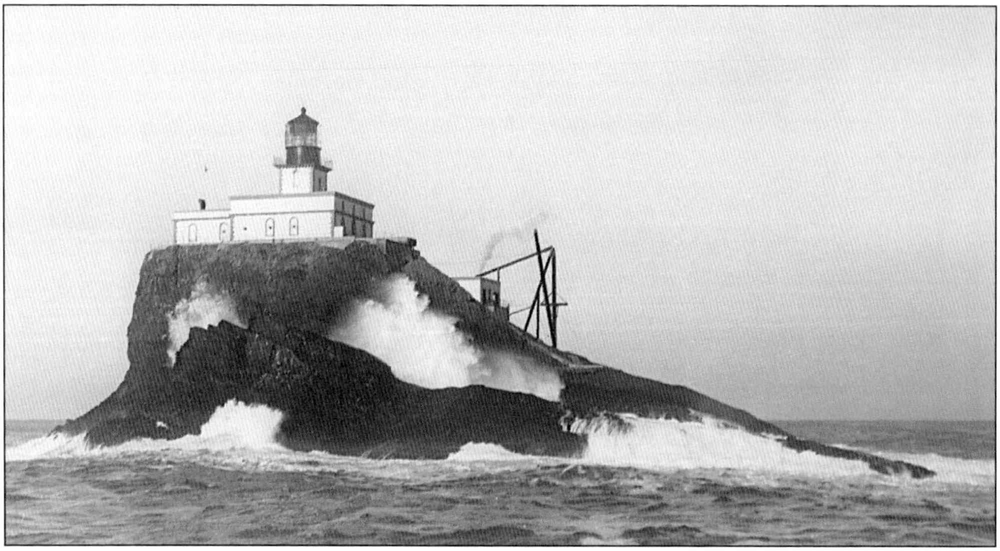

Another recommendation made following the 1934 cyclone was to have the windows on the lighthouse replaced with iron portholes to cut down on the damage from flying rocks during future storms. By 1937, the portholes were in place, featuring heavy glass and iron storm covers, as shown in these photographs taken sometime thereafter. Altogether, the estimated repair bill from the 1934 storm, including the urgent improvements needed to secure the station against further damage, came to $16,000, which, adjusted for inflation, would be almost $300,000 today. This huge expense was another reason the storm was considered the worst that Tillamook Rock Lighthouse experienced in her 76-year operational history. (Above, CCHS; below, USLHS.)

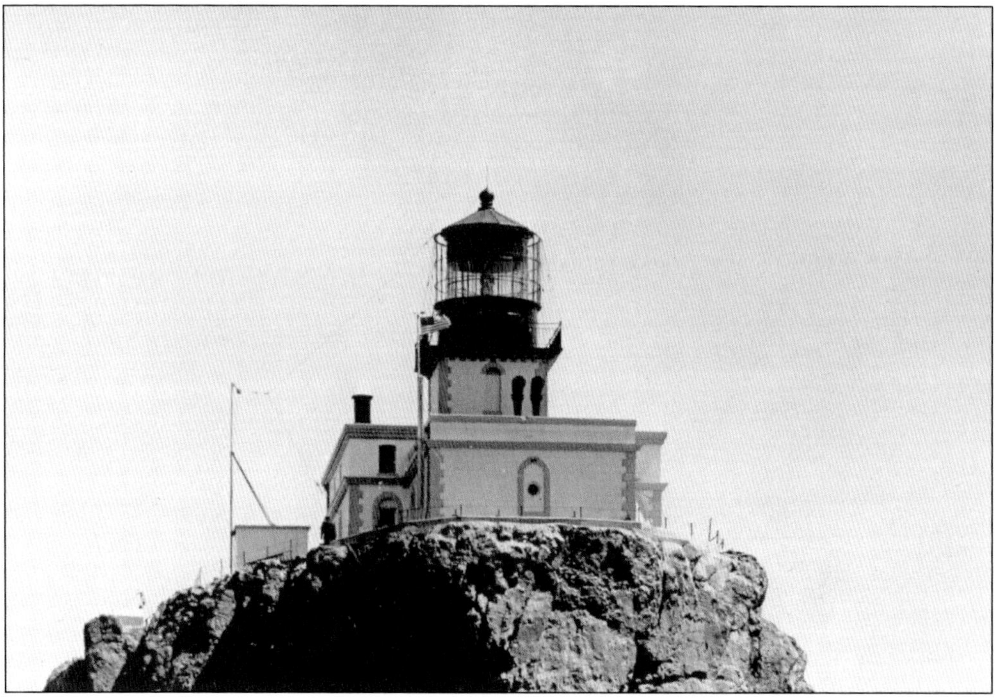

With the derrick operational again (right), and the repairs and recommended improvements completed, life at Tillamook Rock Lighthouse returned to normal by the late 1930s. However, a time of great change was just around the corner. Congress, at the request of Pres. Franklin D. Roosevelt, passed the Reorganization Act of 1939, which consolidated the US Lighthouse Service with the US Coast Guard in an effort to increase the size of the military budget as the nation prepared for war. All former lighthouse vessels, depots, equipment, employees, and coastal lighthouse stations could now be used in the defense of the country against a possible invasion. The early 1940s photograph below shows a new telephone line installed on a cable stand going off the northeast end of the Rock. This was viewed as necessary for national security in case there were any enemy vessels to report. (Right, CGHO; below, USLHS.)

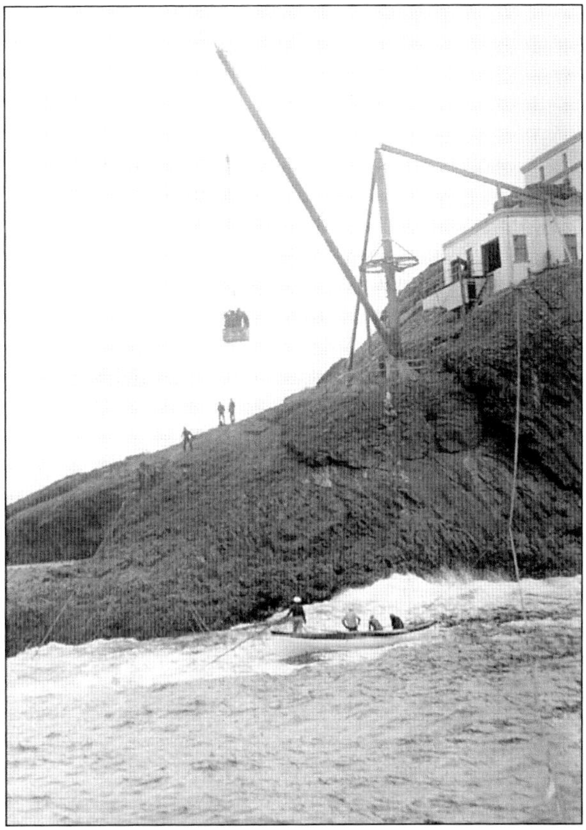

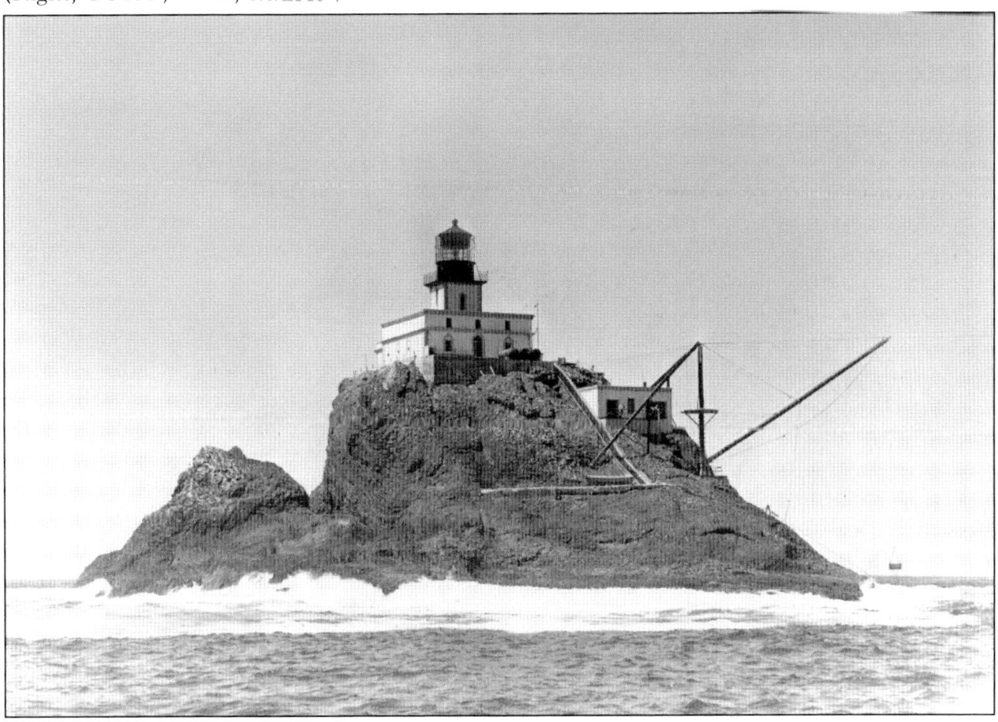

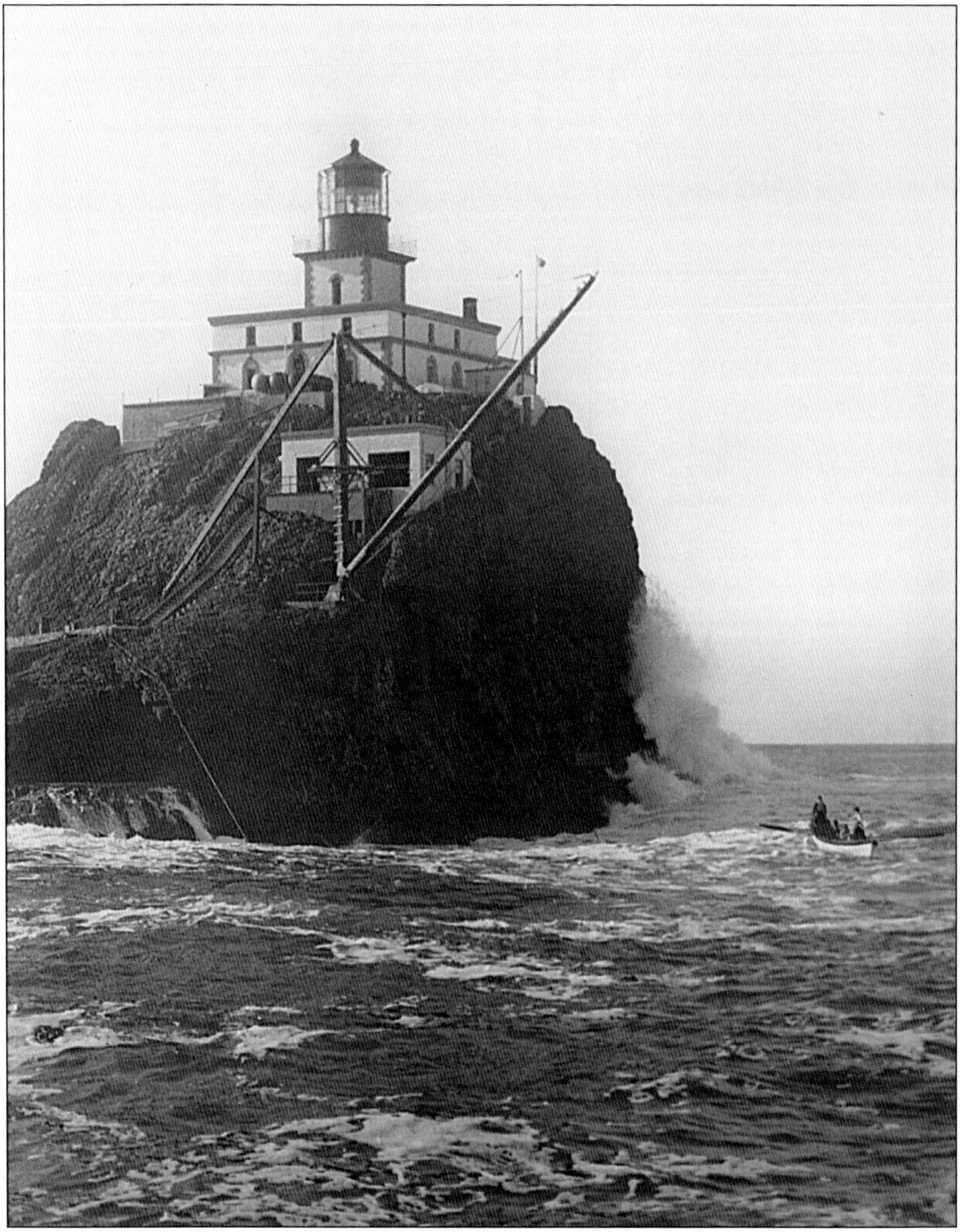

In another 1940s photograph, the basket is lowered in preparation for the imminent arrival of the tender's cargo boat. The outline of the lighting unit can be seen in the tower along with the steel shutters closing off the upper belt of the lantern. The telephone cable stand is again apparent, and there have been some timbers laid across the front of the southwest foundation wall of the lighthouse in order to give support where the rock was washed away. It appears that all of the suggested precautions and improvements did help in the following years, as there were no more accounts in either newspapers or Coast Guard records of tremendous storm damage to the lighthouse. It seems Tilly's wrath was curtailed from this point on, at least in terms of the amount of destruction she could incur. (CCHS.)

Four

Tender Mercies

Of all the thousands of personnel who served in the United States Lighthouse Service, perhaps the least recognized for their invaluable service and courage in the face of adverse conditions were those who served on lighthouse tenders. Without the tenders, few lighthouses, particularly those that were offshore, would have been able to exist. No construction materials would have been delivered to build them, no keepers would have been transported to man them, and no provisions or supplies would have been brought to sustain them. The lighthouse tenders were the lifeblood to isolated stations such as Tillamook Rock, and the lighthouse keepers came to rely on them for their daily survival.

In a letter to former lighthouse keeper Orlo E. Hayward, who had transferred to a shore station, head keeper Robert Gerlof reminded him, "You know how it is out here, no excitement, only every month getting stirred up when the Tender comes around." The Tillamook Rock keepers highly anticipated the tender's regular arrival, as it brought mail and provisions besides the necessary supplies to keep the lighthouse operational. When emergencies happened, such as sickness, accidents, or the occasional case of insanity, the lighthouse tender would brave any seas to get to the Rock as quickly as possible to render vital assistance. The October 1934 storm and subsequent rescue of the sick keepers offer good examples of the tender's response in extremely hazardous conditions. It took a good deal of daring as well as skill for the tender's crew to risk their own lives in saving others.

The lighthouse tenders were also involved in many at-sea rescues of stranded or sinking craft, freeing vessels that were icebound, or providing transport and refuge for people on land during events such as fires. But mostly, the tenders provided the necessary maintenance of the hundreds of unmanned aids to navigation, such as the buoys that marked river entrances and channels. The work they performed in maintaining these necessary markers was just as important as the beacons shining from the lighthouses that gave warning and kept mariners safe.

These next pages are especially dedicated to those stouthearted crews and staunch vessels.

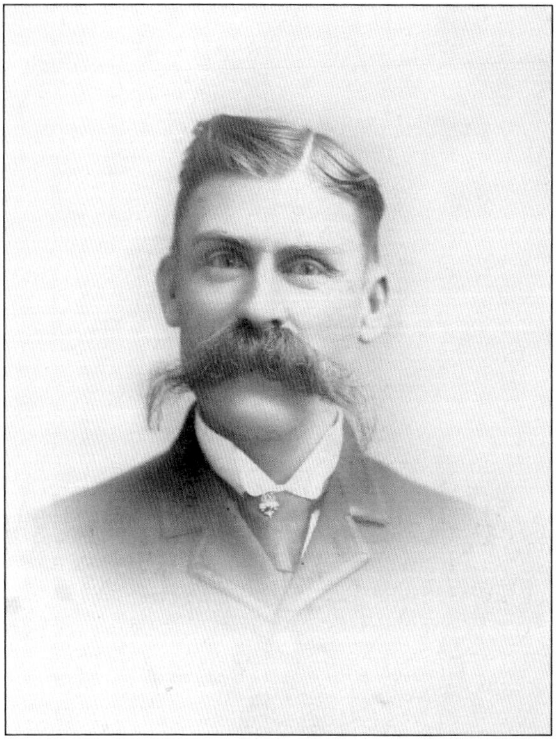

Capt. Charles Richardson (b. 1850), pictured in the 1888 photograph at left, had a very long and notable career in the Lighthouse Service, spanning 44 years on several lighthouse tenders. He started out on the tender *Putnam* in 1874, then came west to serve as mate on the tender *Shubrick* during the time it was involved in construction of Tillamook Rock Lighthouse. When the *Shubrick* was decommissioned in 1886, Richardson became master on the tender *Manzanita* until 1892, when he was sent to bring the new tender *Columbine* out west. He captained her until 1911, when he transferred to the second tender *Manzanita* until his retirement in 1919. The below photograph, taken around 1910 on the fantail of the second *Manzanita*, shows Captain Richardson standing with his son Lee who is holding the ship's telescope. Lee is dressed in a lighthouse uniform sized just for him. (Both, CRMM.)

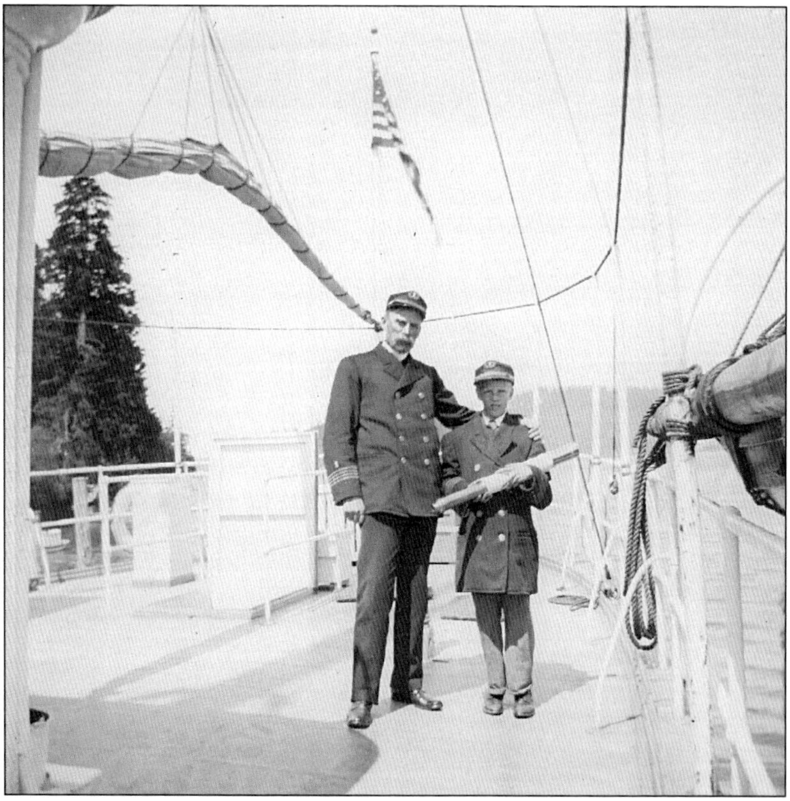

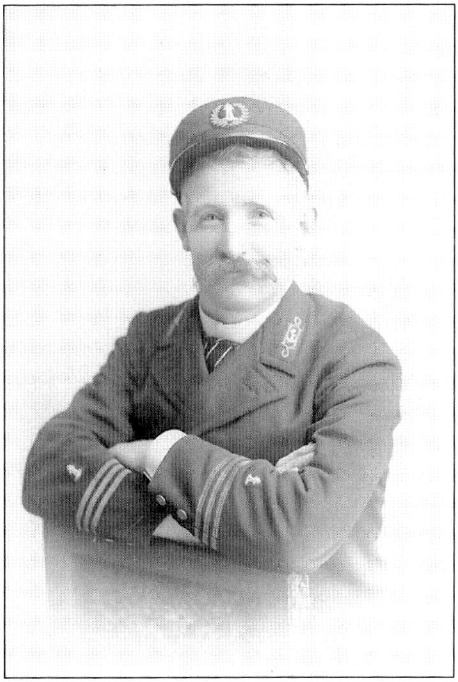

Capt. William E. Gregory (b. 1848) spent over 30 years on lighthouse tenders in Oregon, Washington, and Alaska from the mid-1880s to 1918. From 1886, he was on the tender *Manzanita* servicing Tillamook Rock Lighthouse for 17 years, 11 of which he was captain. In 1903, he took command of the new lighthouse tender *Heather*. He then captained the tenders *Armeria* (in Alaska) and *Kukui* (in Hawaii) before taking the *Columbine* to Maine during World War I. (Michigan Lighthouse Conservancy.)

This illustration, drawn by Fred A. Routledge and published in the *Sunday Oregonian* on April 17, 1904, features Tillamook Rock Lighthouse and the three lighthouse tenders *Heather*, *Manzanita*, and *Columbine*, along with the Tongue Point Depot, the lightship *Columbia*, and a portrait of Captain Gregory. It is interesting that the lighthouse rendering shows only a single level without the attic addition that was put on in 1898. (Used with permission, © Oregonian Publishing Co.)

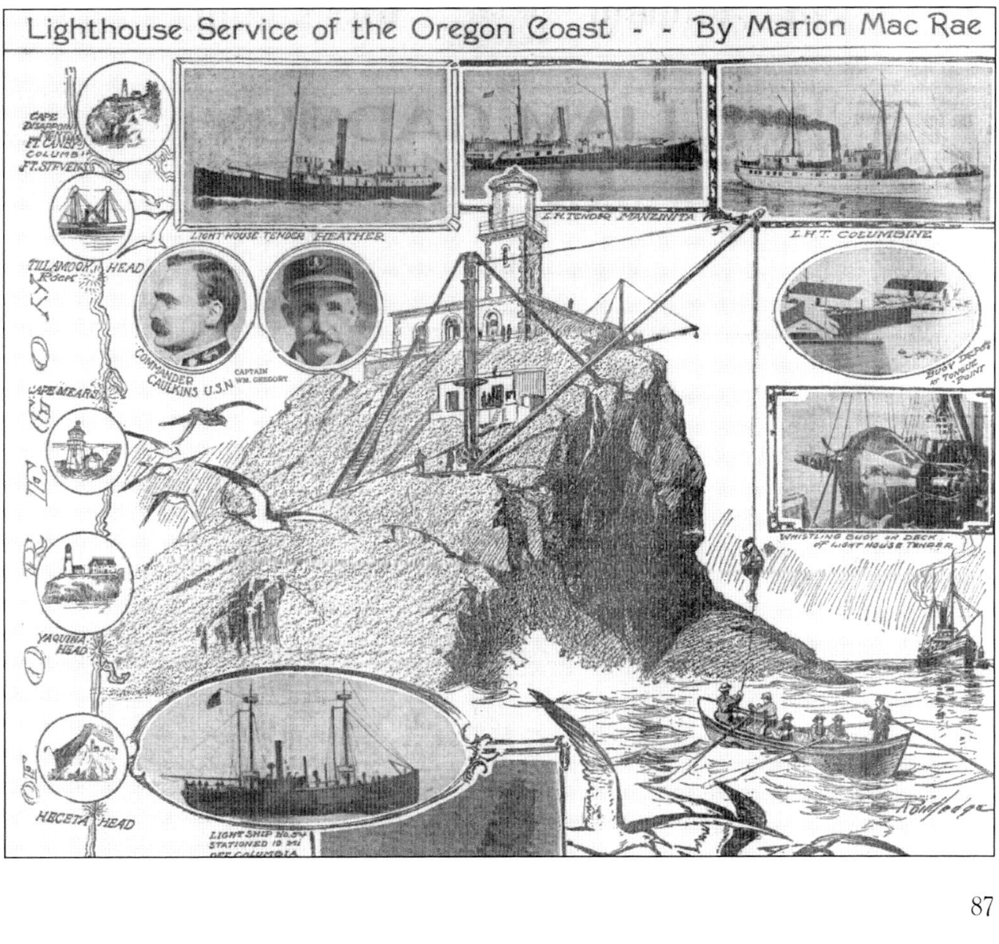

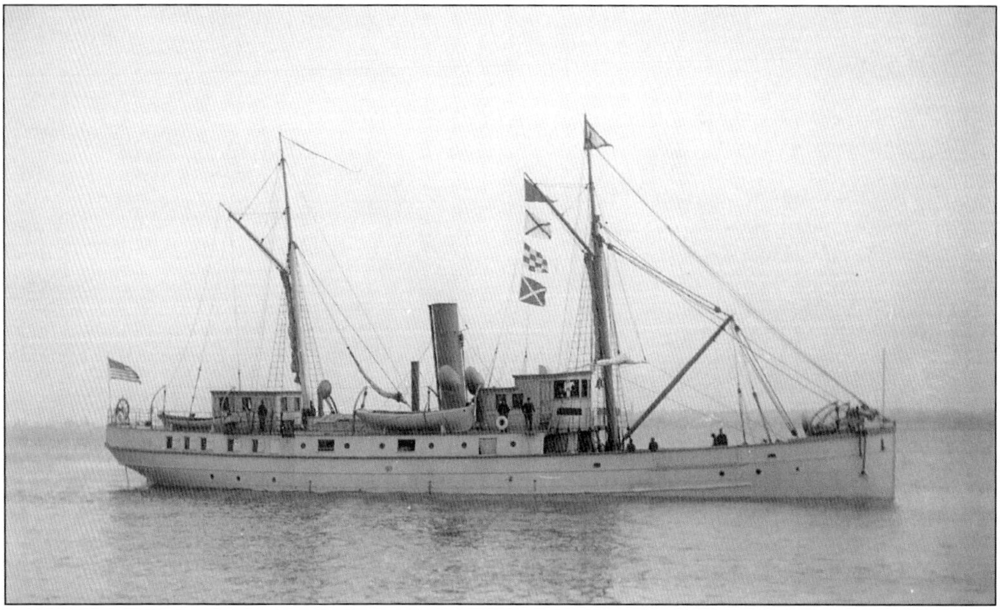

Bedecked in her launch flags, the lighthouse tender *Columbine* is shown leaving New York for the West Coast on October 12, 1892, with Capt. Charles Richardson in command. The *Columbine* served throughout the 13th district for many years, including all the way to Alaska, before later being sent to the 5th, and then 9th, district. (NARA.)

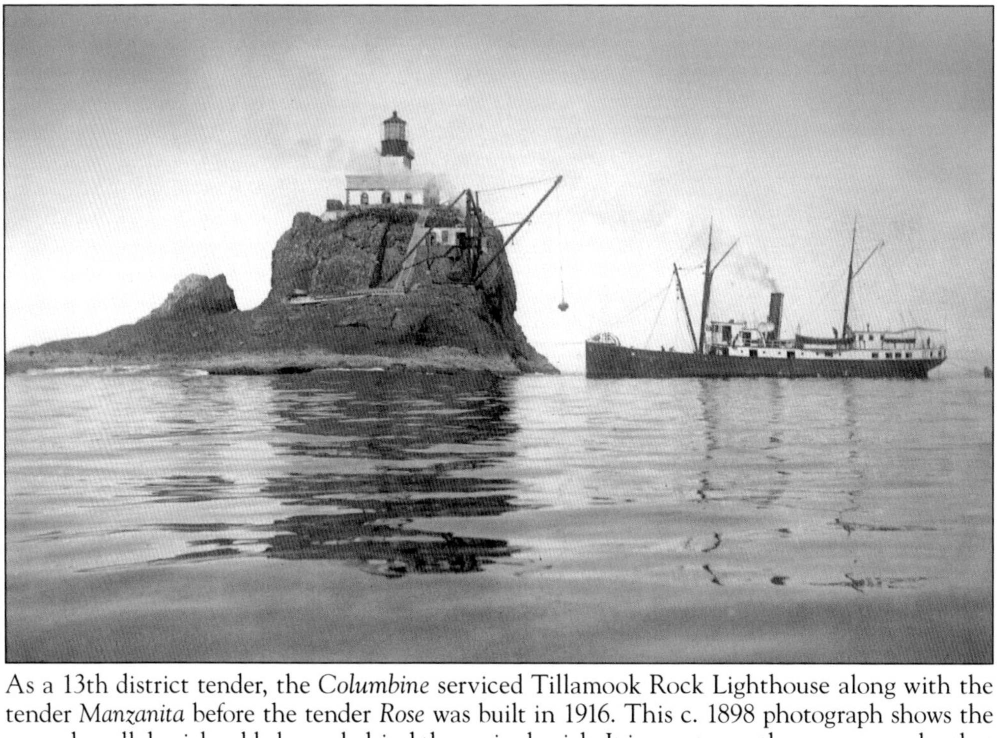

As a 13th district tender, the *Columbine* serviced Tillamook Rock Lighthouse along with the tender *Manzanita* before the tender *Rose* was built in 1916. This c. 1898 photograph shows the second small derrick cable boom behind the main derrick. It is rare to see the ocean so calm that a tender could be moored that close to the Rock within the derrick's direct reach. The tenders usually had to anchor much farther out and use the cargo boat to deliver supplies. (NARA.)

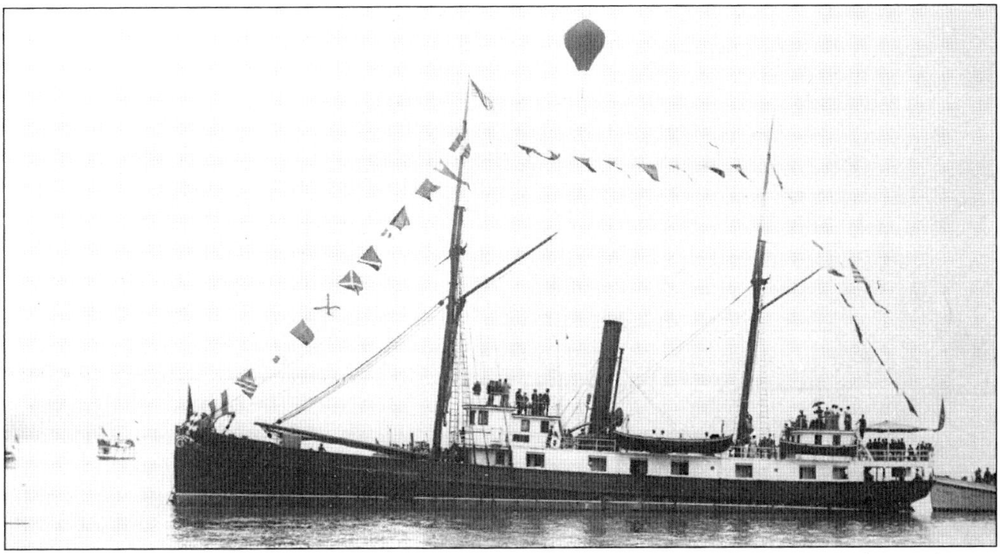

This photograph of the first tender *Manzanita* was taken sometime between 1894 and 1905 during the yearly regattas held in Astoria. In addition to her normal district duties, the *Manzanita* often served as the flagship and judges' boat for the yearly festival. (CCHS.)

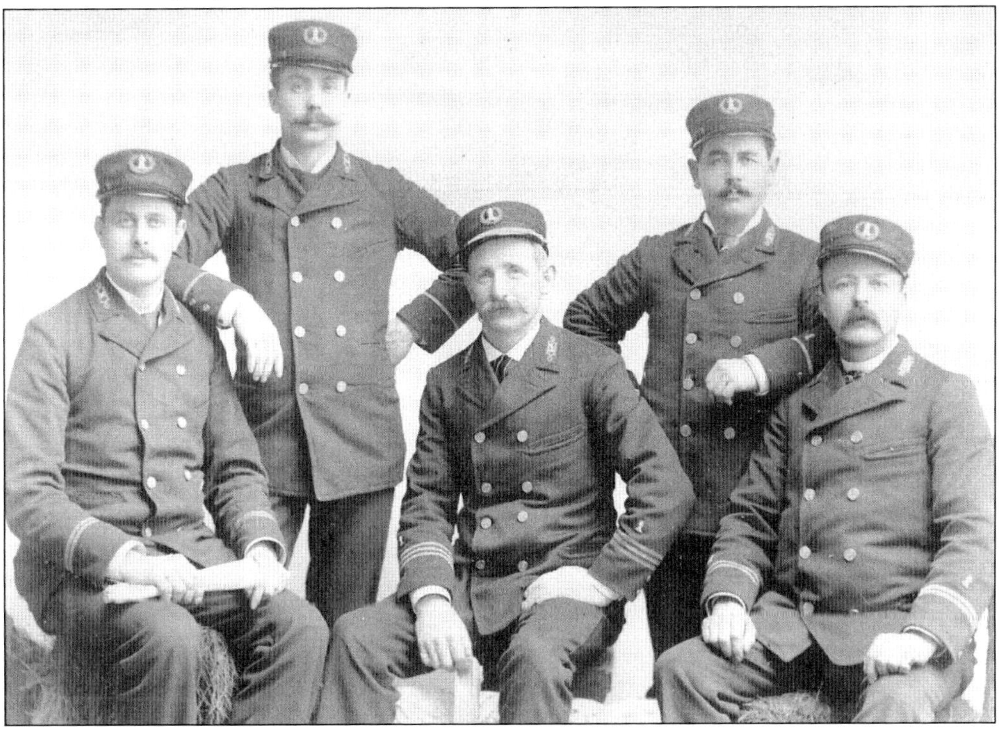

Chief Eng. Albert Rickards (left) sits next to Capt. William Gregory (center) in this c. 1892 tender *Manzanita* crew photograph. US Lighthouse Service uniform regulations help identify officer positions on a lighthouse tender by both the collar insignias of anchors (deck crew) or propellers (engineers) and the emblems or number of stripes on the sleeves. Gregory and Rickards were promoted to take the place of Capt. Charles Richardson and Chief Eng. Lord, respectively, when the latter two left to serve on the tender *Columbine* in 1892. (CRMM.)

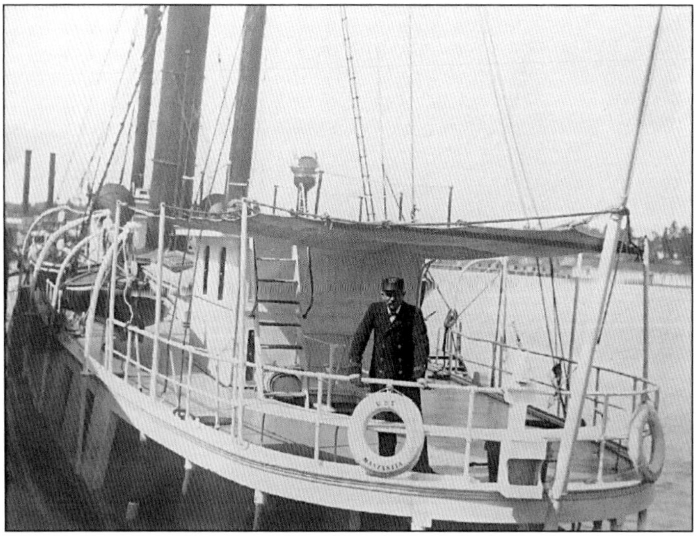

Capt. William Gregory leans on the railing above one of the tender *Manzanita's* life buoys at the stern. Unfortunately, in October 1905, the *Manzanita* sank in a collision with the dredge *Columbia* and tug *John McCracken* in the Columbia River near Puget Island. It was later salvaged and became the tug *Daniel Kern*. It was eventually scrapped and burned in 1939. (Michigan Lighthouse Conservancy.)

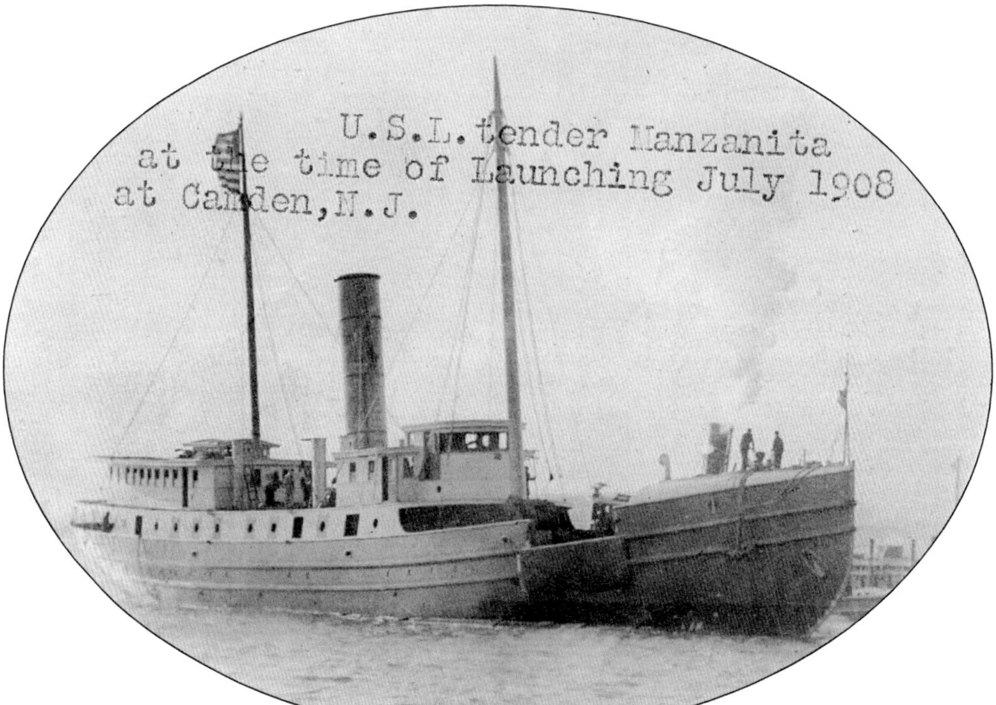

The second *Manzanita*, almost 40 feet longer than the first, was the lead ship in a class of eight vessels of similar construction that included the lighthouse tenders *Sequoia* and *Kukui*, which would also serve in the Pacific coast districts. In 1908, following the same route as the "Great White Fleet," the three lighthouse tenders, along with three lightships constructed at the same time, made the long voyage around Cape Horn to the West Coast. (CRMM.)

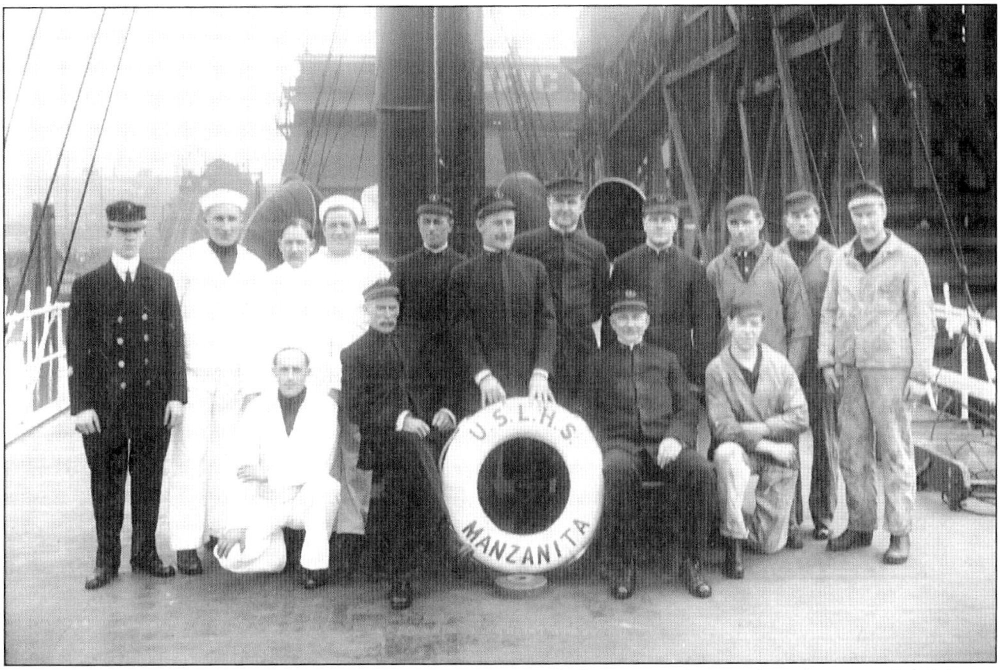

In this c. 1915 image, Capt. Charles Richardson sits at left next to the tender *Manzanita's* life buoy with Chief Engineer Brown sitting on the other side. Among the group of officers standing directly behind them is Carl L. Hagen (standing fifth from left), who would later command the tenders *Fern* and *Rose*; Charles A.A. Modeer, with his hands on the ring buoy, who would captain the *Manzanita* for almost 20 years; and Axel E. Anderson (standing fourth from right), who was in charge of the Tongue Point Lighthouse Depot in Astoria for 35 years until 1955. (CGNW)

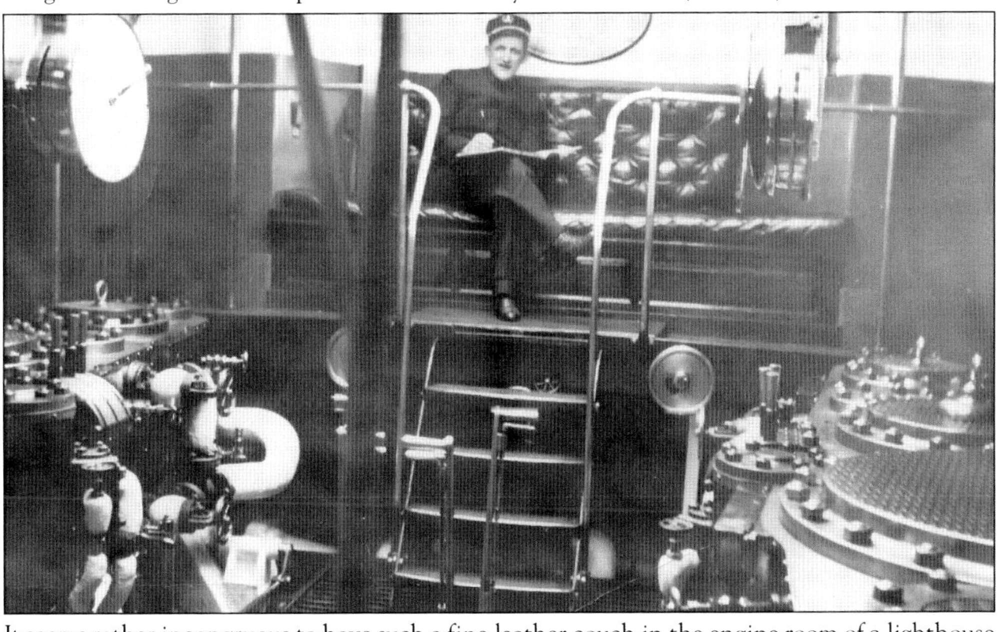

It seems rather incongruous to have such a fine leather couch in the engine room of a lighthouse tender, as shown in this photograph taken on the tender *Manzanita* sometime between 1915 and 1925. The engineer could certainly sit in comfort to write his daily reports. (CCHS.)

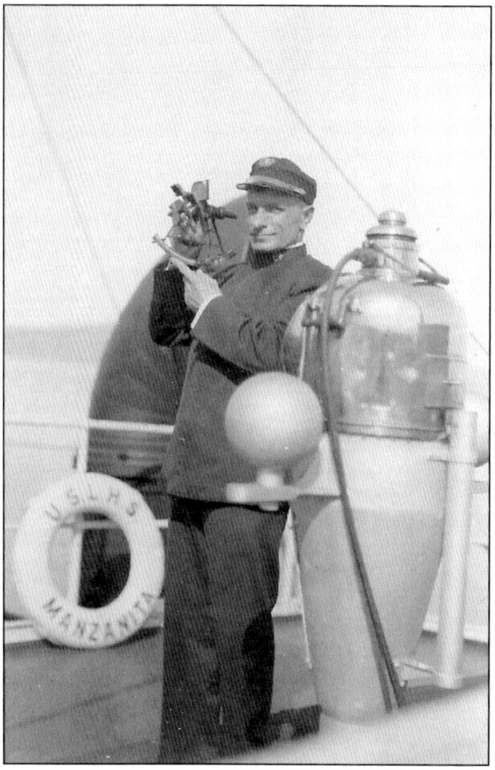

William J.H. Siekemeyer is holding the sextant in this c. 1913 photograph taken on the deck of the tender *Manzanita*. Siekemeyer started out on the lightship *Swiftsure* in 1912 before he changed to the lighthouse tender *Manzanita* until 1918. He was master on the tender *Rose* at some point before transferring in 1925 to be captain on the tender *Kukui* in the Hawaiian Islands for the next 17 years until his retirement in 1942. (Axel E. Anderson collection.)

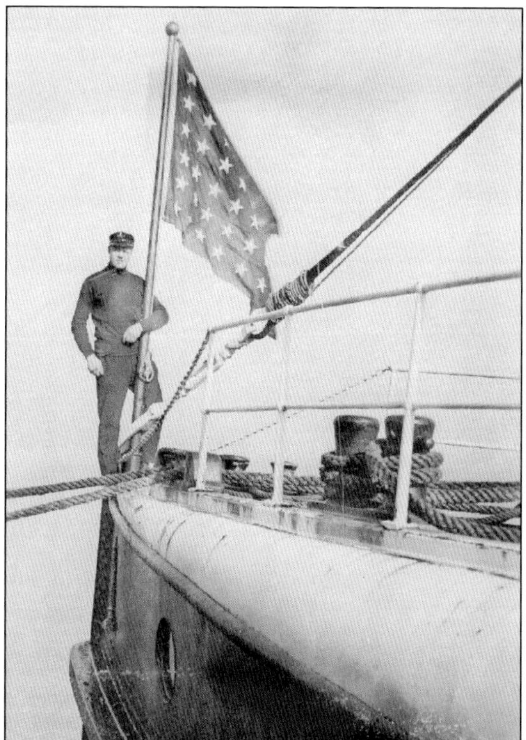

This patriotic 1917 photograph is thought to be of Axel E. Anderson, who stands next to the naval Union Jack on the bow of the *Manzanita* during World War I. The Naval Appropriations Act of 1916 allowed the president to transfer to the War Department "such vessels, equipment, stations and personnel of the Lighthouse Service as he may deem to the best interest of the country." The *Manzanita* was one of the vessels conscripted in July 1917. (CRMM.)

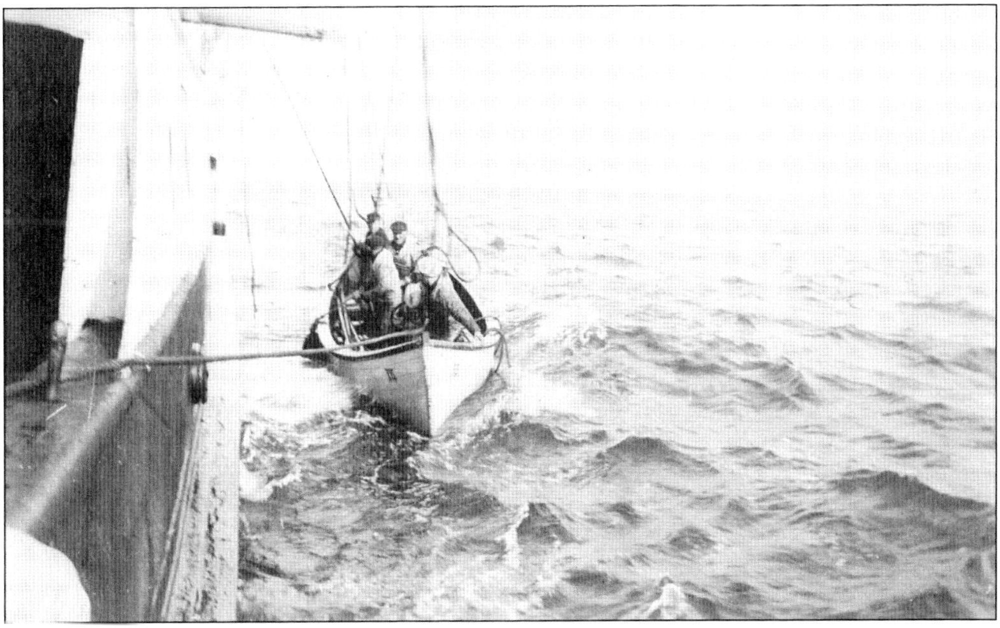

The whaleboat, with one lighthouse tender officer in uniform in the rear and several other crew members aboard, is launched from the *Manzanita* in 1917. The *Manzanita* was on patrol duty at the mouth of the Columbia River during World War I. In addition to its wartime duties, the *Manzanita* serviced buoys and lighthouses in the district, including at Tillamook Rock. (CRMM.)

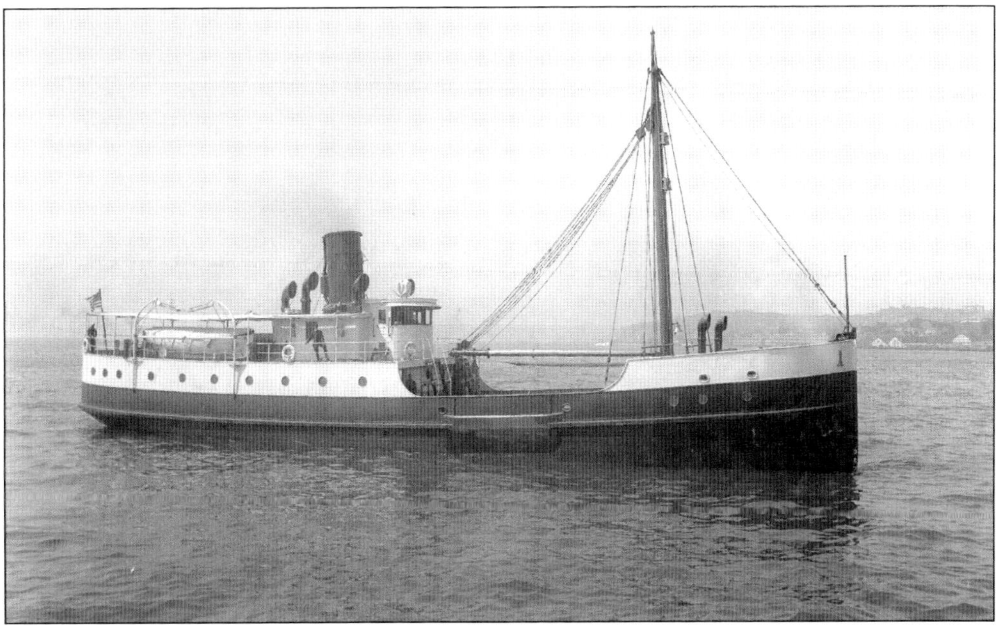

This photograph, taken sometime between 1916 and 1919, shows the lighthouse tender *Rose* that was commissioned in 1916 and brought to Astoria by Capt. Charles A.A. Modeer. It was immediately conscripted into the Navy as another patrol vessel, and Capt. Modeer remained in command of her, serving as a lieutenant commander. After the war, Modeer transferred to the *Manzanita*. The *Rose*, released from military service, then took up the normal duties of a Lighthouse Service tender and was frequently seen servicing Tillamook Rock Lighthouse. (NARA.)

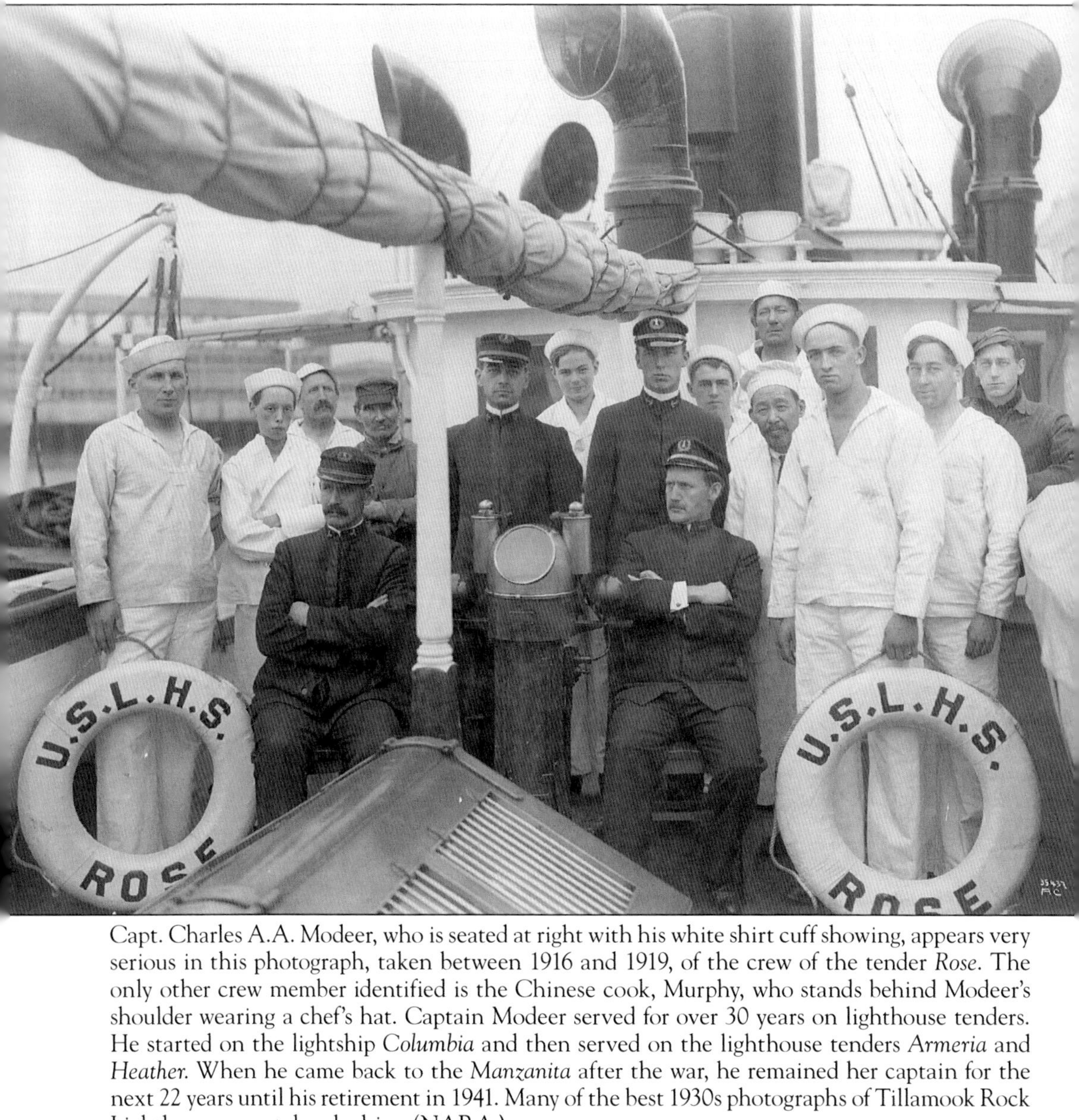

Capt. Charles A.A. Modeer, who is seated at right with his white shirt cuff showing, appears very serious in this photograph, taken between 1916 and 1919, of the crew of the tender *Rose*. The only other crew member identified is the Chinese cook, Murphy, who stands behind Modeer's shoulder wearing a chef's hat. Captain Modeer served for over 30 years on lighthouse tenders. He started on the lightship *Columbia* and then served on the lighthouse tenders *Armeria* and *Heather*. When he came back to the *Manzanita* after the war, he remained her captain for the next 22 years until his retirement in 1941. Many of the best 1930s photographs of Tillamook Rock Lighthouse were taken by him. (NARA.)

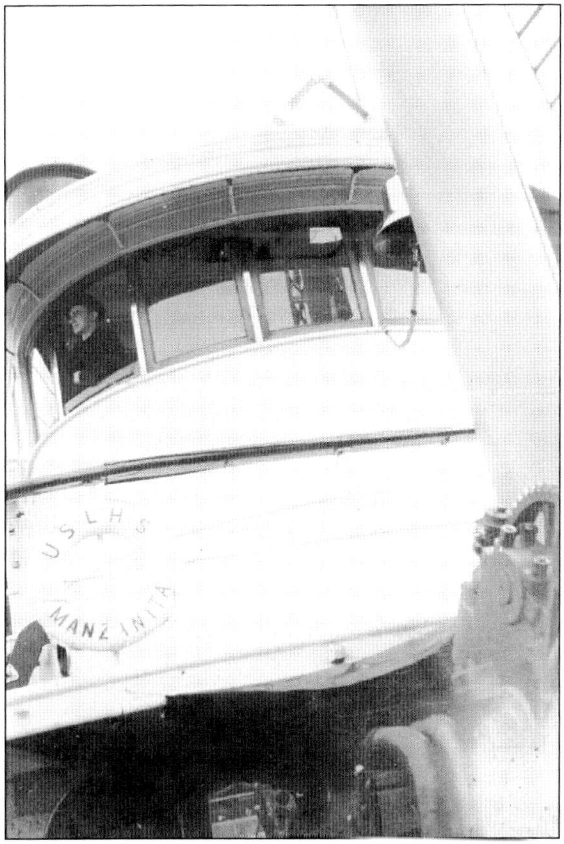

These two photographs, taken on the lighthouse tender *Manzanita* in the 1930s, show Quartermaster John K. Miller peering out of the wheelhouse window and also piloting at the wheel while Capt. Modeer stands with his hand on the engine order telegraph. While it appears that the quartermaster did most of the steering, there were several times that the *Manzanita* was involved in collisions with docks and other vessels, and Captain Modeer was held responsible. His service record is extremely interesting to read, as the entries go back and forth between "commended" and "cautioned" with an occasional "license suspended" due to the assists, rescues, and wrecks that happened over the course of his long career. (Both, CRMM.)

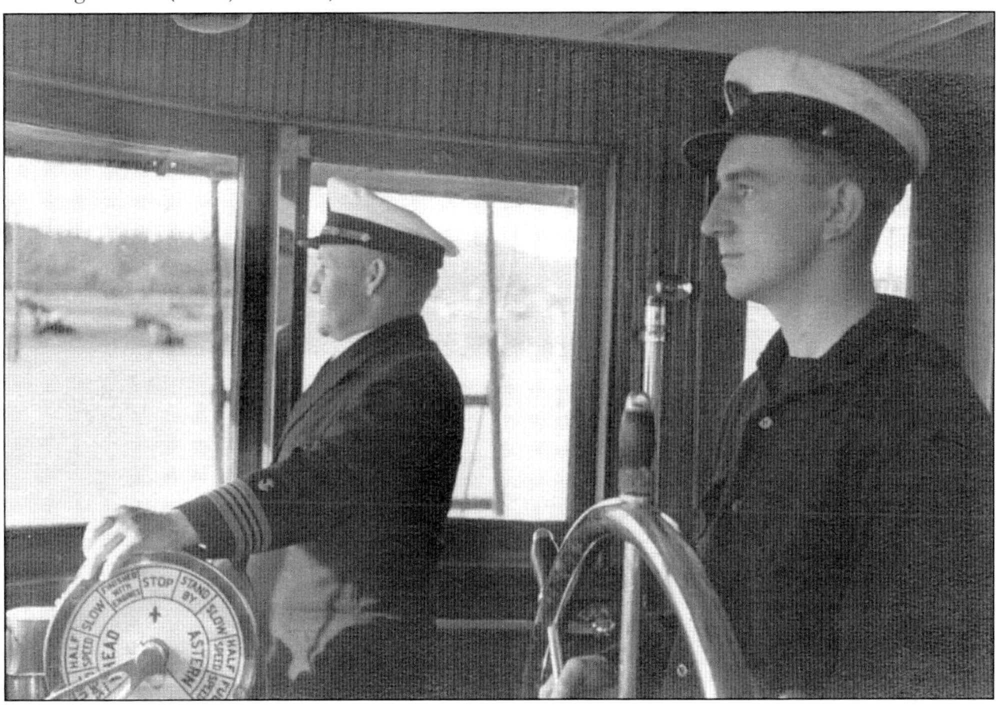

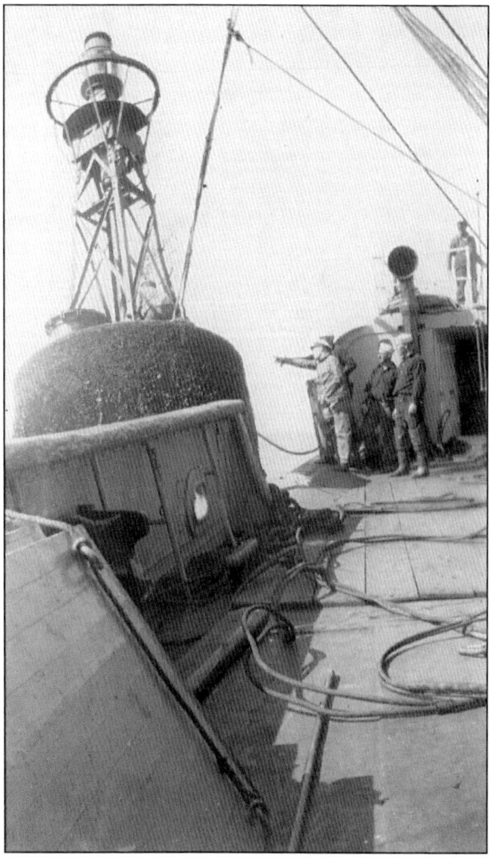

These two photographs, which were taken in the 1930s on the *Manzanita*, are from the album entitled "The Private Rogues Gallery of John K. Miller." They were labeled "Taking on a Big One" (left) and "In She Comes" (below). In a 1934 *Honolulu Star-Bulletin* interview, Capt. William J.H. Siekemeyer, of the lighthouse tender *Kukui*, described what happens to a buoy once brought aboard: "Here the buoy is overhauled, scraped of its marine growth, reconditioned and repainted. We must be certain that the relieving buoy is in its proper place and location shown on mariner's charts. In replacing the renovated buoy, we use sextant angles, sound or otherwise to ensure that the buoys go back to their correct positions. Sometimes the handling of large buoys in unfavorable sea conditions involves the highest order of skill and seamanship." (Both, CRMM.)

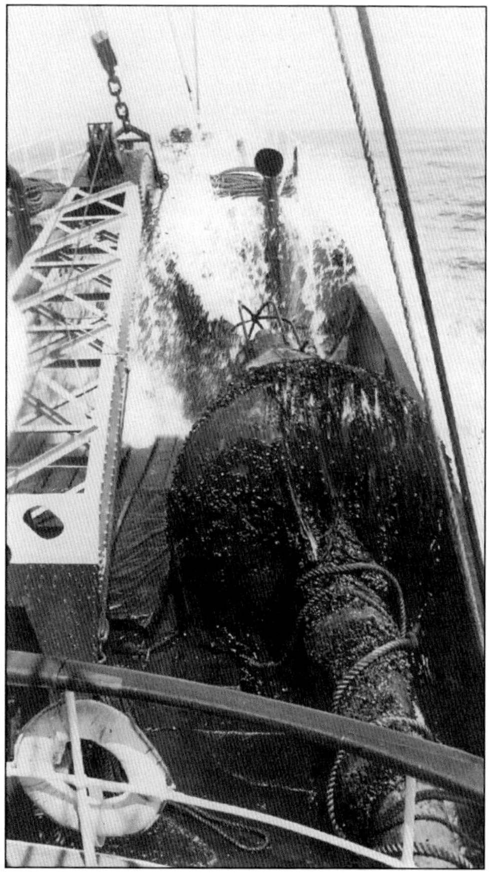

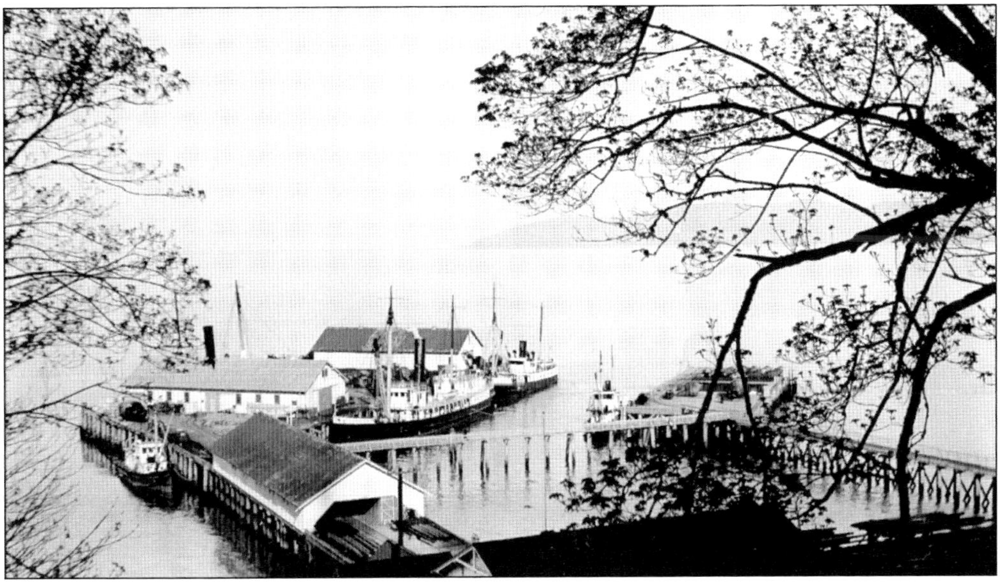

Tongue Point Lighthouse Depot in Astoria was home port for the 17th Lighthouse District tenders. Here they received servicing and upgrades on a regular basis. The above photograph, taken in 1929, shows the stacks of the lighthouse tenders *Rose* (left) and *Manzanita* rising above the far side of the dock, while the large tender *Heather* has the tiny *Larch* moored in front of it on the near side. In the very rare 1935 photograph below, all five district lighthouse tenders are docked. From left to right are the *Larch*, *Manzanita*, *Heather*, *Rose*, and *Rhododendron*. It would be interesting to know why all five of them were called home at once. (Both, Axel E. Anderson collection.)

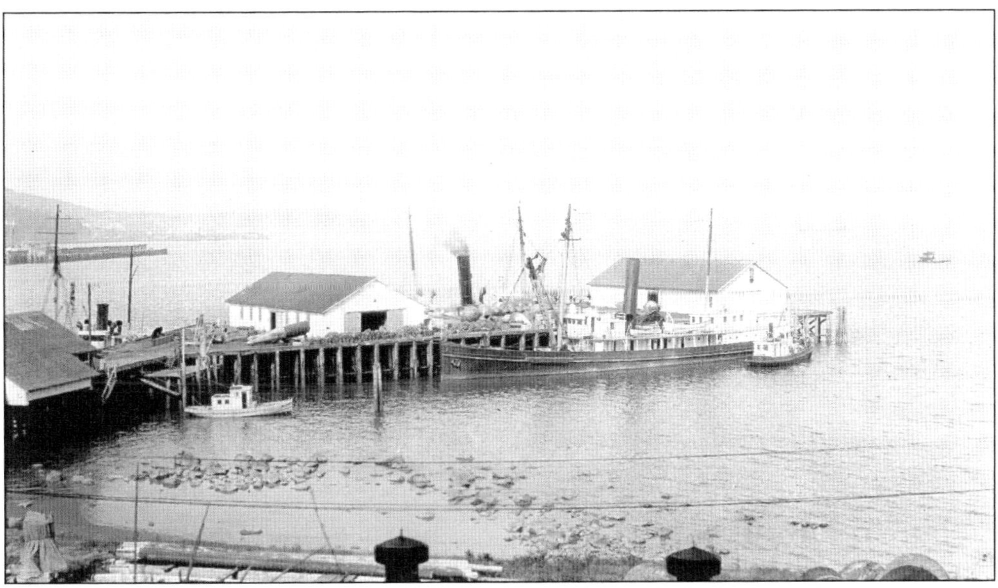

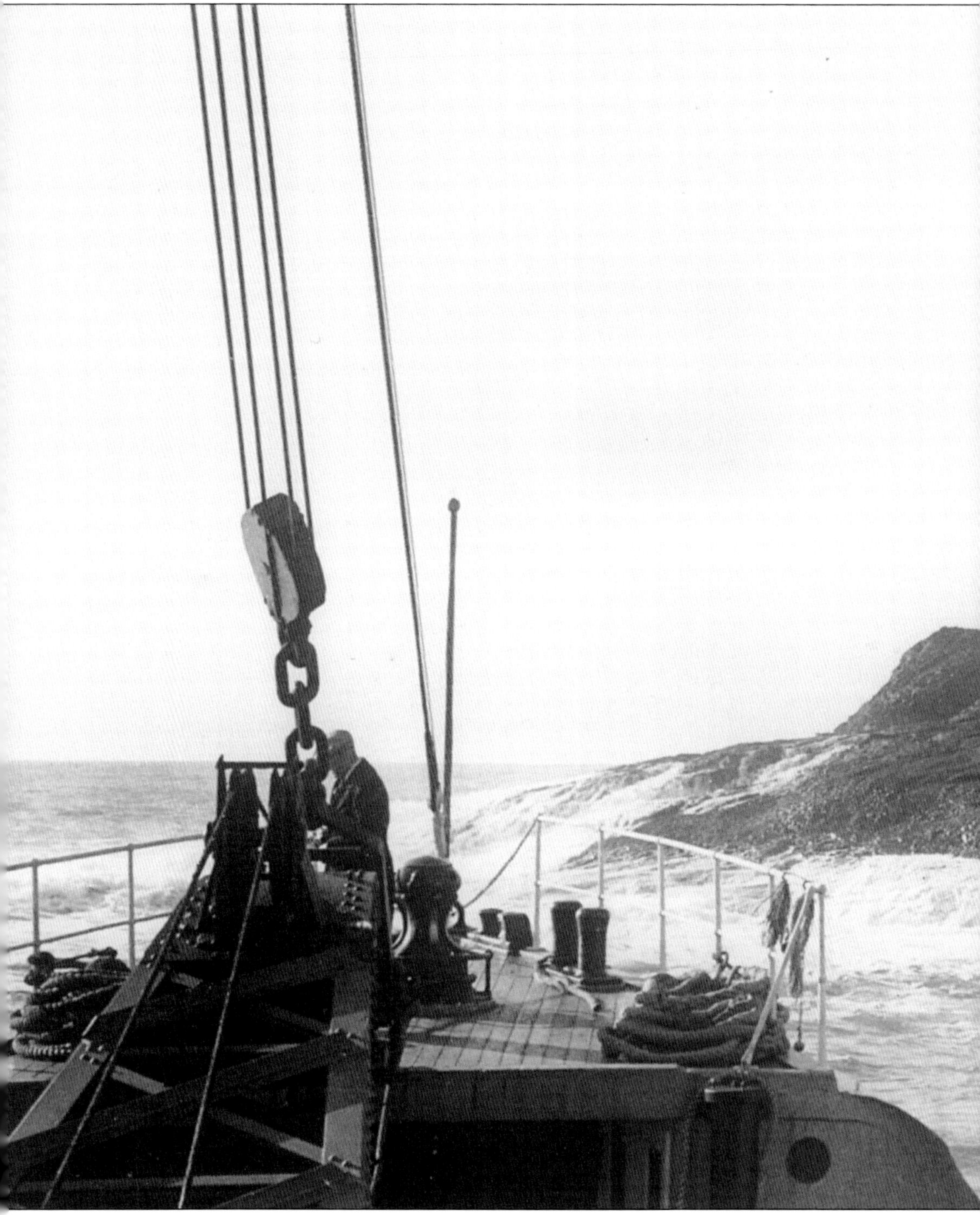

This post-1935 photograph was taken by Capt. Charles A.A. Modeer from the deck of the tender *Manzanita*. Upon the occasion of the 200th anniversary of Boston Light in 1916, US Secretary of Commerce William C. Redfield declared that "the government has a fleet of vessels in its service whose duty it is to go where no other vessels are allowed to go, and which, through storm, darkness

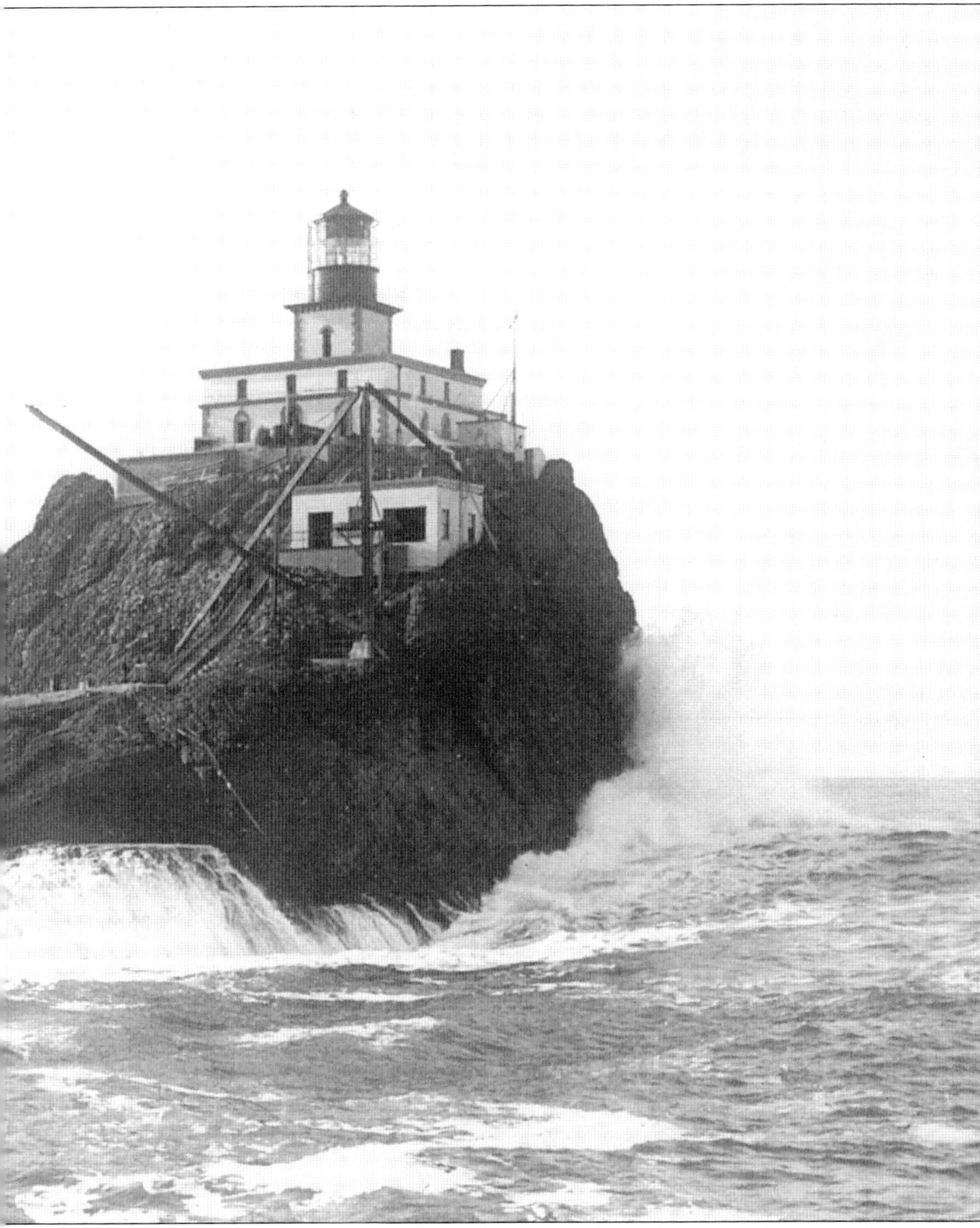

and sunshine, does its work for humanity without boasting, without advertising. The men of this service work with none to trumpet their praises, and with only their own sense of duty to guide them. The story of the Service is full of brave deeds, and I honor the men who have done and are doing these things." (LHD.)

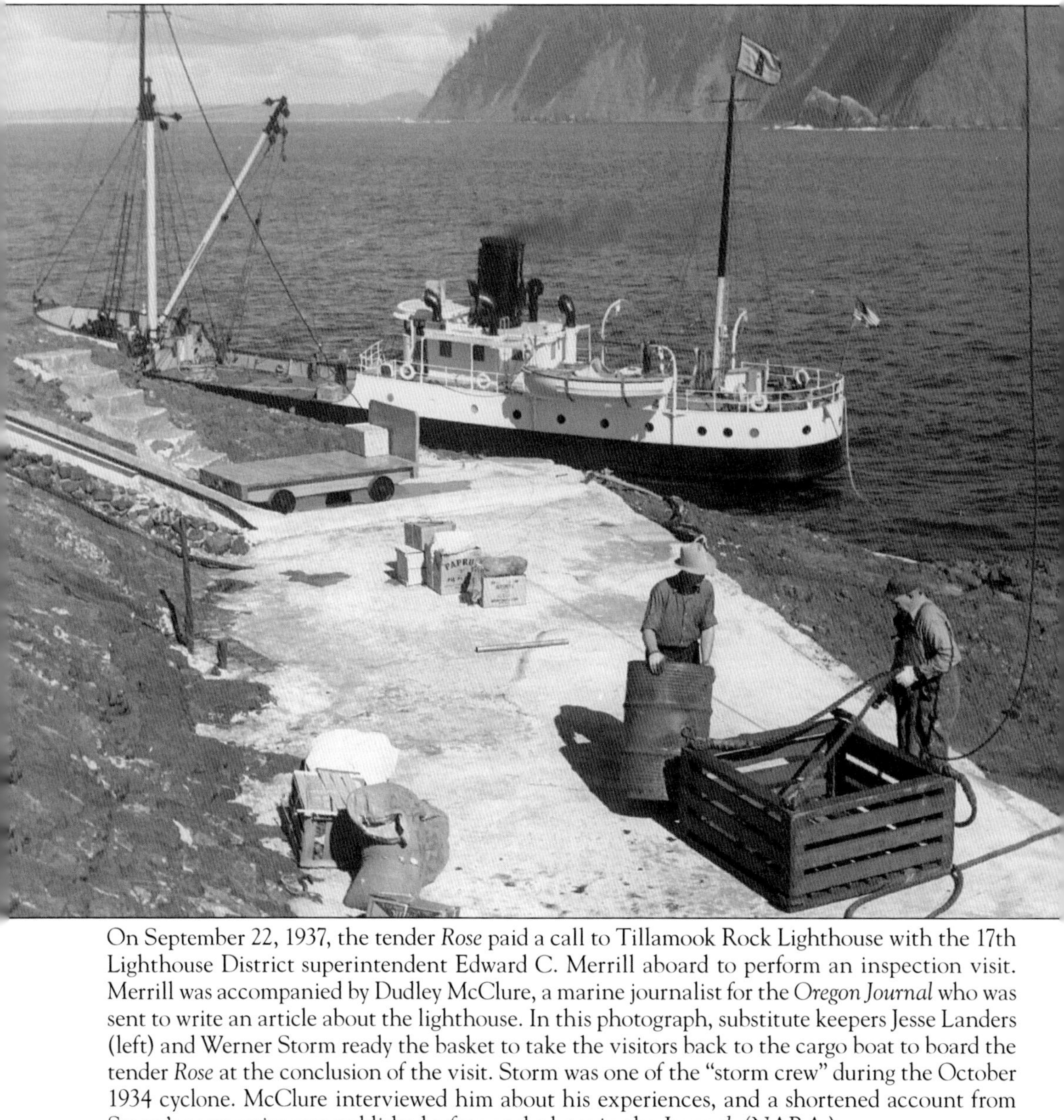

On September 22, 1937, the tender *Rose* paid a call to Tillamook Rock Lighthouse with the 17th Lighthouse District superintendent Edward C. Merrill aboard to perform an inspection visit. Merrill was accompanied by Dudley McClure, a marine journalist for the *Oregon Journal* who was sent to write an article about the lighthouse. In this photograph, substitute keepers Jesse Landers (left) and Werner Storm ready the basket to take the visitors back to the cargo boat to board the tender *Rose* at the conclusion of the visit. Storm was one of the "storm crew" during the October 1934 cyclone. McClure interviewed him about his experiences, and a shortened account from Storm's perspective was published a few weeks later in the *Journal*. (NARA.)

This photograph shows journalist Dudley McClure (left) and Superintendent E.C. Merrill in the basket headed back to the lighthouse tender *Rose*. First Officer Claude Asquith, who had transferred over from the *Manzanita* to the *Rose*, mans the rudder of the whaleboat beneath them. McClure noted in his article that over the 57 years the lighthouse had been in operation up to that point, there were only 175 names signed in the visitors' log, and most of them were Lighthouse Service employees. (CGHO.)

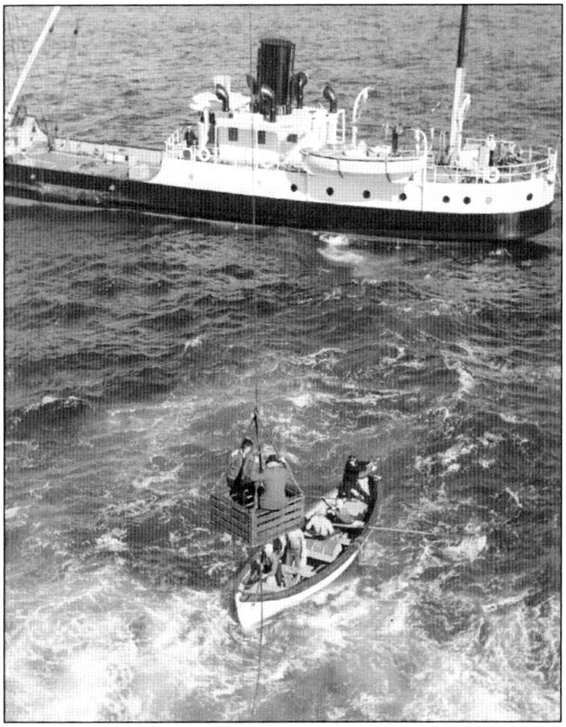

During World War II, which came shortly after the consolidation of the Lighthouse Service and the Coast Guard in 1939, lighthouse tenders were once again used to patrol the ocean waters off the Columbia River. The Monomoy surfboat shown here may have been launched from the buoy tender *Papaw*. (CCHS.)

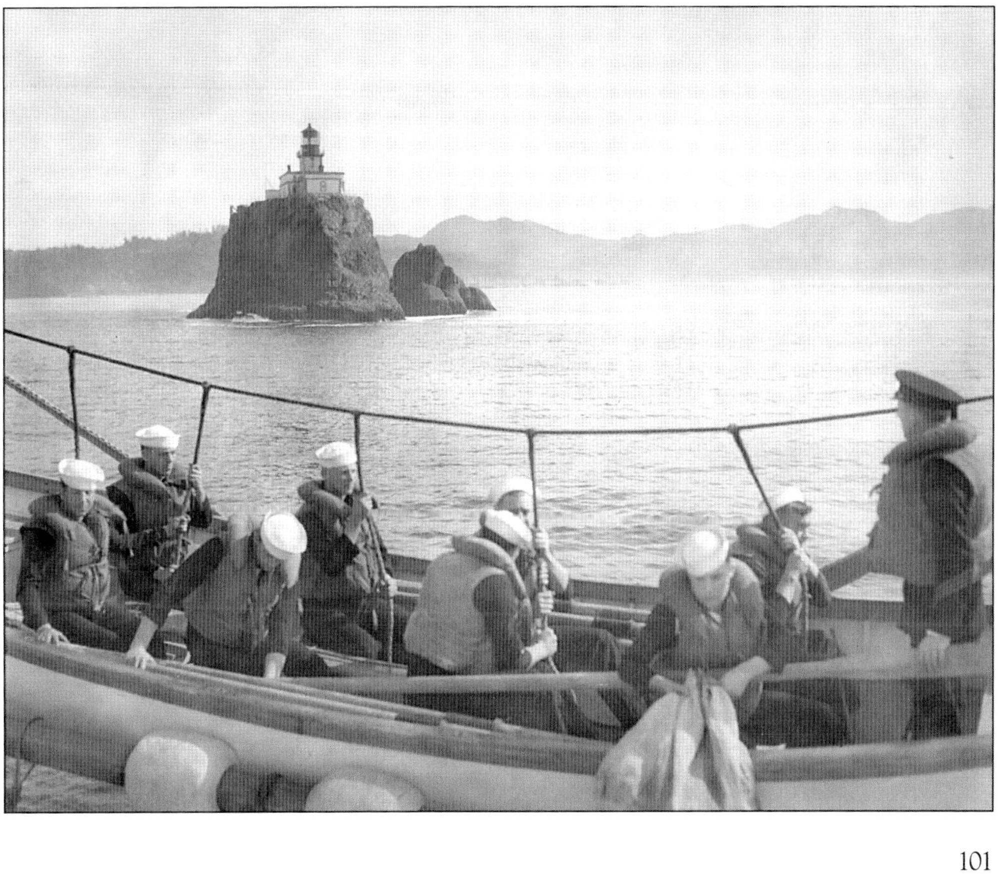

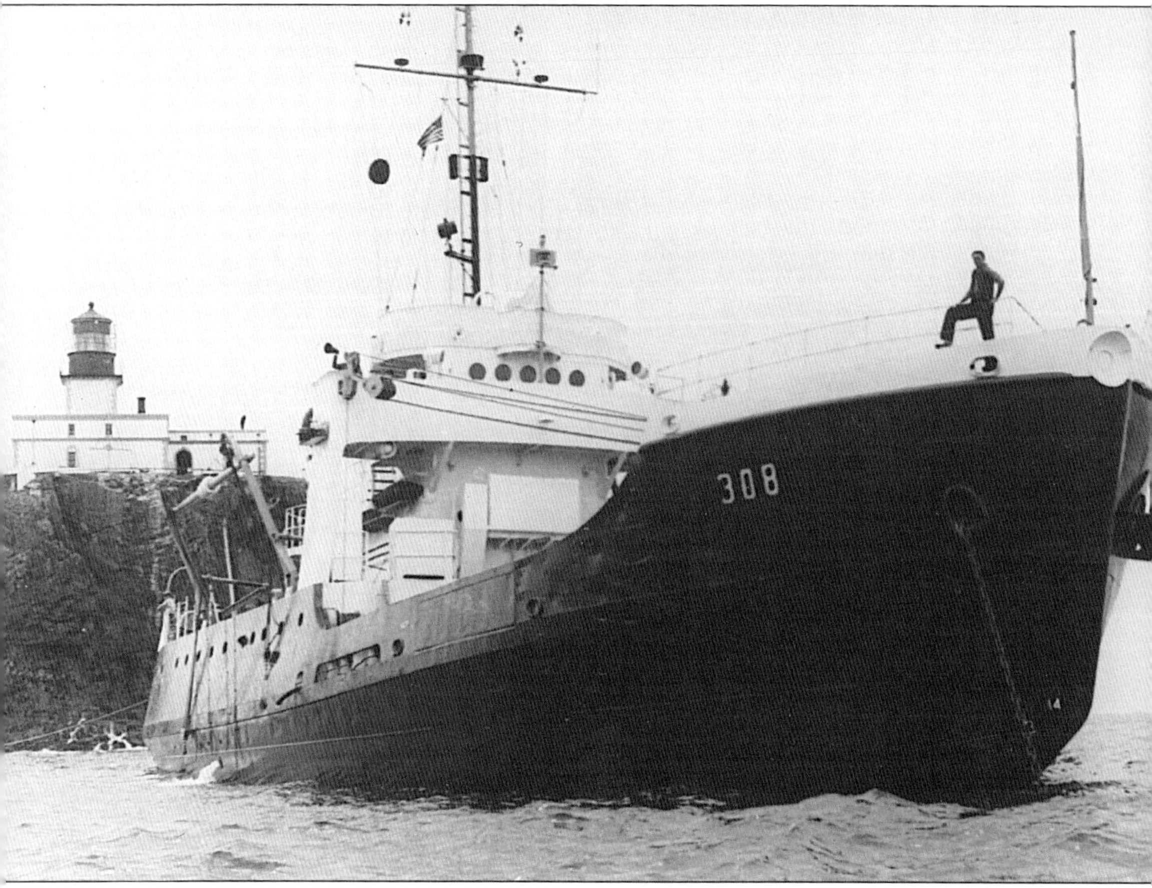

The *Papaw*, buoy tender USCGC WLB-308, was commissioned in 1943 and worked out of San Francisco during the war. When the war ended, its home port was Astoria until 1949, when it went to tend the lights and aids to navigation around the Florida Keys and the Caribbean. The *Papaw* also served in South Carolina, Maryland, Louisiana, and Texas, where she was based until being decommissioned in 1999. This photograph was taken when she was in Oregon, sometime between 1945 and 1949. (CGHO.)

Five

Changing Tides

As a result of the Reorganization Act of 1939, the United States Lighthouse Service was formally dissolved and had its duties officially taken over by the Coast Guard. It was the first time in United States history that a military branch of the government took over a civilian branch of the government. Pres. Franklin D. Roosevelt viewed this as a logical action in the preparation for war, which he felt was inevitable. However, a number of former Lighthouse Service personnel had difficulty adjusting to Coast Guard supervision, and some complained about being mistreated.

During the consolidation, lighthouse keepers were offered the opportunity to stay on as civilian keepers or join the Coast Guard as military keepers and be subject to military rules and possible reassignment at a minute's notice. The keepers were split in their decisions. This worked well for some, but others found it difficult to adapt.

At Tillamook Rock Lighthouse, keepers George H. Wheeler and Oswald "Ozzie" Allik chose to remain on as civilian keepers after the consolidation and war effort. Wheeler had been serving there for 17 years when young Coast Guardsman Jim Gibbs arrived in 1945. Gibbs later wrote, "I had been informed that those who manned this stationary ship were old-time career civil-service employees. . . . Those doughty individuals, as I was later to find out, were better suited to such isolated duty for long periods than were the younger Coast Guardsmen like myself."

In fact, from the frequency of new keeper names mentioned in newspaper articles and official reports in the 1940s and 1950s, it seems that the Rock became a revolving door, as most keepers only stayed a year or two at most before requesting a transfer. Thankfully, head keepers Wheeler and Allik, who served after him, provided the continuity and experience necessary to keep the Rock securely functioning without major incidents during this time.

By 1957, it became apparent that another change was on the horizon. Lighthouses were being automated or replaced by other types of beacons as navigational technology advanced, and Tillamook Rock Lighthouse would soon join the ranks of the abandoned guardians of the sea.

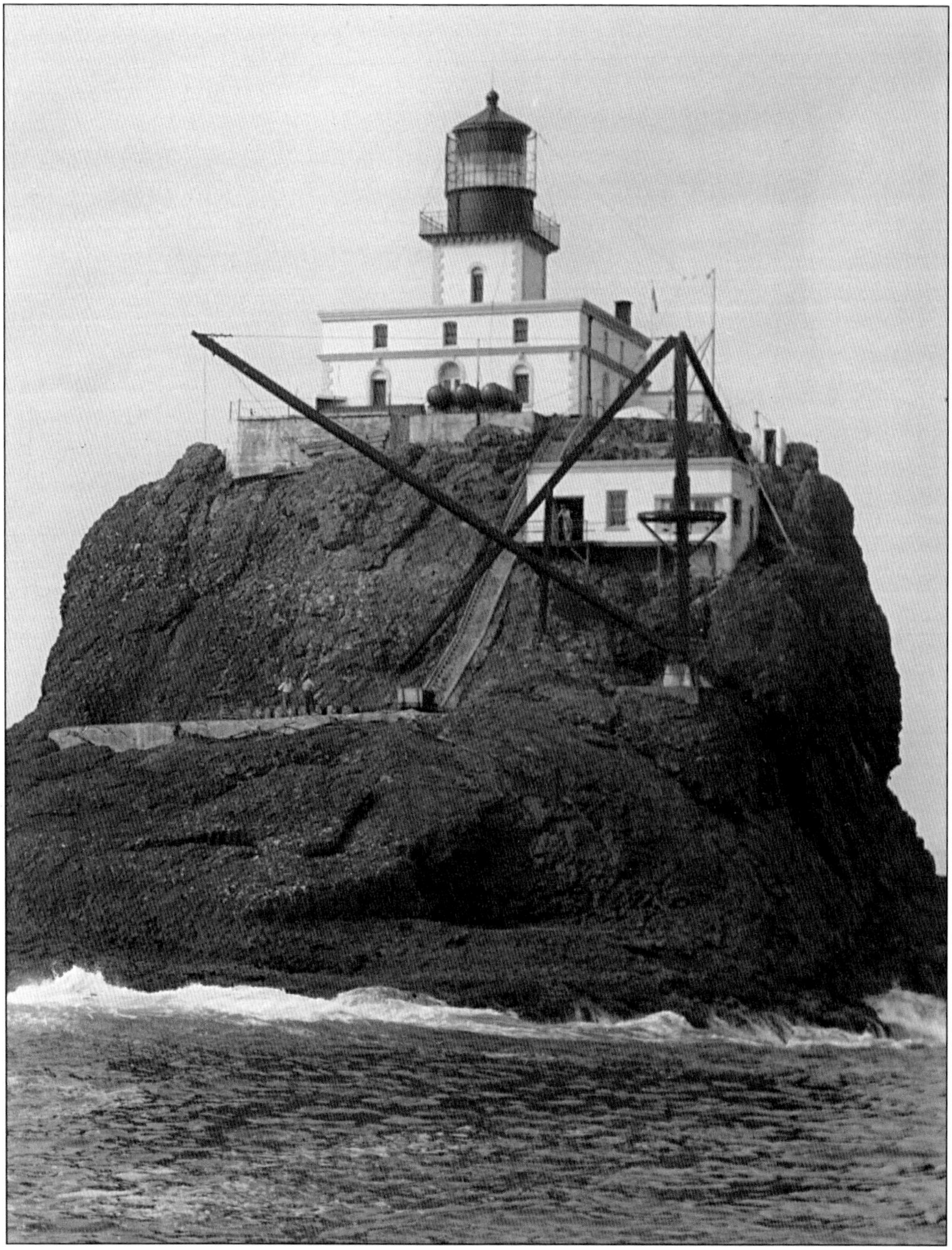

This photograph, which dates to the late 1940s or early 1950s, shows no noticeable change from the previous decade except perhaps that more of the rock was missing on the outer contour of the left edge near the cement foundation corner of the lighthouse. It appears that keeper Ozzie Allik is standing at the railing of the winch house while two other keepers wait on the landing platform below. Allik kept a very tight ship and demanded the established routine be kept, including the daily cleaning schedule. According to Lon Haynes, who served under Allik, "For the most part, each day was pretty much like the day before it, uneventful, boring, drab . . . cleaning of walls, floors, doors, etc., with periodic painting of, walls, floors, doors, etc." (NARA.)

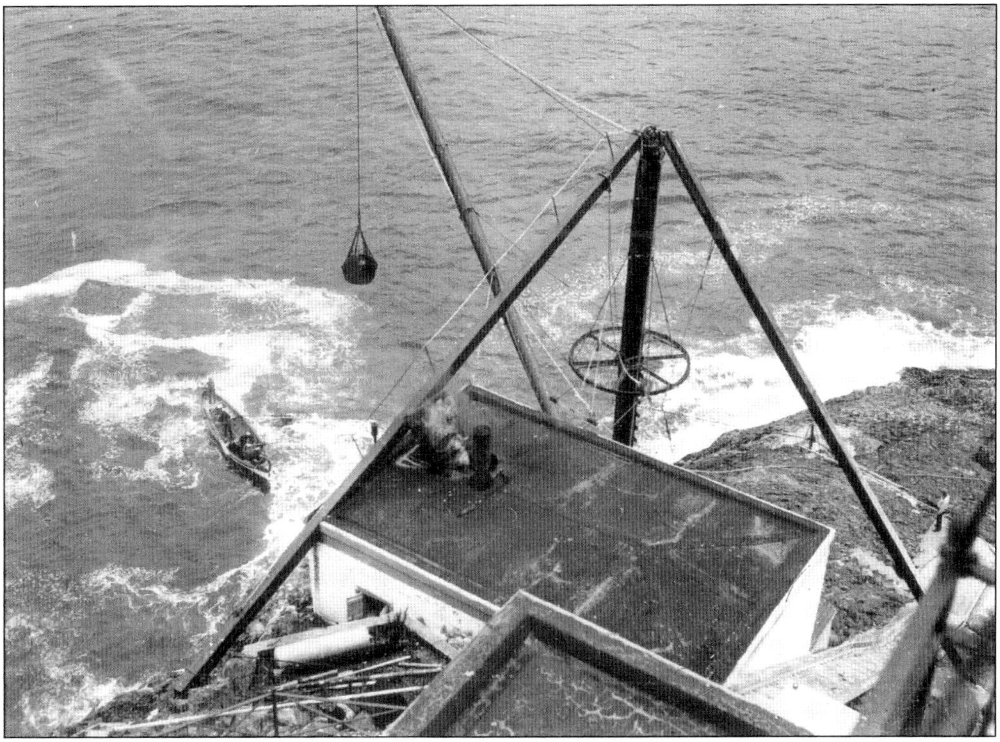

This interesting view from the 1940s is from the lantern deck of the lighthouse looking past the roof of the winch house to the cargo boat below. A nice pile of odds and ends from some project sits outside the iron rail of the cement walkway below, and it is interesting to see how the roof of the winch house is used as a support for one of the stiff derrick legs that passes through its back corner. (CGHO.)

The high sign is being given by the officer manning the steering oar of the whaleboat as the cargo net is being handled by the crew of the tender *Manzanita* in this 1940s image. The photographer was in a rather dangerous place to take this picture—down at the very base of the rock, where waves could have swept him off. (CRMM.)

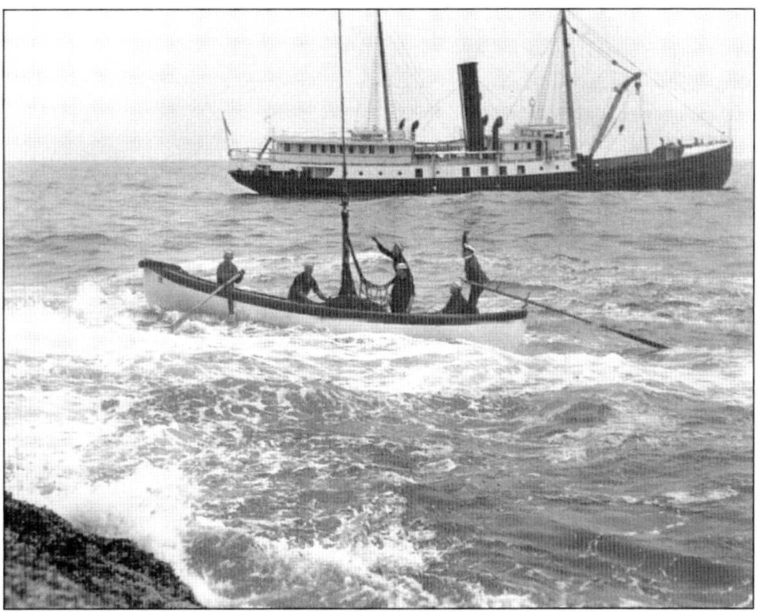

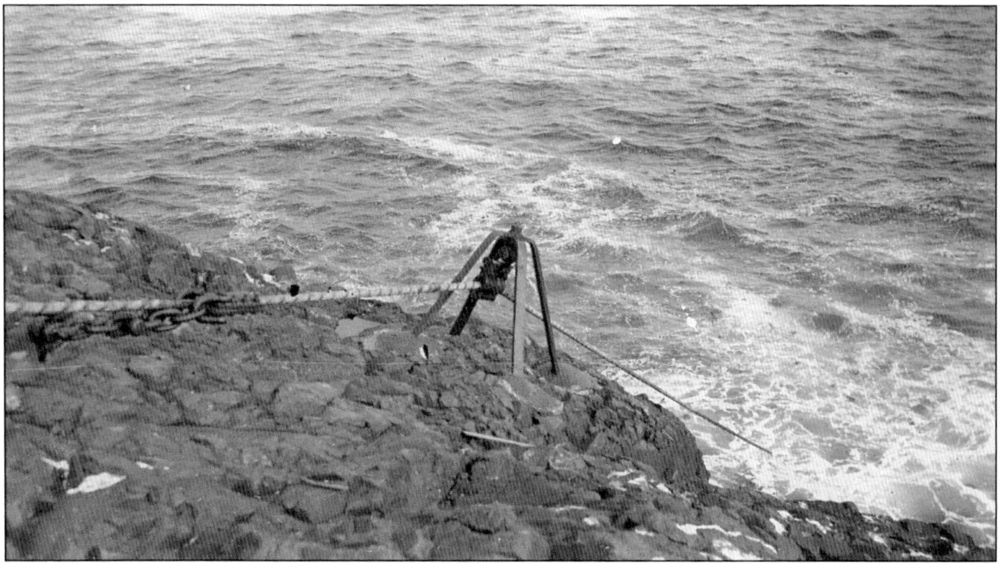

These two photographs were most likely part of a report that had to be submitted after Tongue Point Lighthouse Depot supervisor Axel E. Anderson went out to the Rock to inspect the telephone cable that was once again put into service in 1948. On the backs of the photographs, Anderson wrote that they showed the 48-inch, four-legged cable stand and chain bridle of six or eight links of 1.25-inch chain. The cable stand kept the cable from chafing against the rocks during the normal wave action at the base. Unfortunately, the cables still broke during intense storms. Anderson had originally served on the tender *Manzanita* for three years as a young man in the 1910s, so he was well acquainted with the Rock and most likely made many visits over his long career at the Tongue Point Lighthouse Depot. (Both, CCHS.)

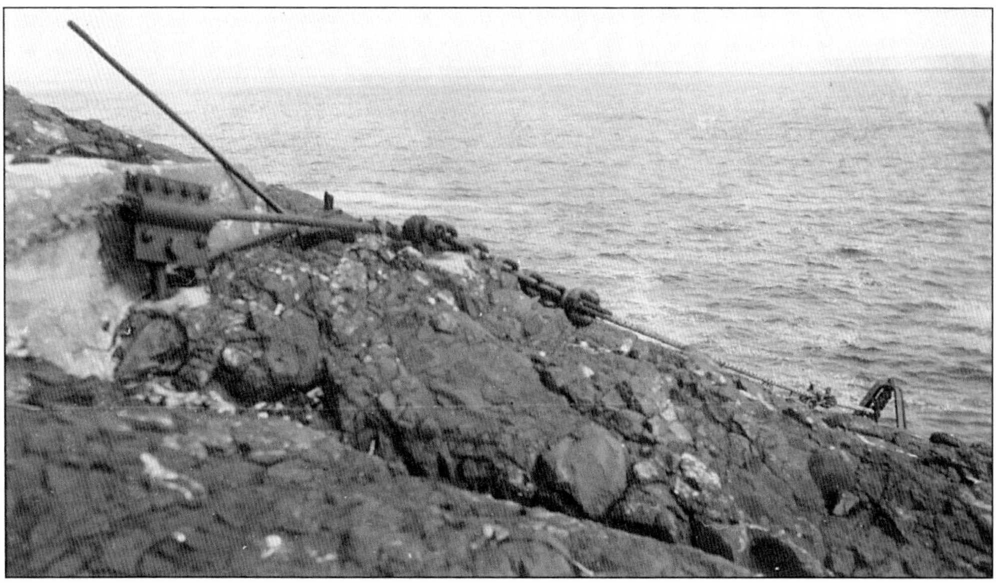

In 1945, James A. Gibbs (b. 1922) arrived at Tillamook Rock Lighthouse to serve for a little over a year at what he once described as "Dante's Inferno." Of his arrival experience, pictured below on the motor lifeboat from the Point Adams Lifeboat Station, he wrote, "my feet went out from under me and I was dragged unceremoniously over the fo'c'sle head, ensconced in the breeches buoy. Over the side I went, floundering in the coldest water this side of solid ice. I thought my death warrant had been signed when with a terrific jerk, I ascended from the depths like a hooked fish—up, up, dangling some 75 feet above the swirling waters boiling against the defiant precipice below." Gibbs's memoir, *Tillamook Light*, is still considered by most historians to be the greatest personal account ever written of the lighthouse. (Right, LHD; below, JGC.)

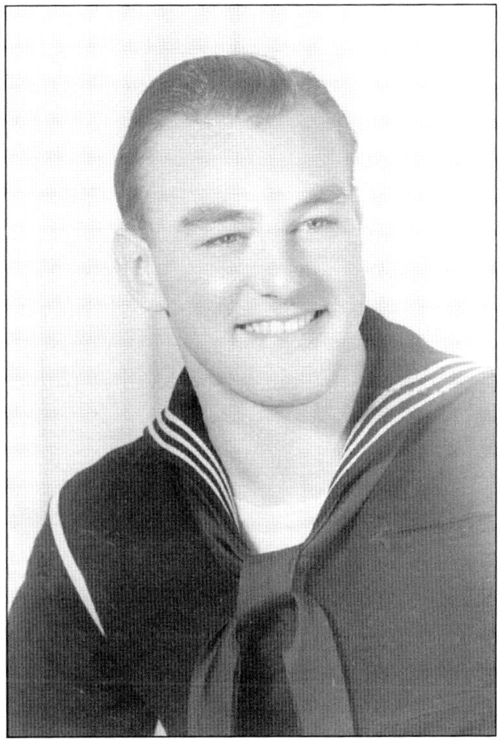

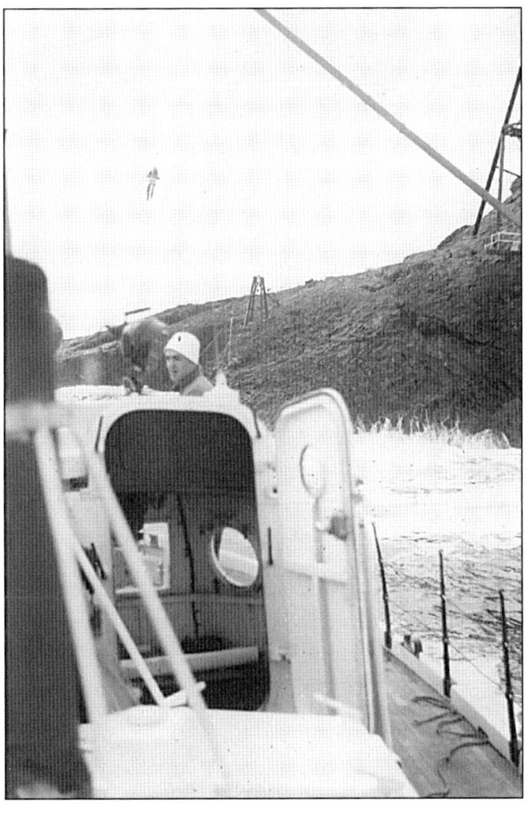

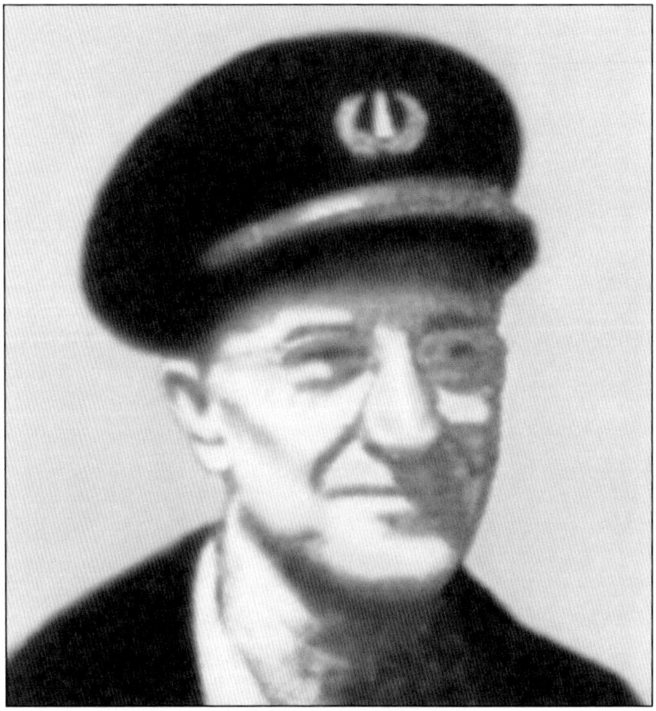

George H. Wheeler (b. 1893) was the second-longest-serving keeper at Tillamook Rock Lighthouse. Wheeler served from 1928 to 1952, except for a three-year stint at Turn Point Lighthouse in Washington. He was head keeper from 1942 onward. He might have surpassed Robert Gerlof's 25-year record had he not tragically died as a result of a boating accident while fishing in 1952, presumably while on his normal shore leave. (LHD.)

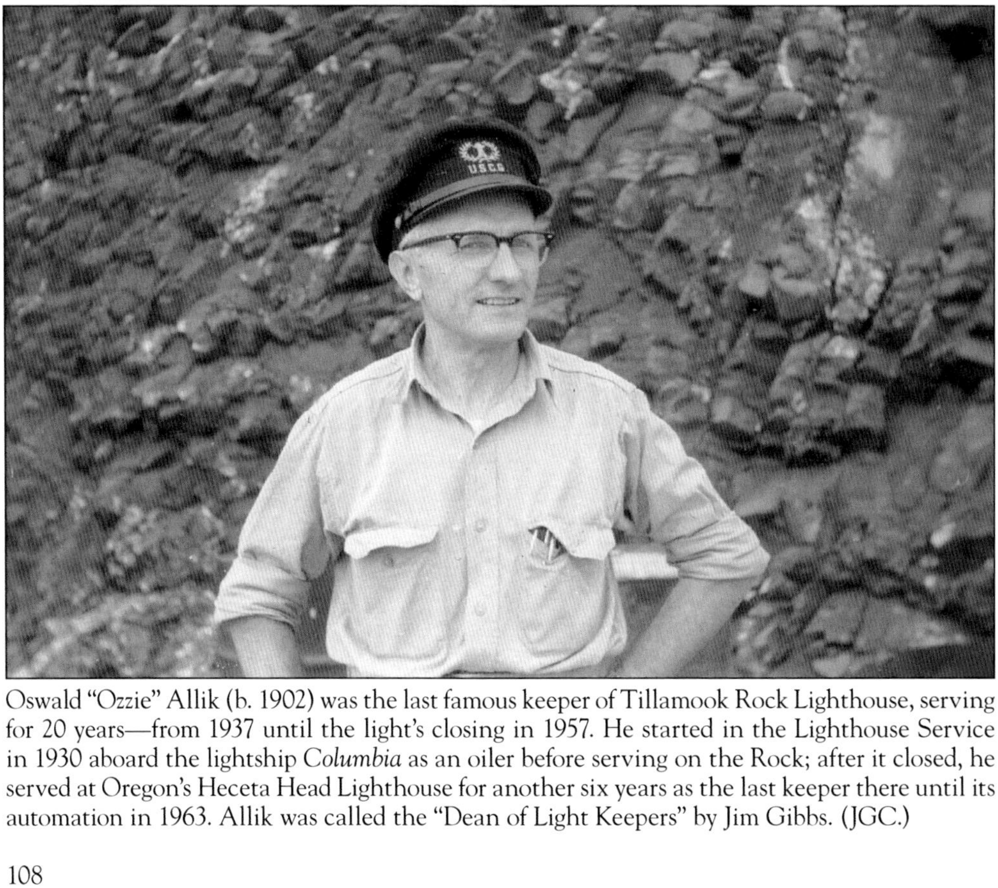

Oswald "Ozzie" Allik (b. 1902) was the last famous keeper of Tillamook Rock Lighthouse, serving for 20 years—from 1937 until the light's closing in 1957. He started in the Lighthouse Service in 1930 aboard the lightship *Columbia* as an oiler before serving on the Rock; after it closed, he served at Oregon's Heceta Head Lighthouse for another six years as the last keeper there until its automation in 1963. Allik was called the "Dean of Light Keepers" by Jim Gibbs. (JGC.)

Lon Haynes (b. 1936) served at Tillamook Rock Lighthouse from 1954 to 1956 under head keeper Ozzie Allik. At age 81, Haynes is one of the last surviving keepers who can tell personal stories of his time on the Rock. When he accepted his assignment, he did not realize that the lighthouse would be offshore and was quite shocked when he first saw it and had to ride in the breeches buoy to get to it. (LHC.)

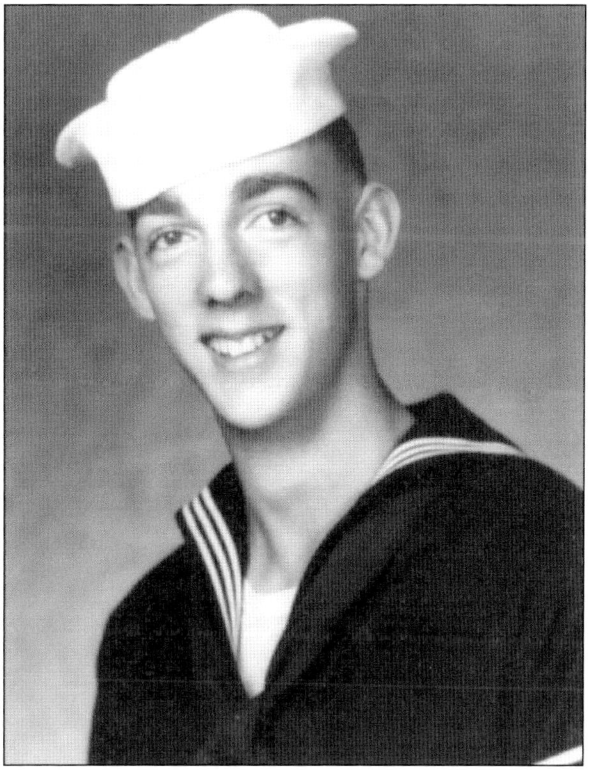

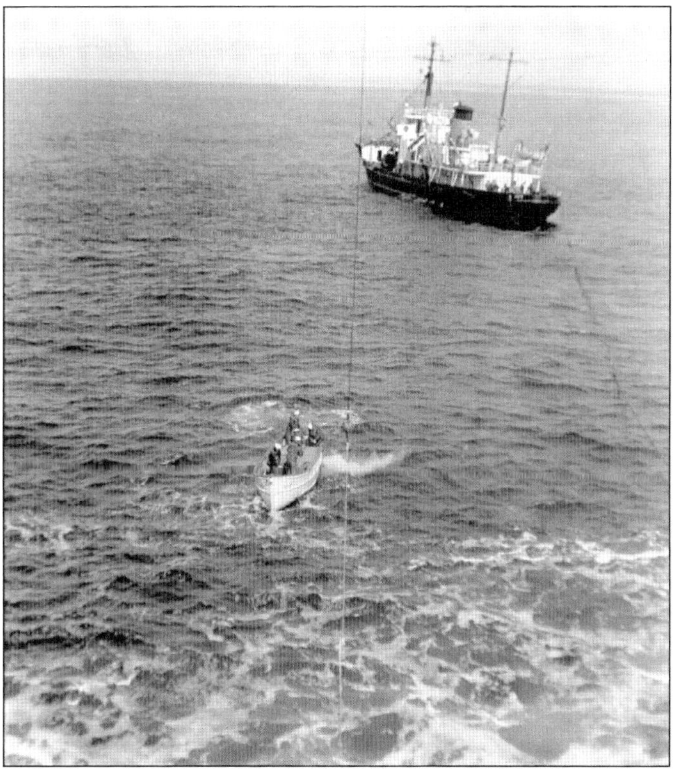

In 1954, the tender *Ivy* was servicing Tillamook Rock Lighthouse and delivered Lon Haynes to his new duty station. The *Ivy* was originally commissioned as the Navy mine-layer *Barbican* during World War II before being transferred to the Coast Guard in 1946. She was the fourth tender to be named *Ivy*, and from 1951 was home ported in Oregon. (LHC.)

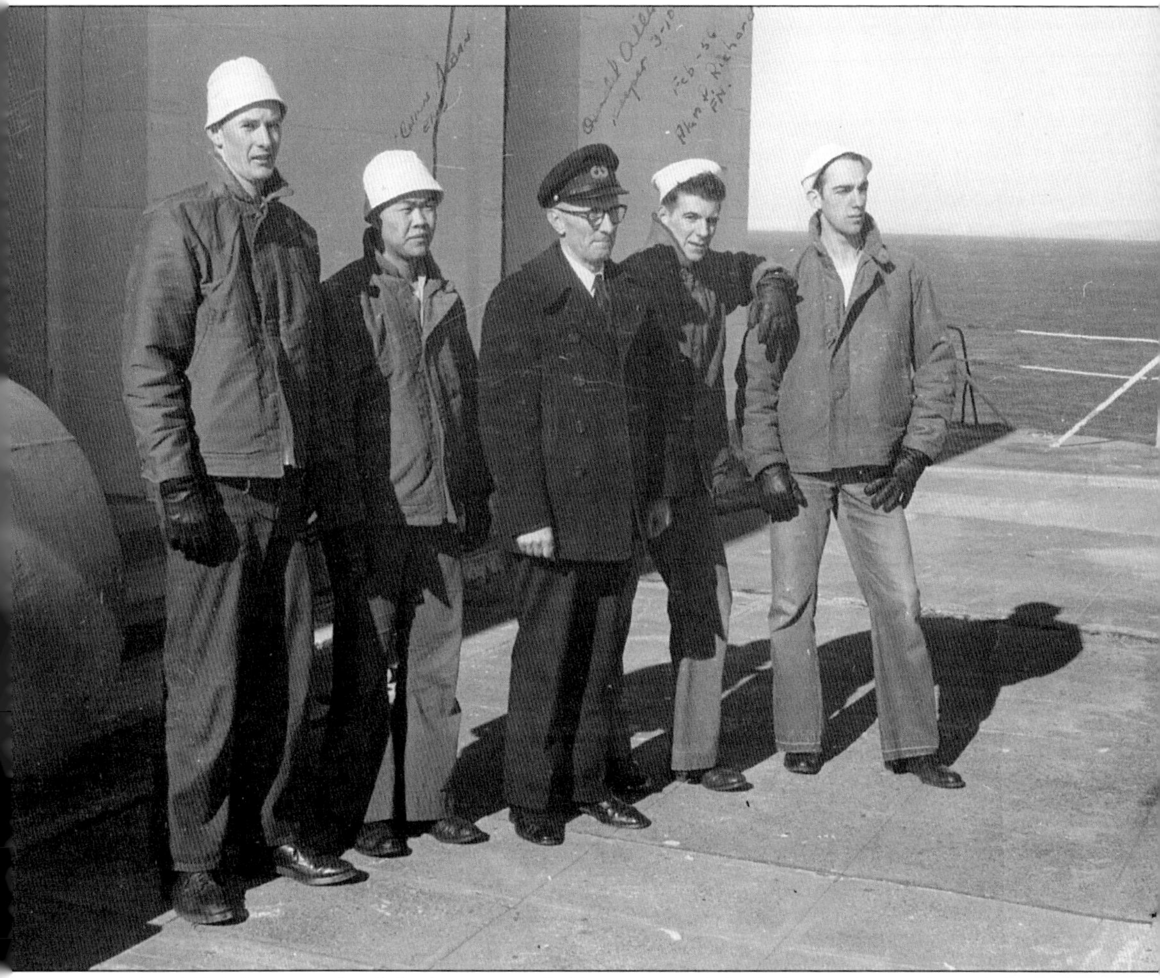

This 1956 photograph of the keepers at Tillamook Rock Lighthouse shows, from left to right, James Jack, Alban Chinn, Oswald Allik, Alan D. Richards, and Lon Haynes. In an *Oregonian* interview, Allik talked about what the keepers did from day to day: "We keep busy on the Rock. We have to keep the four diesel engines, two compressors, two generators and other equipment operating. That is enough to keep the men busy during regular working hours. When they have spare time, the younger men usually study for advances in rating to enginemen or boatswain's mate." (LHC.)

This photograph shows head keeper Ozzie Allik standing in the doorway at Tillamook Rock Lighthouse. Allik did not talk a lot. Lon Haynes described him as having "a stoic personality and I don't think I can remember him ever smiling. This is not to say anything negative about the man, he just never displayed emotion of any kind, it just wasn't in his nature." (JGC.)

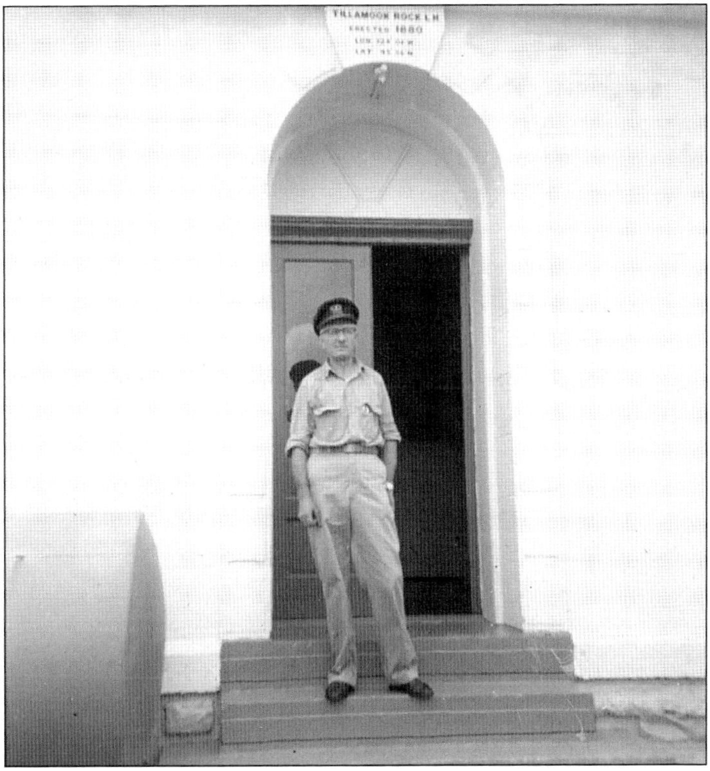

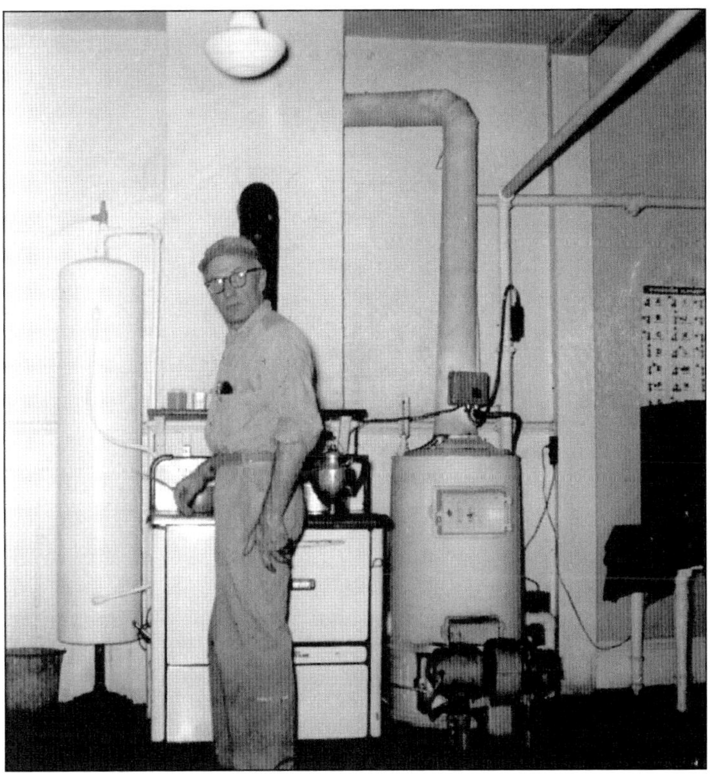

However, valiant service was in Ozzie Allik's nature. After 33 years of faithful dedication in keeping the light to safeguard others' lives, he ironically died through a final act of service. He had a heart attack while trying to save the lives of two motorists in a highway incident 12 years after retiring from lighthouse duty. It was not surprising that Allik had received the federal government's Albert Gallatin Award for his long and stalwart service to others. (LHC.)

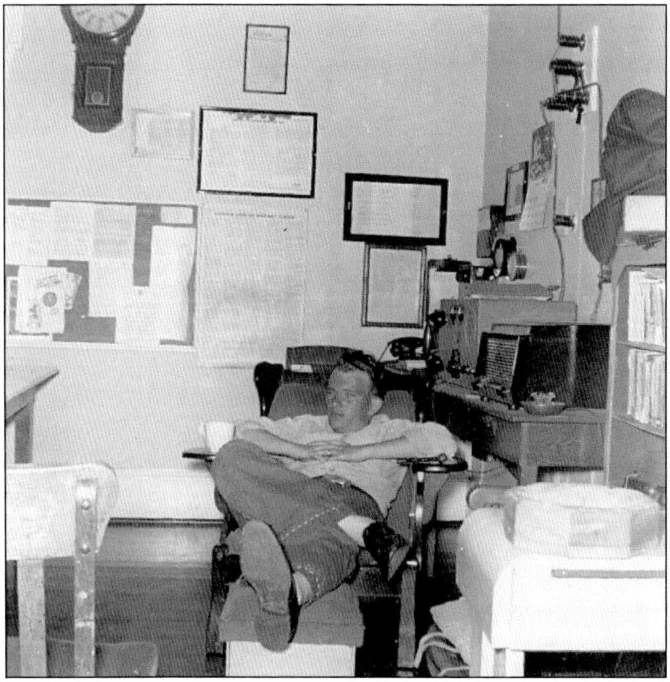

Seaman Greenly is shown relaxing in the day room of Tillamook Rock Lighthouse, where a television set was able to receive two local channels. Keeper Lon Haynes tells of playing jokes on the second-in-command, who would watch *The Voice of Firestone*, a show no one else wanted to see. Haynes and his cohort, keeper Al Richards, would turn the antenna (pictured below) just enough so that the reception would come in and out on the television set just to annoy the man. That was much more entertaining to them than being forced to watch a program they had no interest in. (Left, LHC; below, JGC.)

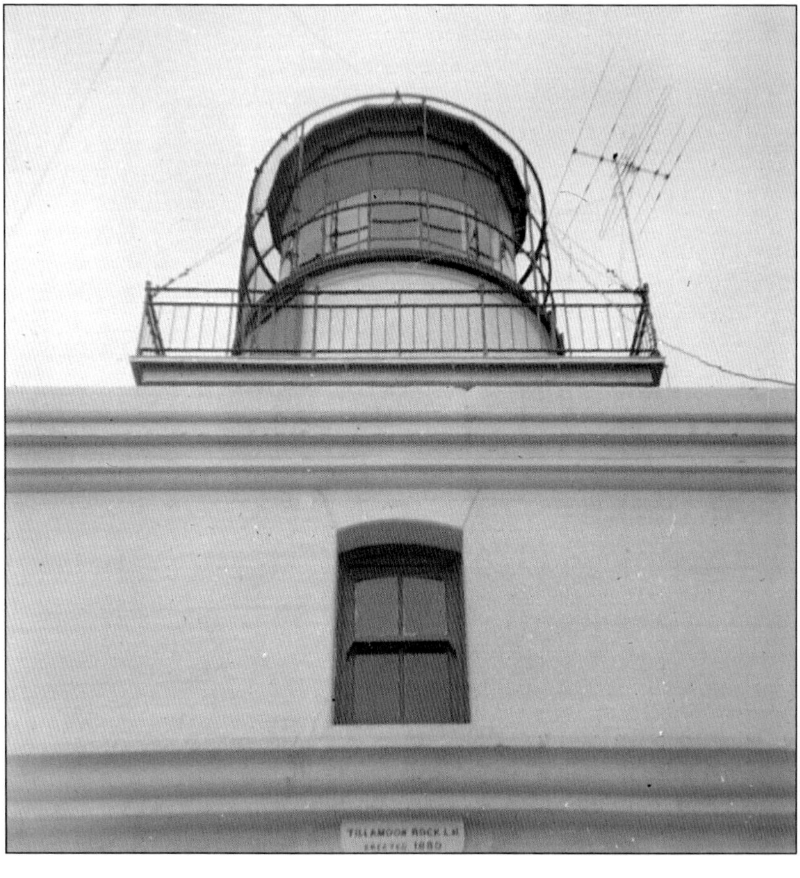

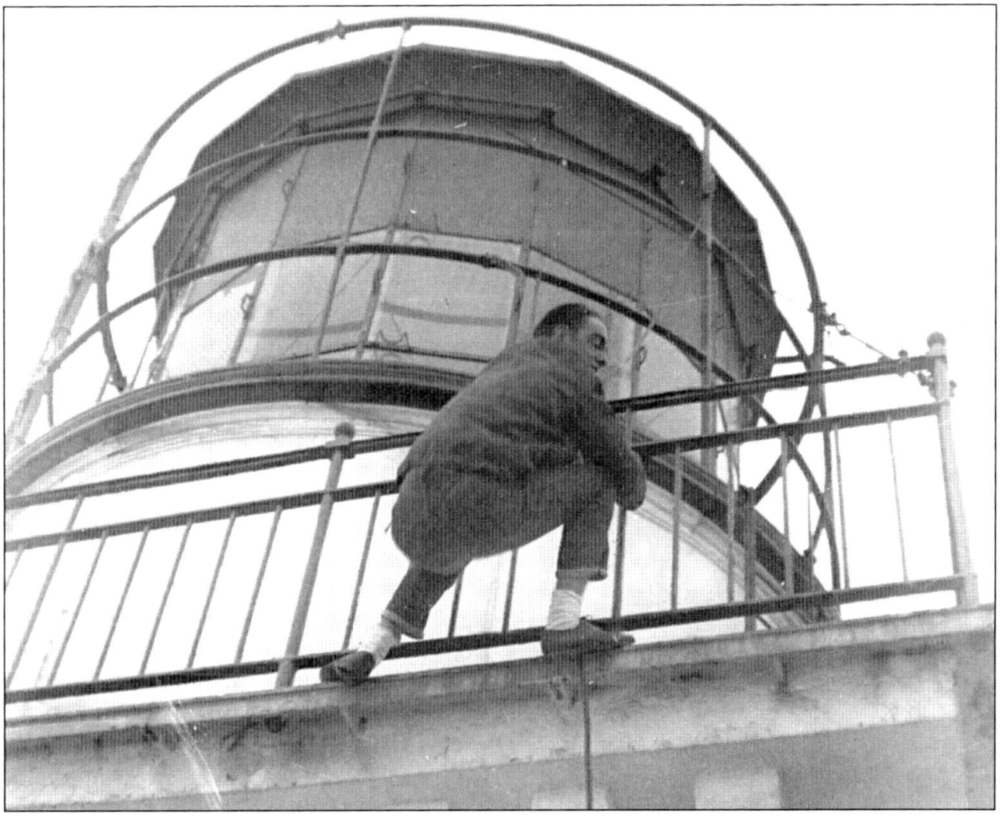

In 1955, keepers Lon Haynes (above) and Al Richards (right) show their tower-climbing and rope-dangling skills, somewhat reminiscent of the Fearless Foursome's antics some 35 years earlier. Besides tower climbing and watching television, keepers in the 1950s played a lot of cards, including pinochle, poker, and cribbage, during their recreational hours at the lighthouse. Haynes also mentioned bringing his violin and guitar to the lighthouse to play in his room, the walls being too thick to bother others with the sound. But Haynes was still bored serving there. Tired of being wet and cold after 20 months, he transferred off the Rock to what he thought would be a warm tropical paradise in Hawaii but instead ended up on the Coast Guard tender *Blackhaw*, breaking ice in Alaska. (Both, LHC.)

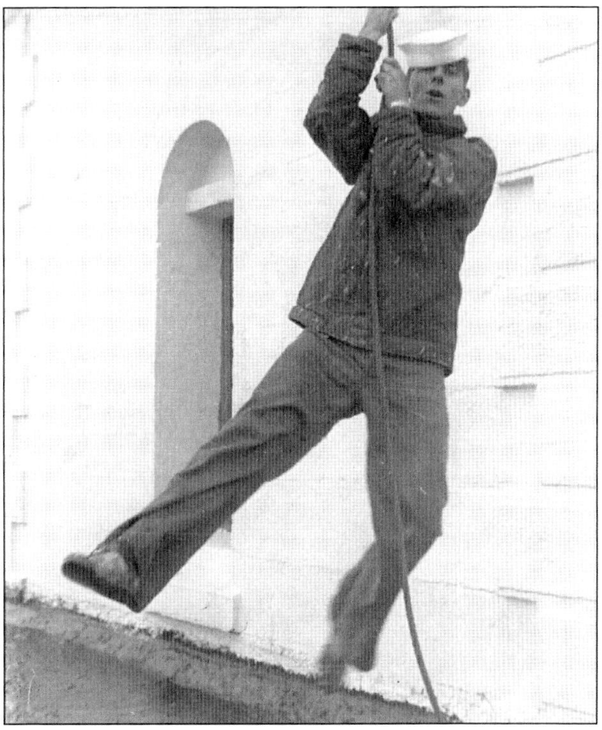

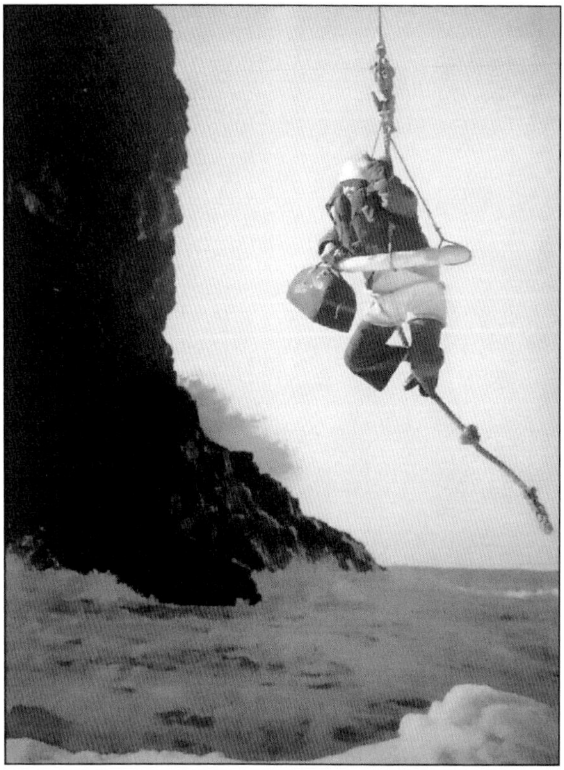

Keeper Alban Chinn rides the breeches buoy up to the lighthouse in 1956. Chinn was in the Coast Guard for three years before coming to Tillamook Rock Lighthouse at age 22. His claim to fame on the Rock was his excellent cooking. Even though all keepers were supposed to rotate kitchen duties, if someone knew how to cook well, they were given the permanent assignment. Lon Haynes had it until Chinn showed up and usurped him because of his superior culinary abilities. (USLHS.)

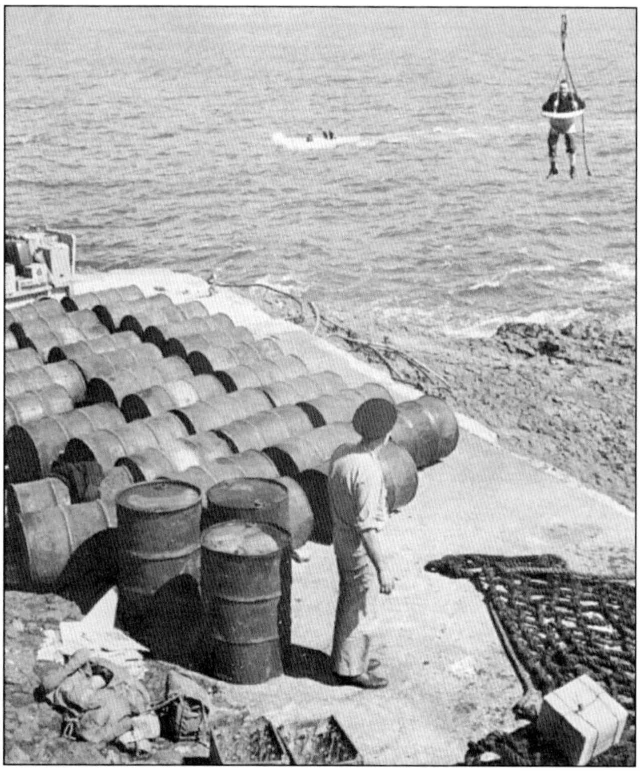

Ozzie Allik stands on the landing platform waiting for the last delivery of the day—one of his keepers. All supplies had to be hoisted from the platform up to the lighthouse, including the drums containing the diesel fuel necessary for the engines and compressors that ran the fog-siren and derrick hoist engine and generated electricity for the lighting unit and keepers' quarters. (USLHS.)

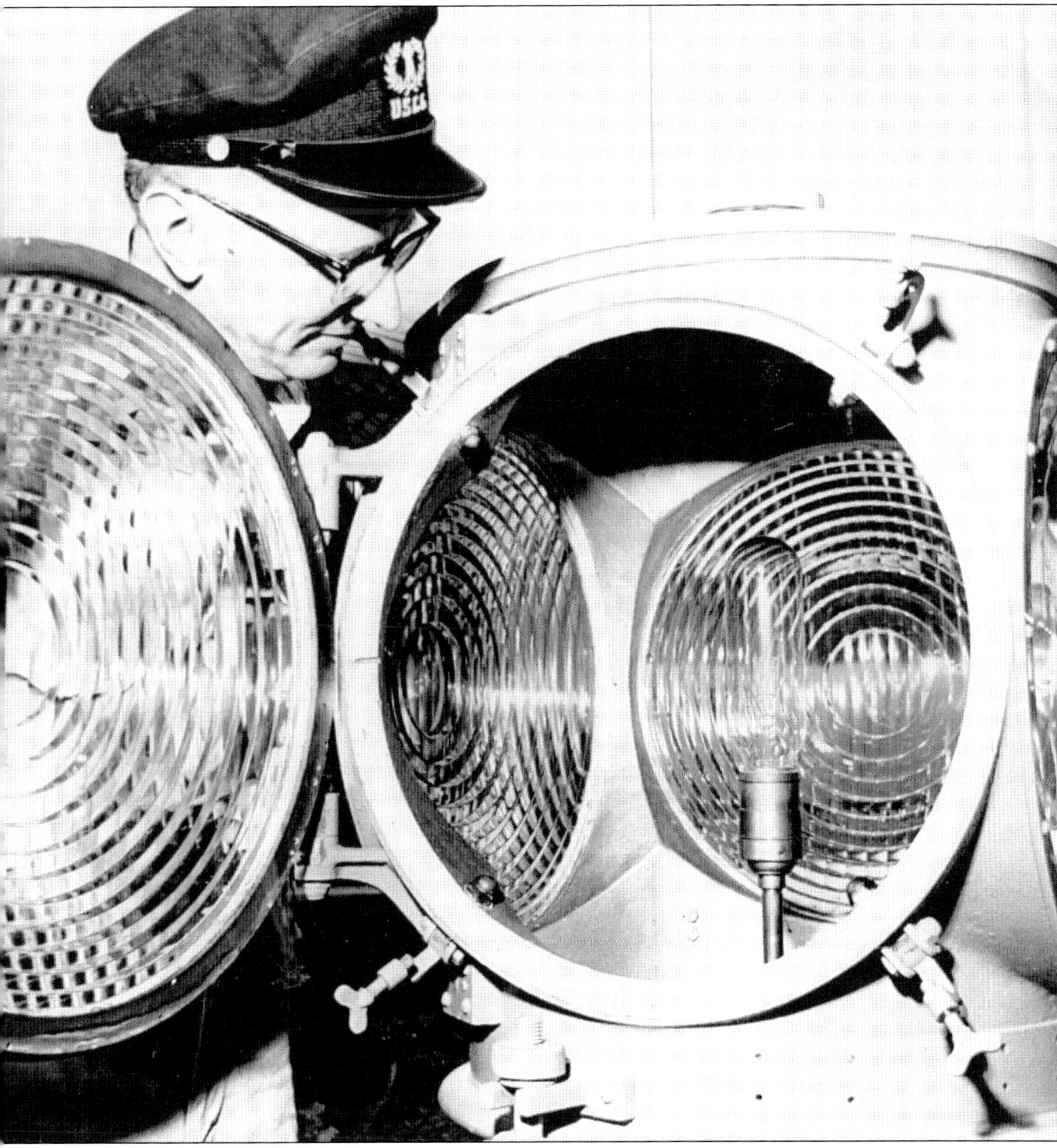

Head keeper Ozzie Allik shows off the interior of the Type B Revolving Duplex Composite Lighting Unit. Each tier utilized a 500-watt T-20 lamp. Lon Haynes commented that the young Coastguardsmen were never allowed to clean or touch the unit; Ozzie always did that himself. Because the longest an assistant Coast Guard keeper would stay was usually the 18-month minimum, perhaps Allik felt it was not necessary to have them trained in lens maintenance. Or maybe it was his high sense of responsibility and consistency that would not allow him to delegate it to the "kids," as he called them. However, according to Haynes, the second-in-command was always an engineman who was qualified to service and repair the engines for the compressors and generators, should the need ever arise. (CGHO.)

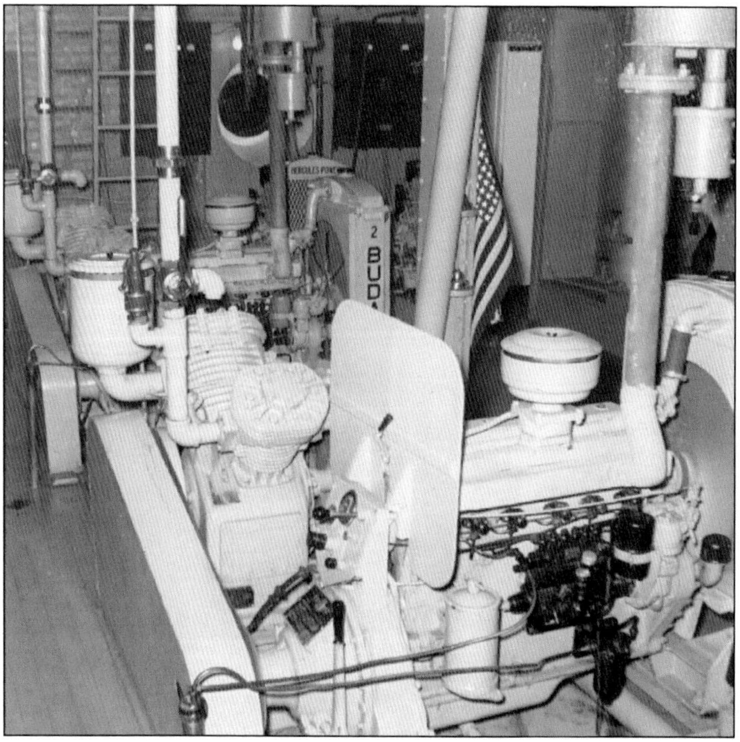

Keeper Ozzie Allik kept a pristine station. The fog-signal room (pictured here) almost looks like it could be a showroom for new lighthouse equipment with how perfectly clean and polished the dual sets of engines and compressors appear. (LHC.)

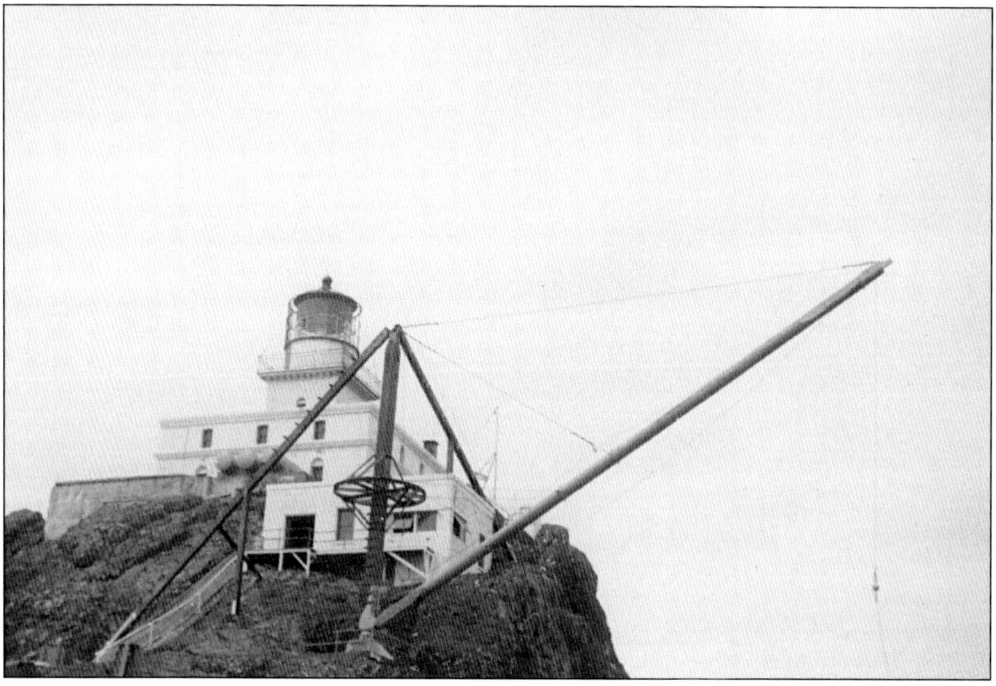

This 1950s photograph of the lighthouse shows it in a coat of immaculate white paint, and there does not appear to be a nut, bolt, or rock out of place. Keeper Ozzie Allik must have put all the energies of his young Coast Guard assistants to good use to keep up such an appearance. It also must have made any inspection visits a pleasure to write up with such spotless cleanliness. (JGC.)

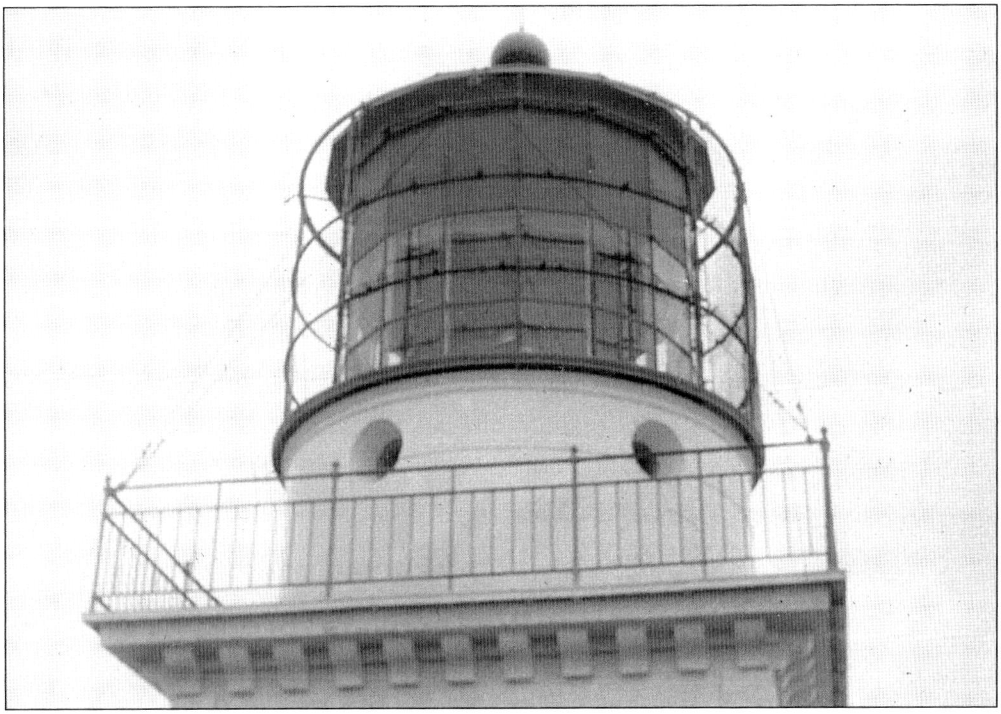

Sometime in the early to mid-1950s, the bottom section of the lantern of Tillamook Rock Lighthouse was painted white. In this photograph, the dark curtains protecting the lighting unit are clearly visible as well as the upper belt of metal shutters that replaced the glass panes after storm improvements were made in 1935. (JGC.)

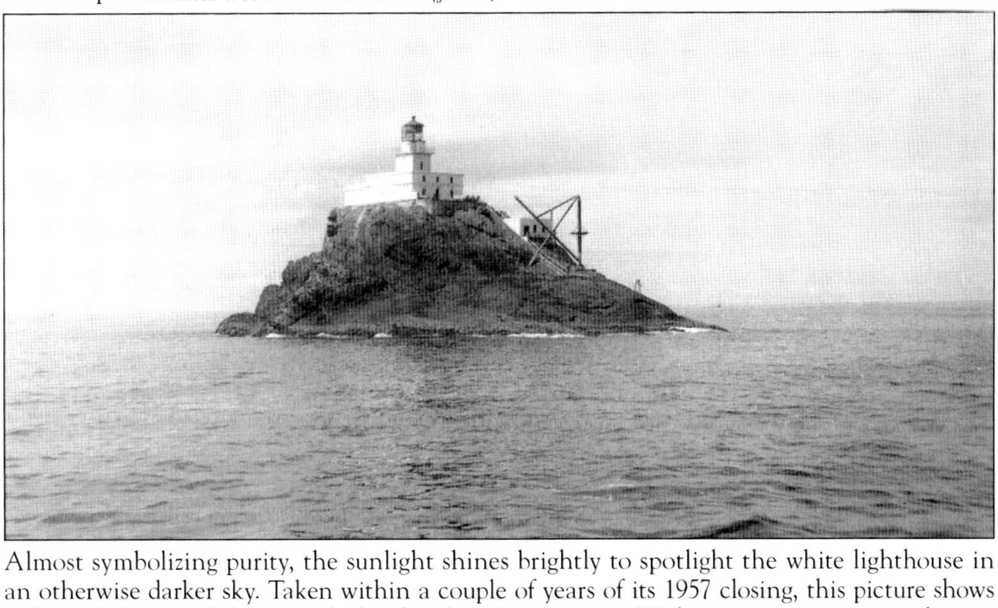

Almost symbolizing purity, the sunlight shines brightly to spotlight the white lighthouse in an otherwise darker sky. Taken within a couple of years of its 1957 closing, this picture shows Tillamook Rock Lighthouse at the height of its 76-year career. With newer equipment, good storm precautions, and an efficient head keeper, the light shone brightly during the last few years of its working life. Unfortunately, with the advances of navigational technology, the cost of maintenance and manpower was deemed too high, and a final change was soon to arrive. (JGC.)

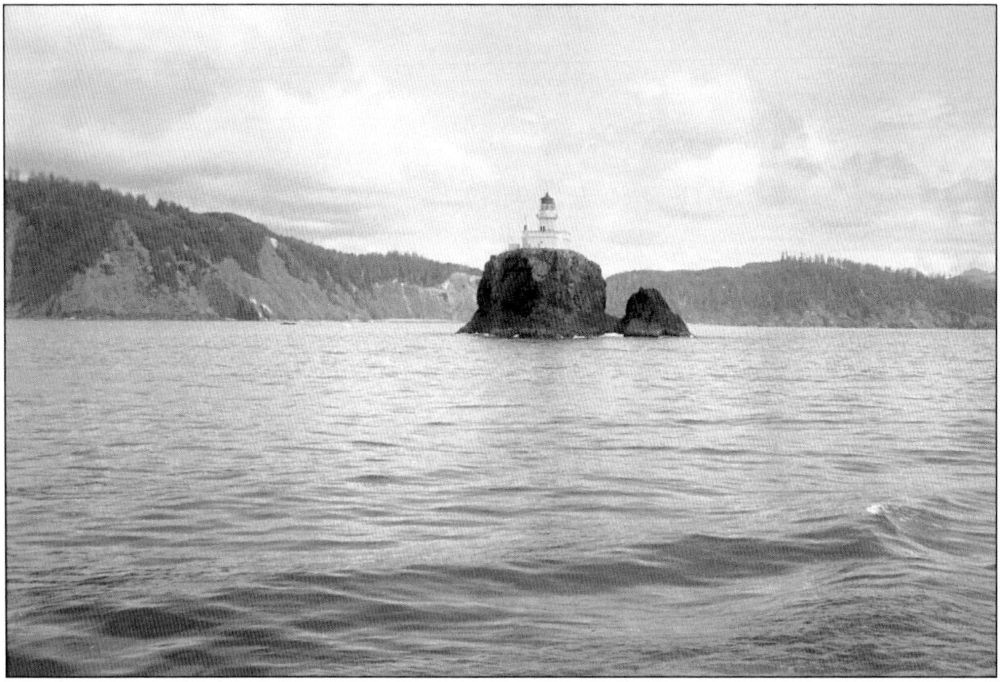

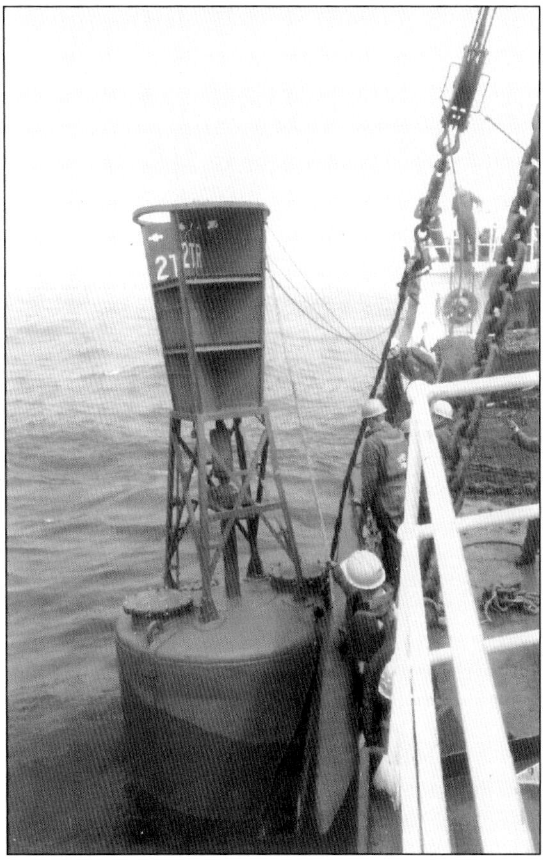

According to a Coast Guard press release, "Before Tillamook Light was discontinued, the U.S. Coast Guard held a public hearing at City Hall in Astoria on March 1, 1956. There were groans of disapproval from various of the public for sentimental reasons. Reasons for discontinuance were that the light was considered remote, difficult and dangerous to support, expensive to maintain, and the present coastwise stream track passing the Rock today goes 9 miles to the westward going well beyond the range of the fog-signal, therefore, the light was no longer justified. The light station, which displayed an 80,000 candlepower light visible for 18 miles, and the fog-signal, were discontinued on Sept 1, 1957. Replacing this aid to navigation is a '2TR' whistle buoy [pictured at left], radar reflector type, 16 feet high, set in 28 fathoms of water, .5 miles west of Tillamook Rock. It has a 440 candlepower red light, visible at 9 miles." (Both, USLHS.)

Six

Silent Sentinel

Since its decommissioning in September 1957, Tillamook Rock Lighthouse has changed hands many times. It has been purchased by parties who wanted to repurpose it into a purported gambling casino, family summer home, restaurant, or vacation retreat. But in all cases, the plans went awry after it was found to be too difficult to restore or maintain to any degree.

In 1980, it was purchased by a group of investors who turned it into the Eternity at Sea Columbarium, where cremated remains could be stored for those who wanted to rest at sea. When the columbarium's license was revoked in 1999 by the Oregon State Cemetery Board for improper records and not having proper storage niches, no more urns could be interred beyond the 30 or so already placed there. In 2005, another attempt was made to renew the license, but the application was again rejected.

In 1994, the US Fish and Wildlife Service purchased a conservation easement in perpetuity for Tillamook Rock's inclusion in the Oregon Islands National Wildlife Refuge. Under the existing agreement, the lighthouse can continue as a columbarium with the stipulation that no one goes ashore during the annual seabird breeding season between March 15 and September 1.

Aerial surveys are flown annually by refuge biologists to photograph the Rock and document its modern inhabitants—sea lions and seabirds—but no maintenance has been done by Eternity at Sea for more than two decades, and the lighthouse is in an ongoing state of permanent decay. Recent drone footage shows cracks expanding in the outer walls and the iron lantern rotting, with huge holes widening as winter storms wash away more of it each year.

For the past 25 years, *Lighthouse Digest Magazine* has published the "Doomsday List of Endangered Lighthouses" that are in danger of being lost forever. Sadly, Tillamook Rock Lighthouse has been on that list for most of those years. It will be a very sad day when those who visit the Oregon beaches of Ecola State Park look out and see only a ruin of what was once the most famous lighthouse of the Pacific coast.

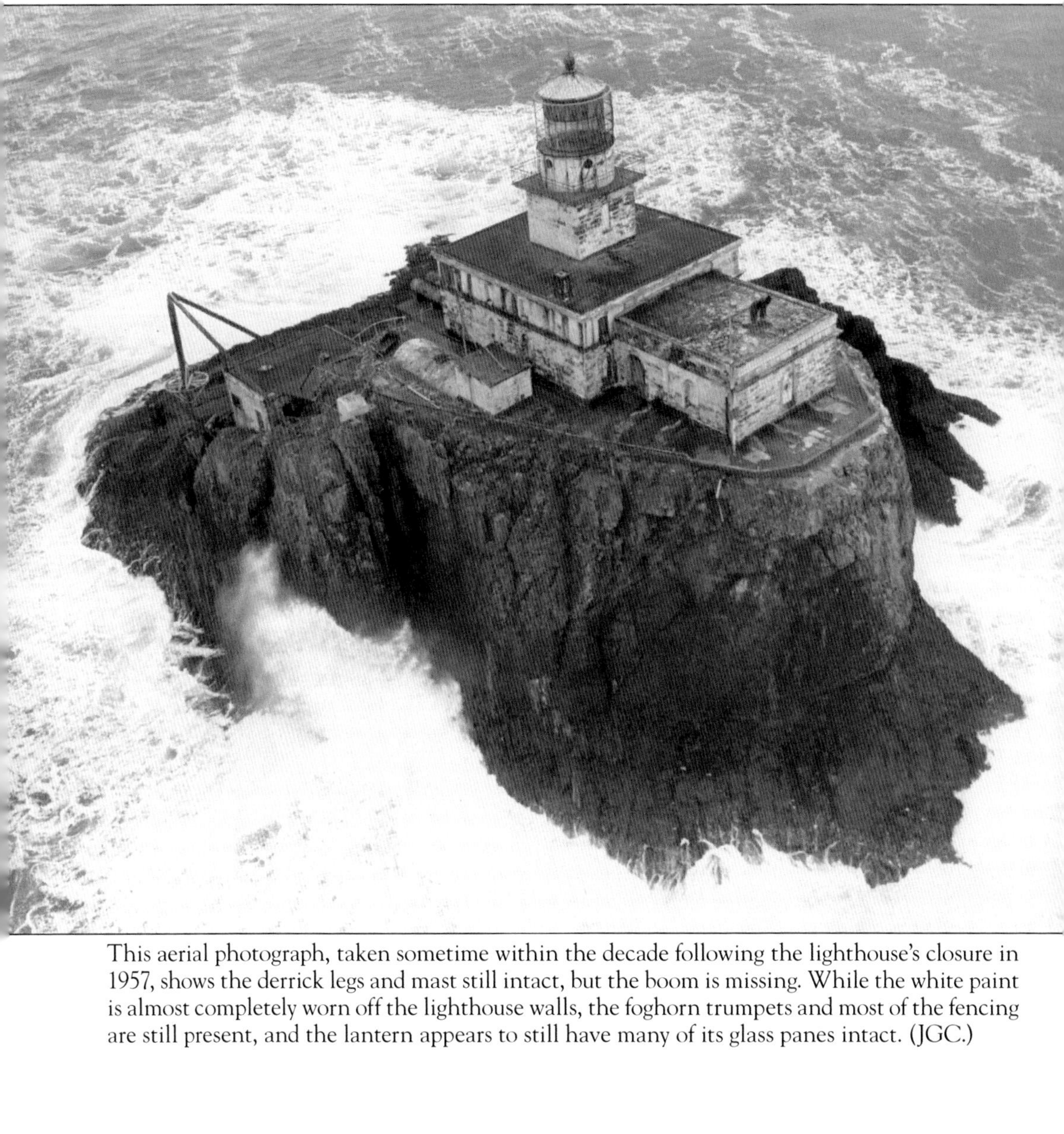

This aerial photograph, taken sometime within the decade following the lighthouse's closure in 1957, shows the derrick legs and mast still intact, but the boom is missing. While the white paint is almost completely worn off the lighthouse walls, the foghorn trumpets and most of the fencing are still present, and the lantern appears to still have many of its glass panes intact. (JGC.)

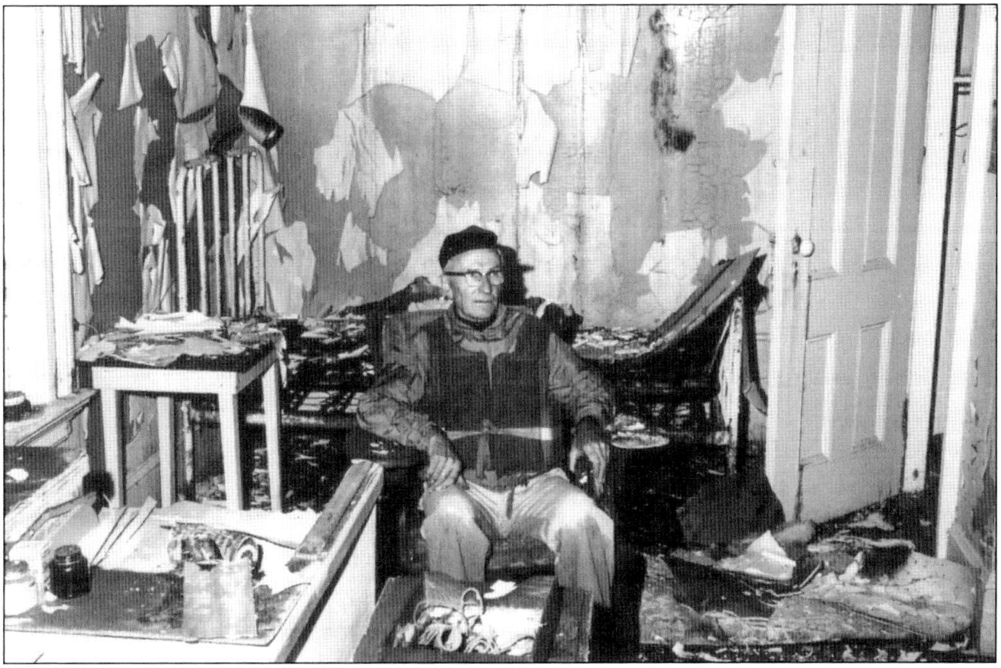

In 1969, retired keeper Ozzie Allik returned to Tillamook Rock Lighthouse 12 years after he turned off the light for the final time. Surrounded by debris, peeling wallpaper, and mildew damage, Allik sits in what was once his office. It must have been a heart-wrenching experience for him to see the state of the lighthouse where he had spent 20 years of his life keeping it spotlessly clean while diligently maintaining the light every night. It was said that he was proud of the fact that in all those years, the light was never dark for any reason. He had done his job well. How devastating, then, for him to return to this scene of utter dilapidation through neglect. (Both, LHD.)

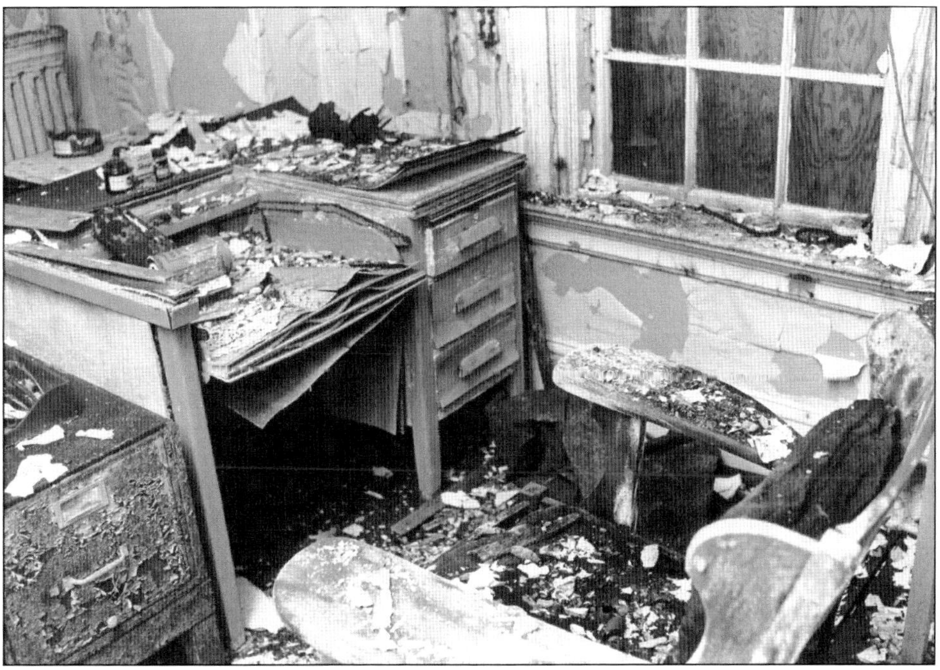

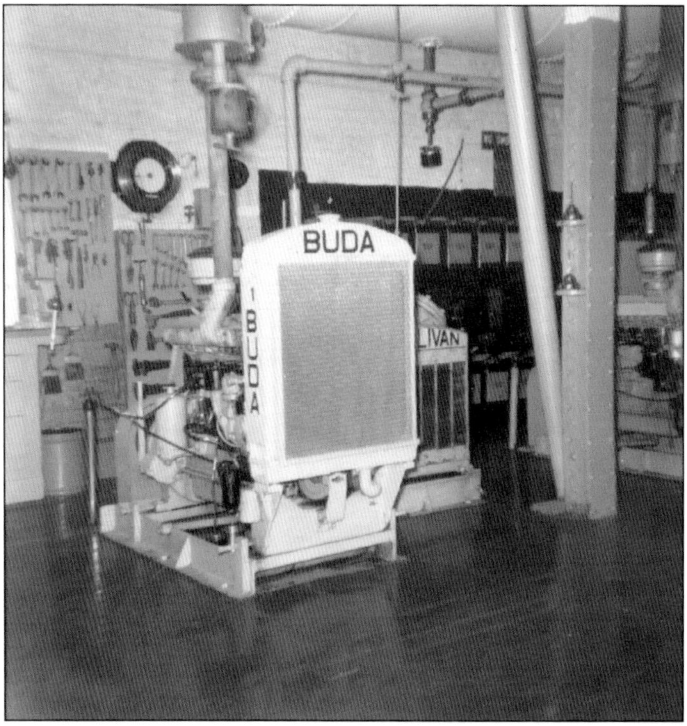

During former keeper Ozzie Allik's return visit, in every part of the station, the state of advanced deterioration was evident. In the fog-signal room, the machinery that was abandoned in 1957 because it was too old or heavy to remove was rusting and rotting due to the saltwater environment. Compare the 1945 photograph that Jim Gibbs took when he first arrived on Tillamook Rock (left) with the one from 1969 (below) showing the same Buda brand engine from the matched pair. (Left, JGC; below, CCHS.)

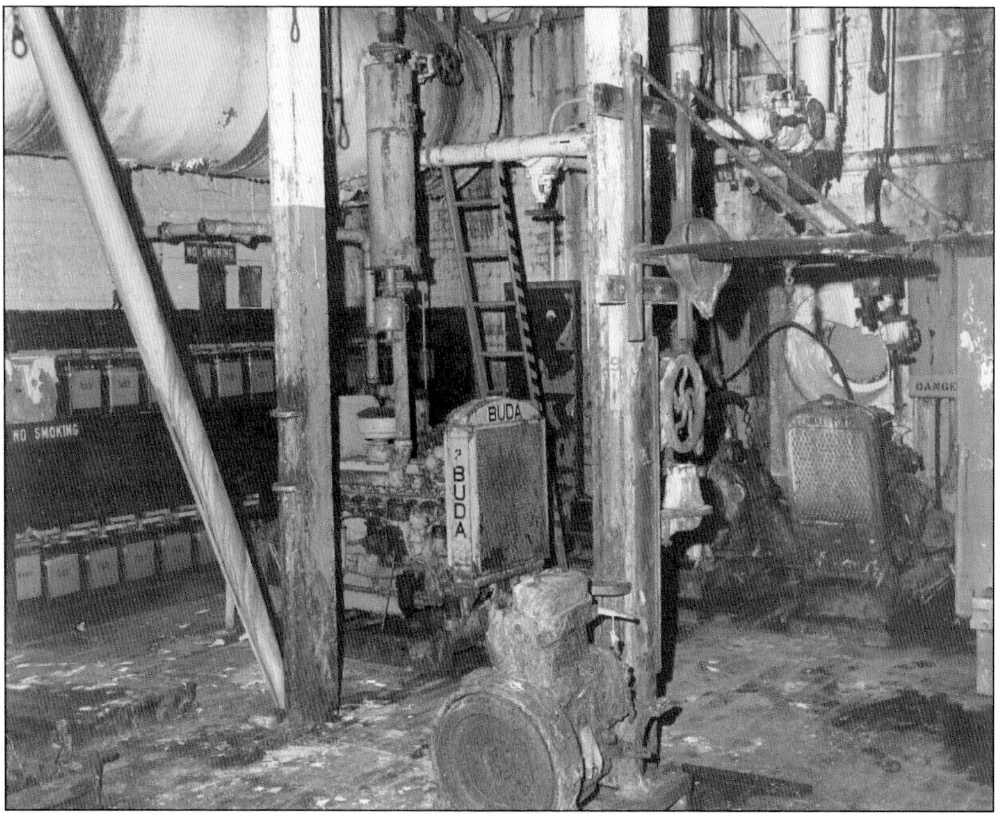

Another set of before-and-after images of the fog-signal room equipment tells the tale in very graphic terms of the state of decay of Tillamook Rock Lighthouse after only a decade of neglect. This 1955 photograph of matched engines in pristine condition was taken by Lon Haynes when he was serving on the Rock. (LHC.)

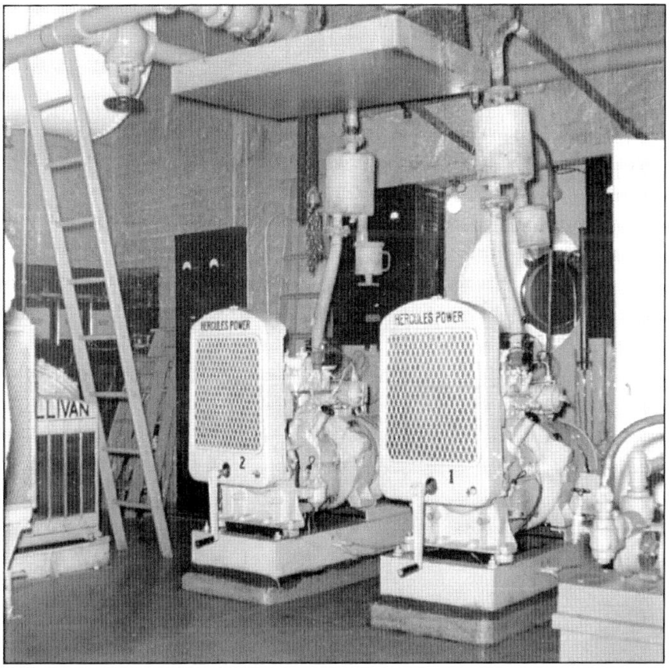

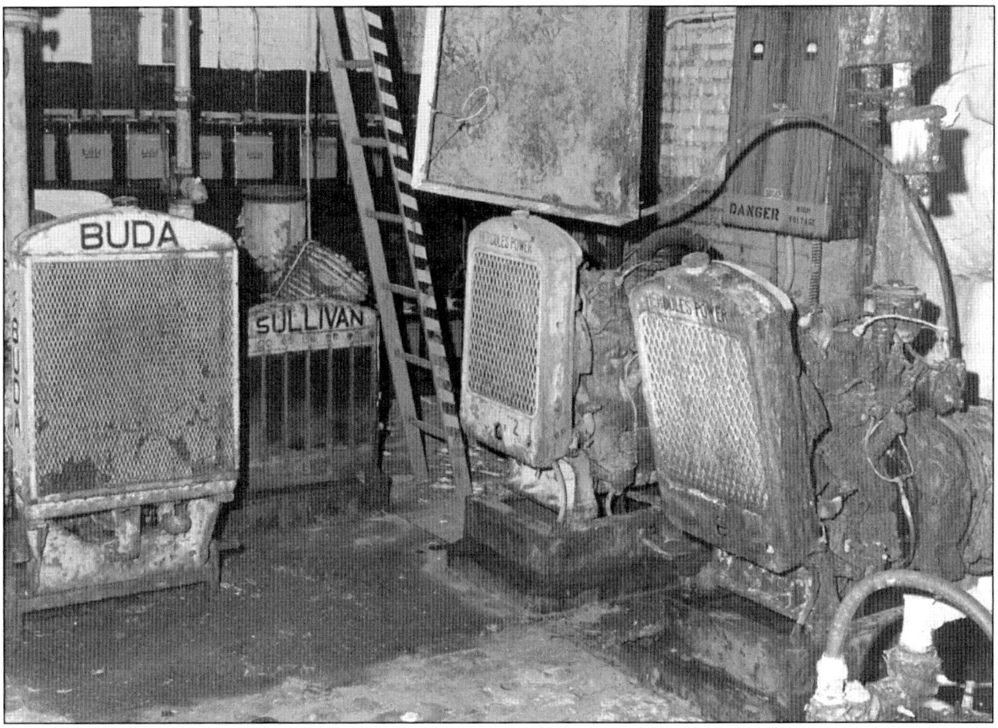

This 1969 photograph, taken from almost the exact same angle as above, offers a stark contrast and shows the ruination and wreckage of the equipment. The angle of the radiator on the right is reminiscent of an old tombstone that is ready to fall over in a forgotten, unmaintained cemetery. It symbolizes all the historic lighthouses across America that have already fallen or are in a similar state today due to abandonment. (JGC.)

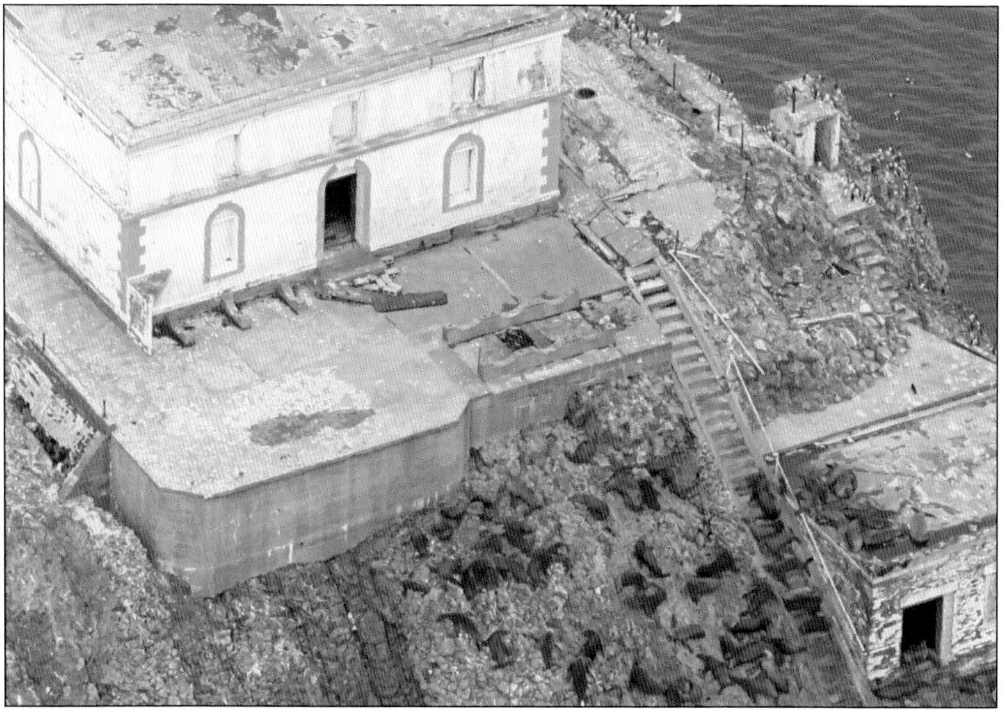

This 2010 aerial view of Tillamook Rock Lighthouse shows the front doors lying askew and huge cracks running from the headers in the attic windows up to the roof. The concrete walkway above the stairs is torn up, and sea lions and seabirds are resting on the rock slopes, stairs, winch house, and outhouse. (USFWS.)

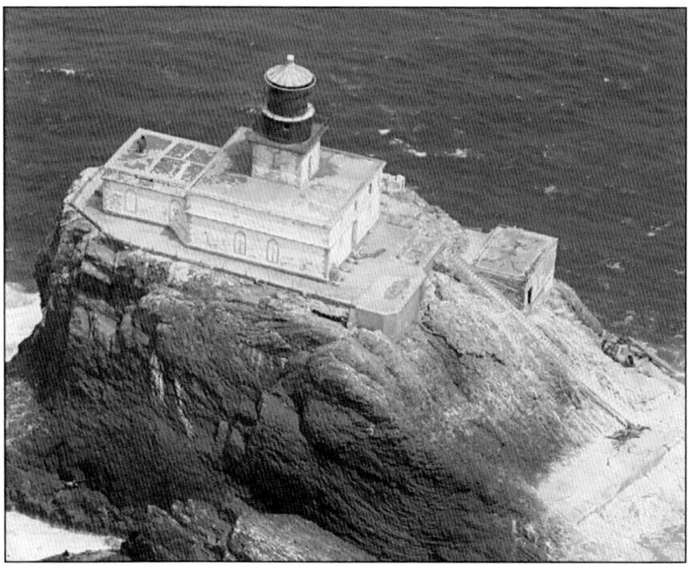

In this aerial view from June 2017, it is almost as if Tillamook Rock Lighthouse is weeping for its fate. The portholes set into the bricked-up windows on the south side above the crevice have dark stains that are seeping down in a straight line from the center of the porthole. In the color photograph, they, as well as the rusted lantern, are blood-red. The remains of the broken derrick mast are falling off the rock edge toward the sea. (USFWS.)

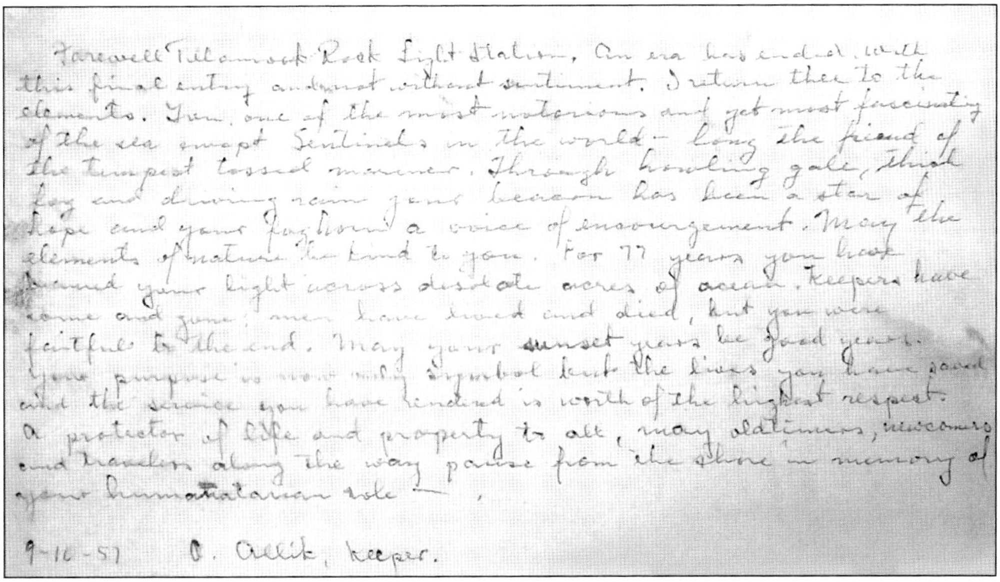
Farewell Tillamook Rock Light Station, An era has ended. with this final entry and not without sentiment. I return thee to the elements. You, one of the most notorious and yet most fascinating of the sea swept Sentinels in the world – long the friend of the tempest tossed mariner. Through howling gale, thick fog and driving rain your beacon has been a star of hope and your foghorn a voice of encouragement. May the elements of nature be kind to you. For 77 years you have beamed your light across desolate acres of ocean. Keepers have come and gone; men have lived and died, but you were faithful to the end. May your sunset years be good years. Your purpose is now only symbol but the lives you have saved and the service you have rendered is worth of the highest respect. A protector of life and property to all, may oldtimers, newcomers and travelers along the way pause from the shore in memory of your humanitarian role —

9-10-57 O. Allik, keeper.

Former keeper Jim Gibbs composed this poetic final entry transcribed by Ozzie Allik into the logbook on September 10, 1957, which reads, in part: "Farewell Tillamook Rock Light Station. An era has ended. With this final entry and not without sentiment, I return thee to the elements. You, one of the most notorious and yet one of the most fascinating of the sea swept Sentinels in the world — long the friend of the tempest tossed mariner. . . . May your sunset years be good years. Your purpose is now only a symbol, but the lives you have saved and the service you have rendered is worthy of the highest respect. A protector of life and property to all, may oldtimers, newcomers and travelers along the way pause from the shore in memory of your humanitarian role." (Above, LHD; below, USFWS.)

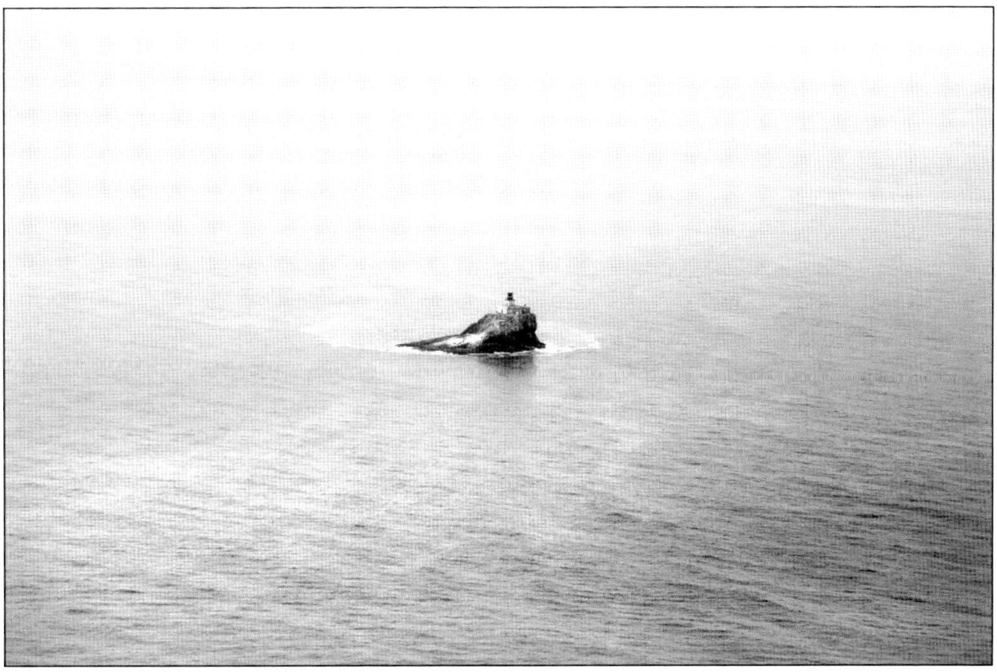

Known Keepers of Tillamook Rock Lighthouse

Allik, Oswald (1937–1957)*
Amundsen, Lars F. (1898–1905)
Andresen, Axel E. (AL 1915)
Barker, James F. (1895)
Bearman, Charles H. (AL 1915–1916)
Beemon, Lewis M. (1886)
Bergen, Michael F. (1906–1907)
Beyer, Albert (AL 1917–AL 1918, 1927–1928)
Bjorling, Charles (1883–1884)
Booker, Ernest F. (1888)
Brien, Daniel H.O. (1882–1883)
Brodie, Edward E. (1896–1898)
Burchall, Joseph (1894–1896)
Burroughs, George L. (1924–1928)
Cameron, Archie G. (1930–1931)
Clark, Daniel W. (AL 1913)
Coe, Henry A. (1885)
Collins, Stephen H. (1881–1883)
Cook, Henry C. (1890–1893)
Cosper, Fred B. (1882)*
Crawford, George G. (1893, 1896–1898)
Dahlgren, William (1901–1919)*
Dahlin, Olaf (AL 1913)
Davis, Charles H. (1885–1887)*
Dibb, Roy P. (AL 1940, 1945)
Doody, James (1884)
Farrington, Grady (1935)
Flynn, John M. (1887–1888)
Fogg, Robert E. (AL 1934)
Forty, John L. (1911)
Gadsby, William (1933–1934)
Gerlof, Robert (1903–1928)*
Gibbs, James (1945–1946)
Gibson, Thomas (1899–1901)
Graham, Charles F. (1884)
Hall, Charles B. (1931)
Hammond, Frank C. (1911–1916)
Hansen, Howard L. (AL 1919–AL 1921)
Hansen, Olaf L. (1894–1896)
Hanson, Hugo (AL 1934–1937)
Haynes, Lon (1954–1956).
Hayward, Orlo E. (1920–1921)
Heagney, John (1901–1902)
Hedden, Phillip E. (1923–1924)
Hill, William (AL 1930–1936)*
Hiller, Floyd H. (1931)
Hodge, Gordon (1930–1931)
Hornung, Joseph (1884–1887)*
Howe, Nels A. (1938–1939)
Hunt, George A. (1887–1892)*
Hurlbut, Daniel R. (1900)
Ingvold F. (1884–1885)
Jansen, Gust (1903–1907)
Jenkins, Henry (1933–1935)

Johnson, Albert H. (1930–1931)
Jones, Nathaniel (1884–1885)
Jones, Thomas (1881–1882)
Jones, Thomas (1911)
Justen, Charles (1905–1906)
Kissell, William F. (1894–1896)
Kussman, Jack (1938)
Langlois, William T. (1896–1899, 1903–1910)*
Laschinger, Ed (1937–AL 1940)*
Lawrence, Walter T. (1919–1921)
Lee, George A. (1907–1909)
Leonard, Joseph W. (1903)
Lund, Raymond (1933–1934)
Martin, Guy C. (1911–AL 1912)
Martin, James H. (1885–1888)
Mauley, Lewis J. (1881)
Milkowski, Teofil (AL 1924, 1929)
Miller, Charles (1912–AL 1913)
Monette, W. (1909–1910)
Nielsen, A. (1908–1910)
Nikander, Gustaf A. (1898–1903)
Oakley, Harry (1924–1925)
Patterson, John P. (1881–1882)
Pesonen, Alexander K. (1892–1898)*
Petersen, Rasmus (1887–1894)*
Quigley, William C. (1951–1952)
Quinn, Edmond (1883)
Roeder, Albert (1881)*
Rousseau, Charles N. (AL 1924)
Rowe, George M. (1881–1882)*
Rustad, Axel (1893–1900)*
Sanders, Alex (1907–1908)
Sandstrom, John (1883–1884)
Sauer, Louis C. (1889–1890)
Schechert, Glenn M. (1952–1953)
Score, Hans P. (1890–1893)
Shaw, James E. (1912)
Solverson, Arthur (1929–1930)
South, Benjamin F. (1884–1885)
Stark, J.N. (1881)
Stark, W.H. (1910–1911)
Stillwell, George H. (1898–1903)*
Stith, Edward C. (1941–1947)
Storm, Werner (AL 1934)
Stream, Marinus A. (1882–1883, 1894)*
Themiley, John C. (1885)
Tibbetts, Gardner (AL 1917)
Tronsen, Ingvold F. (1885)
Umdenstock, Richmond E. (1932)
Varnum, C.D. (1882–1884)*
Walker, Fred H. (1936)
Waters, Criss C. (1923)
Way, George W. (1883–1884)
West, Howard W. (1939–1940)
Wheeler, George H. (1928–1932, 1935–1952)*
Whitehead, Charles D. (1924)
Wiren, Oscar (1900–1901)
York, Henry C. (1889)
Zauner, Christian (1886–1889)

* denotes head keeper
AL = at least

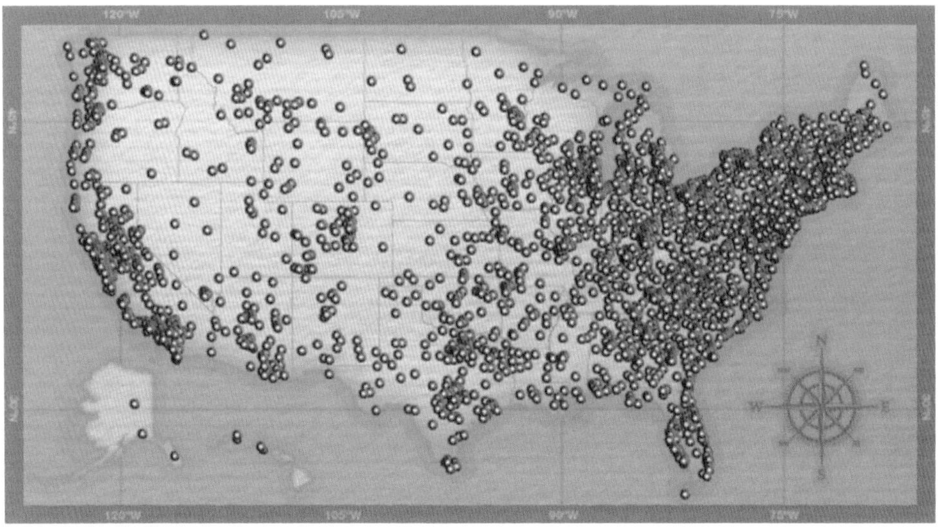

Consistent with our mission to preserve history on a local level, this book was printed in South Carolina on American-made paper and manufactured entirely in the United States. Products carrying the accredited Forest Stewardship Council (FSC) label are printed on 100 percent FSC-certified paper.

MADE IN THE USA